THE DINOSAURS

The Dinosaurs

W. E. SWINTON

B.Sc., Ph.D., F.R.S.E.
Centennial Professor in the University of Toronto
and Senior Fellow of Massey College
Formerly in charge of Fossil Amphibians
Reptiles and Birds, British Museum (Natural History)
Director, Royal Ontario Museum

LONDON. GEORGE ALLEN & UNWIN LTD
NEW YORK. JOHN WILEY AND SONS INC

FIRST PUBLISHED IN 1970
Second Impression 1971

© *George Allen and Unwin Ltd 1970*

British ISBN 0 04 568001 9

Library of Congress Catalog Card Number: 75-113605

PRINTED BY OFFSET IN GREAT BRITAIN
BY ALDEN & MOWBRAY LTD
AT THE ALDEN PRESS, OXFORD

Dedication

DINOSAURS

They built no cities, shaped no great empires
Knew naught of wisdom, had but few desires.
They lived each day as life itself compelled,
Marked no tomorrow for all it might have held.
Friendless in life and all alone in death
They left but dust—yet men have given it breath.

W.E.S.

PREFACE

The thirty-four years that have passed since I wrote a previous book on the subject have seen a wave, almost a tidal wave, of publications on dinosaurs and related groups of reptiles and on their environments. Many excellent monographs and books have appeared and to attempt to keep up to date with this flow of information has become a full-time task. This book differs in many respects from the earlier one, in concept, arrangement and in the text. It is virtually a new book.

The intervening years have also been fruitful in that I have been able to visit almost all the main collections of dinosaurs in the world and have seen many of the historical excavation sites, especially in North America. Many hitherto unknown facts about the early history of dinosaur discovery have been unravelled and are presented here.

In a world torn by dissension and distrust it is pleasant to be able to repeat what I said earlier about scientists and museum officials. The years intervening have been marked by close association with and great kindness from many fellow workers, which I record with gratitude and recall with pleasure. I hope that some of this pleasure may prove transmissible and will reach the reader.

But the passage of the years has deprived me of many friends referred to in the text; especially do I regret the loss, now many years ago, of Vernon Edwards whose line restoration-drawings and three-dimensional models for photography did so much to enliven the earlier book. Since that time Mr Neave Parker has produced many a notable restoration scene for me and would have illustrated this edition but death has claimed him too.

Toronto, June, 1968   W.E.S.

CONTENTS

ILLUSTRATIONS

FIGURES

These plates were drawn by Neave Parker with the collaboration of the author and are reproduced from *The Illustrated London News*.

CHAPTER I

Introduction

Interest in dinosaurs is widespread, even if in the case of the general public it often rests on serious misconceptions. The dinosaurs are often thought to have been a series of giant and fierce animals that dominated the earth and then quite suddenly and mysteriously disappeared. The facts that many dinosaurs were small and harmless and that some kinds were becoming extinct all through dinosaurian history are unknown or apparently uninteresting to that public. Many cartoonists on paper, on film and on television are determined to associate dinosaurs with men, so that all too often fact struggles ineffectively with fiction in this branch of palaeontology.

Despite all this, for those of more serious intent the story of dinosaurian discovery is fascinating; the men involved and their expeditions were often part of the history of land settlement and civilization. Hundreds of specimens and thousands of bones have been found and have been studied as closely as clues in a detective story, often to yield a clear picture of much scientific value.

Bones give clues to size and to relationship and also bear witness to the muscles that once invested them or were attached to them. It is thus possible to make illustrations of regions of the body covered in their muscles (see Fig. 1). Imprints of the skin pattern are occasionally found, and eggs have been known for many years from England and France as well as from the more recent and more spectacular discoveries in the Gobi Desert of Mongolia.

Sometimes the bones bear evidences of accident or disease.

17

Now and then it is possible to make casts of brain cavities and thus assess the relative, if not the actual, development of the senses. A knowledge of reptilian anatomy and physiology makes it plausible to suggest certain similarities of perception or behaviour in dinosaurs. Plant remains in the same deposits give a clue to the background of vegetation, and other fossils disclose at least a part of the contemporary animal life. The pitting of old rocks by rain drops and the ripple marks of now-vanished seas all help to complete the complex picture of the life of the past and its environment.

FIG. 1. Restoration of musculature of *Chasmosaurus*. (From L. S. Russell) 1935.

Such a rounded appreciation of the life and geography of dinosaur times is absolutely necessary if we are to avoid thinking of dinosaurs as over-dominant or virtually alone on the lands. The dinosaurs were not just precursors of mammals and men on the same kind of geological stage. The Mesozoic Era, that well-known Age of Reptiles, was vastly different in its geography, climatology, atmosphere and in the temperature range of its lands and seas from the ages that succeeded it. Indeed these physical conditions were integral parts of the making of the Age of Reptiles and their modification was largely responsible for subsequent changes in fauna and flora and in genera and species.

One can ask such questions—and expect nowadays to find answers to them—as what was the general distribution of oxygen and carbon dioxide in the Mesozoic? What was the effect of ultra-violet light in those days, the temperature tolerance of large reptiles and indeed the possibility of their

18

being homoiothermal, in the general background as revealed by palaeotemperature analysis? How is dinosaurian distribution related to the theories or the facts of continental drift and how is their topography revealed by recent studies of palaeomagnetic fields? Only as a result of such questionings and studies is it possible to give a satisfactory account of the evolution of dinosaurs and of the contemporary rise of the mammals. The inauguration of the Trias and the close of the Cretaceous are more than marks on a geological calendar and they are separated by more than years.

The main purpose of the text must be the descriptive palaeontology of the dinosaurs themselves, to which we can now add the early history of the discovery and recognition of their remains and the story of international dinosaurian exploration. With this general background of knowledge one can hope to discuss meaningfully the life of dinosaurs, the question of growth rates, individual age, the evidence of accident and disease and eventually, of course, the problem of extinction.

Details of the most important localities for finding dinosaurs are given. In reference to this one may stress here the importance of training in handling the materials, such as is acquired in museums. In saying this one does not imply that students or experts on dinosaurs are all in museums but one must warn against the assumption, which is all too frequently made, that a zoologically or geologically qualified person is automatically competent to hunt, find, excavate, prepare, repair and exhibit dinosaur (or any other) bones. There is a great deal of specialized technique in these matters that is best acquired in museums where there are facilities for appropriate training from persons of long practical experience. Many specimens of potential value have been ruined by bad collecting, insecure shipping, or unskilful development (preparation) in the laboratory.

Finally, there must be lists of the principal collections throughout the world where the prizes of skilful collection and treatment are on display. The list of British dinosaurs, which was an appendix to my earlier book, has been omitted as these dinosaurs have been very considerably revised and dealt with elsewhere. They are referred to here when appropriate.

19

Throughout these pages, wherever it is practicable, I refer to or quote original sources. This is because of the difficulty, in many parts of the world, of gaining access to original descriptions, especially in those universities and museums of recent foundation. The benefits of a good research library cannot be sufficiently stressed.

CHAPTER II

The Discovery of Dinosaurs

There is no history; only biography
EMERSON *History*

Dinosaur remains are now known from every continent except Antarctica and their wide distribution in Mesozoic rocks must surely mean that the chances of their discovery must for long have been great. It can be assumed that over the years many men have been familiar with bones and footprints that were sufficiently striking to be noteworthy, but whose origin and meaning were unknown to the observers. We are not likely to discover now what they thought about the remains though some local legends may well derive from such observations. We can, however, assume that they were not the founders of such hardy superstitions as the dragon myths, which seem to have arisen in many countries and are highly characteristic. Moreover, these dragon myths have been largely explained by Professor Elliot Smith without the aid of the dinosaurs.

We do know that American Indians spun some exciting stories based on fossil tree trunks, which they thought were bones, and red coloured lava flows which they considered to be congealed blood. Many of the large bones could, of course, have been those of other large animals, such as mammoths, and not necessarily of dinosaurs. Yet, dinosaur bones must have become familiar to the rising tide of pilgrims to America's golden West. Even today the tracks of the pioneers can be seen and the ruts made by wagon wheels on the Californian trail still clearly mark journeys made over dinosaurian country in the great Mid-West. Perhaps the coming of the railroads did most to bring the bones to notice and, of course, to facilitate their collection. It is, therefore, natural that some of the picturesque

THE DINOSAURS

names of middle-west townships and whistle stops have become
familiar to the student of dinosaurs. This is especially so along
the Union Pacific Railroad that crosses Wyoming and Colorado
and reminds us of discoveries at Bone Cabin, Como Bluff,
Green River, Medicine Bow and Laramie.

Dinosaur history is, however, older than this in the United
States. Dr G. G. Simpson has quoted from a record of the
American Philosophical Society: 'Oct. 5, 1787, (*Proc.*) A large
thigh bone found near Woodbury Creek in Glocester [*sic*]
county, N. J. (perhaps a Hadrosaurus), was described in a paper
by Mr Matlack and Dr Wistar; who, with Dr Rodgers, were
requested to search for the missing part of the skeleton.'
Dr Simpson adds: 'If the Secretary's conjecture bracketed in
the printed version is correct, as it may be, this was the first
dinosaur found in North America, or probably in the world, but
verification is now impossible and this cannot be a true
discovery.'

It can only be added that this is an intriguing record. The
name *Hadrosaurus* was not in use until 1858, so the Secretary's
comment must have been made much later. As we shall see
there is an earlier English record that is more substantial.

Footprints, as compared with bones, have long been well
known, and those discovered by Pliny Moody of South Hadley,
Massachusetts, are well documented. Pliny Moody was a farm
boy and the tracks he found were thought to have been made
by large birds, like ostriches, and some, with even more
imagination, called them prints of 'Noah's raven'. South
Hadley has become a famous locality both for prints and bones
in the red Triassic sandstones of which Hitchcock wrote with
great enthusiasm and which are also fully described in Lull's
Triassic Life of the Connecticut Valley. In these publications it
was, of course, recognized that the so-called bird footprints and
bones were those of dinosaurs.

Bones appear to have been found first in the United States
at East Windsor, Connecticut, in 1818, and these have been
identified as *Anchisaurus*, a large prosauropod named in 1885.
However, the earliest remains of dinosaurs in the United States
for which we have continued records of discovery, description
and availability for re-examination, were obtained on expedi-

22

THE DISCOVERY OF DINOSAURS

tions by Dr Ferdinand Vandeveer Hayden to the area in northern Montana where the north-running Judith river meets the Missouri. Dr Hayden, a surgeon, found some teeth in 1855 that were described in the following year by another medical man, Dr Joseph Leidy, of the Academy of Natural Sciences in Philadelphia, where Dr Leidy was also Professor of Anatomy in the University of Pennsylvania.

The teeth produced the type-specimen of *Trachodon mirabilis*, a hadrosaur (tooth registered No. 9260, Philadelphia Acad. Nat. Sci.), and a tooth of a ceratopsian later identified as *Monoclonius*. A little later Dr Hayden found two vertebrae and a toe bone from a locality on the Grand River which is now in South Dakota. These specimens, the two caudal vertebrae and the phalanx, became the type-specimens of Leidy's *Thespesius occidentalis*, also a hadrosaur. These bones are preserved in the United States National Museum (Nos. 219–221) and were refigured by Lull and Wright in 1942, p. 151.

These discoveries, it will be noted, were all of isolated bones or teeth and the first partial skeleton of a dinosaur to be discovered in the United States was unearthed in 1858 at Haddonfield, New Jersey. This town is only a few miles east of Philadelphia, over the River Delaware. A Philadelphia man, Mr W. P. Foulke, was visiting the district and heard that bones had been discovered earlier in a pit in a field belonging to a farmer, Mr John E. Hopkin. He found that the bones had disappeared but persuaded Mr Hopkin to reopen the pit. In this operation nine teeth, a lower jaw, small parts of upper jaws, twenty-eight vertebrae and the bones of fore and hind limbs were excavated. These were all sent to Dr Joseph Leidy at the Academy of Natural Sciences in Philadelphia, where they still are (No. 10005 ANSP; 9201–9203 ANSP). They were named *Hadrosaurus foulkii*.

It is interesting to note that Mr Waterhouse Hawkins, the English sculptor who made the Crystal Palace models in London in 1854, visited the United States thereafter and, in 1868, set up the Haddonfield bones, with a considerable amount of plaster, as a skeleton. This was dismantled during the last war. The curious skull was mainly the invention of Waterhouse Hawkins. The original bones—limb bones, vertebrae and teeth—

23

amounting to about one-third of the whole reconstruction are now shown in a small case in the Academy.

Farmers and railroaders, pioneers and professors have since found bones and even skeletons, and have uncovered footprints that are now famous. Some of the bones became doorstops, others were incorporated into the walls of cabins, while those collected with such vigour by the great Othniel Charles Marsh of Yale and Edward Drinkwater Cope, of Philadelphia, are the main pillars on which much of the dinosaurian story rests, and of those historic excavations and expeditions that are recounted in later pages.

In Canada the story is not quite so old, the early activity not so great. Neither pioneers nor railmen contributed much to the discoveries. The first alleged dinosaur bone was found, however, under interesting circumstances. Lieutenant Sherard Osborn was in command of the steam tender *Pioneer*, which was part of the expedition under Admiral Sir Edward Belcher in the search for Sir John Franklin in 1853, when he found a vertebra in Triassic beds at Rendezvous Mountain at the north end of Bathurst Island, in what is now the North West Territories. The specimen was given or sent to Professor A. Leith Adams in Trinity College, Dublin, and was described as a cervical of a new genus and species of dinosaur, *Arctosaurus osborni*, in 1875. The specimen is still in Dublin but a cast of it has long been in the British Museum (Natural History) in London where it is registered as R.1611 in the Department of Palaeontology. It was regarded for many years as evidence of a prosauropod dinosaur but more recent opinion is that the vertebra is chelonian and thus the Canadian Arctic loses its lone representative.

Another Canadian 'dinosaur' had a short-lived history. This was the jaw fragment collected in Prince Edward Island in the 1850s that came into the possession of J. W. Dawson, of Pictou, Nova Scotia, and into the knowledge of Sir Charles Lyell, the great geologist. Lyell mentioned the specimen to Dr Leidy, of the Academy of Natural Sciences, Philadelphia, and several members of that institution, including Leidy, subscribed to buy it. On the supposition that it was another of these creatures which made tracks like those in the Trias

THE DISCOVERY OF DINOSAURS

Connecticut Valley, Leidy mistook its age as Trias and named it in 1854 *Bathygnathus borealis*. Since that time it has been recognized as a pelycosaurian reptile of Permian Age, with affinities in Texas rather than in New England. The specimen is in the Academy of Natural Sciences, Philadelphia (No. 9524).

On the mainland of Canada, Dr George Mercer Dawson was the first person to discover dinosaur remains of undoubted authenticity. Dawson was a remarkable man, the second son of the great Canadian geologist, Sir William Dawson, and was educated at McGill University, where his father was Principal, and at the Royal School of Mines in London, where he came under the influence of Thomas Henry Huxley, among other great teachers. Returning to Canada in 1873 young Dawson was appointed a geologist and naturalist on Her Majesty's North American Boundary Commission and became engaged in mapping part of the 49th parallel in collaboration with a United States party.

In the middle of 1874, when the parties were in the neighbourhood of Wood Mountain, in what is now Saskatchewan (approx. 49°N, 106°W), Dawson found fossil bones that were subsequently identified by Professor E. D. Cope as including a hadrosaurian. The locality of this historic discovery is more firmly fixed by L. S. Russell (1966) as in Morgan Creek, six miles west of Killdeer. The bone may be in the National Collections in Ottawa, though at the time of its discovery Dawson was not a member of the Geological Survey. A little later, in July 1874, Dawson made a second discovery, on the Milk River, in what is now south-western Saskatchewan. These bones and teeth were also sent to Professor Cope and were the basis of the evidence for Cope's *Cionodon stenopsis*, a hadrosaurian whose name is now regarded as a synonym of *Thespesius*. The specimens are supposedly now in the American Museum of Natural History, New York, with the rest of the Cope Collection.

Despite the richness of the subsequent collections made in the United States and Canada and the number and distinction of workers in the field of vertebrate palaeontology, it is to England that we must go for the authentic origin of dinosaurian history. Much of this is now well known but interest in dinosaurian history as history is relatively recent and some of the discoveries are described in these pages for the first time.

The earliest record of a dinosaur bone of which I am aware is that figured and described by Dr Robert Plot, first keeper of the Ashmolean Museum and Professor of 'Chymistry' at Oxford University, in *The Natural History of Oxford-Shire* (first edition, 1677, tab. VIII, fig. 4, and p. 131). Referring to 'Stones', Dr Plot says, 'I have one dug out of a quarry in the Parish of *Cornwell*, and given me by the ingenious Sir *Thomas Pennyston*, that has exactly the Figure of the lowermost part of the *Thigh-Bone* of a *Man* or at least of some other *Animal*, with *capita Femoris inferiora*, between which are the *anterior* (hid behind the *sculpture*) and the larger *posterior Sinus* the seat of the strong *Ligament* that rises out of the *Thigh*, and that gives safe passage to the *Vessels* descending into the *Leg*: and a little above the *Sinus*, where it seems to have been broken off, shewing the marrow within of a shining *Spar-like* Substance of its true Colour and Figure, in the *hollow* of the *Bone*, as in *Tab. 8. Fig. 4.* In Compass near the *capita Femoris* just two Foot, and at the top above the *Sinus* (where the *Thigh-Bone* is as small as any where) about 15 inches; in weight, though representing so short a part of the *Thigh-Bone*, almost 20 pounds.'

He goes on to talk of petrifaction, and of plastic powers but comes to the conclusion that 'this Stone of ours . . . must have been a real *Bone*, now *Petrified*', and considerably later in his argument 'that it must have belonged to some greater *animal* than either an *Ox* or *Horse*; and if so in probability it must have been the *Bone* of some *Elephant*, brought hither during the Government of the *Romans* in *Britain*.' He then spends much time in arguing about the movements of elephants in Roman times.

The bone did not escape the notice of John Phillips in his *Geology of Oxford* (1871, p. 164) who says 'it may have been the femur of a large megalosaurus or small ceteosaurus'. Phillips also points out 'that the reference [on Plot's plate] to paragraph 155 of Chap. V is wrong; the description being in paragraph 157'. This is correct so far as Plot's *second* edition (London 1705) is concerned. The figure in the first edition has no reference to a paragraph.

I have no knowledge of the present resting place of the bone and I have not been able to trace the effects or descendants of the 'ingenious Sir Thomas Pennyston'.

Another interesting specimen, also part of a thigh bone and from Oxfordshire, is that described by Joshua Platt. In 1755 Joshua Platt, of Oxford, had found three large vertebrae and had sent them to the well-known Quaker mercer and naturalist, Peter Collinson, who lived in the Lake District. Mr Collinson was much more than a local figure. He was a botanist of international repute and was much in communication with the scientists of America. His experience was wide and it is therefore not peculiar that Mr Platt should have sought his advice.

Alas, there is no evidence as to the opinion on the vertebrae but late in 1757 Joshua Platt made another discovery, that of a fossil thigh-bone at, presumably, the same site in the Stonesfield Slate near Woodstock, Oxford. The news of this discovery was given in a letter from Mr Platt to Peter Collinson: 'About three years ago I sent you some vertebrae of enormous size found in the slate-stone pit at Stonesfield, near Woodstock in this county. I have lately been so lucky as to find a thigh bone.' This he did not send, for the bone and the stone in which it was partly embedded weighed 200 pounds. But Mr Platt had a very good drawing of it made (by J. Mynde) and he gave a brief description of it. This letter, with the drawing, was published in the *Philosophical Transactions of the Royal Society* (Vol. 50, 1758, pp. 524–7, Pl. XIX) at the instance of Mr Collinson who was a Fellow of the Society.

The bone fragment was an incomplete left femur 29 inches long, with a maximum width of 8 inches and a minimum width (across the shaft) of 4 inches. The shape and proportions are very much those of the left femur figured and described in John Phillip's *Geology of Oxford* (p. 281) and referred to as *Cetiosaurus oxoniensis* in the *Catalogue of Fossil Reptilia and Amphibia* in the British Museum (Lydekker, 1888, Vol. 1, p. 138) but Platt's specimen seems to have been proportionately a little longer. The bone was found by the slate miners who worked the Stonesfield Slate by the 'stoop and room' method; he saw it on the roof of one of the cleared areas (room) among

27

the shells of many sickle-oysters (*Ostrea acuminata*) as the workmen call them.

Contemporary opinion was, or Mr Platt presumed, that the fossil was the remains of one of the victims of the deluge. He compared it with the leg of elephants and noted the differences and he came to the conclusion it was perhaps a hippopotamus or a rhinoceros bone. Others, more geologically famous, were to reach similar conclusions about other dinosaur bones in later years.

Much of Joshua Platt's collection went to Christopher (later Sir Christopher) Sykes of Wheldrake, Yorks. The collection was catalogued in 1772 and republished in *The Naturalist* in 1934 by C. Davies Sherborn. There the thigh bone appears priced at four shillings. Some twenty pieces from the collection eventually passed to the British Museum in 1933, but the thigh bone and vertebrae were not among them.

Joshua Platt's record and illustration leave no doubt that this well-authenticated specimen is an identifiable dinosaur bone and is the second earliest record in England. Even this may seem strange because the Oxford Jurassic deposits were long known to be fossiliferous and interesting. As we have seen, Dr Robert Plot was interested, and his successor in the museum, Edward Lhwyd, who became curator in 1690, compiled a work entitled *Lithophylacium Britannicum* describing the fossils he had in the museum, but no large bones are mentioned.

More than sixty years after Platt had found the bone of *Cetiosaurus* we come to the foundation of real and continuing interest in what were to be the dinosaurs of England. There are two contenders for the paternal role: Gideon Algernon Mantell and James Parkinson. Each published, in 1822, descriptions or comments on what we now know to be dinosaurs.

Slender priority goes to Gideon Mantell who published *The Fossils of the South Downs; or Illustrated Geology of Sussex* in London in May, 1822. In this work the author describes and figures some teeth found by his wife at the side of a country road in Sussex. Dr Mantell was a medical practitioner who lived at Lewes in Sussex. A hard working, ambitious man, he travelled considerable distances to see his patients and yet found time to be archaeologist, botanist, geologist, writer and diarist. Early in 1822 he visited a patient in the Cuckfield district of Sussex. Mrs Mantell had travelled with him in his carriage and, while the doctor made his medical call, she wandered along the country road, stopping at a pile of road-metal, the term in Britain for broken stone for mending roads and filling ruts. The stone was Tilgate Stone, a hard calcareous grit that is found in the Wadhurst clay of the Sussex weald. It seldom occurs in great thickness and there are also sandstones in the same formation.

On pieces of the grit she saw some teeth embedded, which she collected and showed to her husband. He realized with remarkable prescience that she had found parts of an animal new to science. The specimens were figured in the book published a few months later. Mantell was puzzled by the identity of the animal. The teeth were those of a herbivorous creature, but in 1822 there were rather restricted ideas on the age of the deposits and the time range of reptiles and mammals. It was highly desirable to discover more specimens and especially bones.

The Fossils of the South Downs has a plate of a Sussex quarry and this has been reproduced recently in Plate 5 of Dr E. H. Colbert's *Dinosaurs* (New York, 1961). In the upper left-hand corner of that plate the spire of Cuckfield Parish Church is clearly seen, so that the location of the quarry could be discovered. However, the text informs a careful reader that the quarry was filled in before the publication of the plate. There is, however, ample proof that Mantell was very active in searching for materials in quarries near Cuckfield and his diary records frequent visits.

In an endeavour to locate the scene of Mantell's quarry, which he never revealed in case rivals invaded his field, the present writer made intensive searches in Mantell's manuscripts and diaries. These searches brought little but they did lead to a visit from a lady who most unexpectedly produced the original of a drawing of the quarry. This drawing had been made by Mr K. W. Cooke, R.A. on August 21, 1872 and showed a party from the British Association visiting what was clearly described as Mantell's Quarry, near Cuckfield. In that year the Association held its Annual Meeting in Brighton and it is clear that there was no mystery about the quarry's location in 1872.

This illustration was reproduced by E. Casier in *Les Iguanodons de Bernissart* (1960, p. 34). In the late 1950s things were different. There was no such quarry and no convenient windmill as a guide. I was none the less attracted to an obviously filled-in region near Wightman's Green where I knew Mantell had been, and to an old quarry further to the west. It was while visiting the latter one day that I felt bold enough to visit a large house nearby and discovered it was called Mill House; but no one remembered a windmill or a quarry. With the help of my former British Museum colleague, Thomas Wooddisse, who came to live in Cuckfield, we discovered a very old man, in his nineties, who remembered that as a boy he had seen a windmill where the house now stood and as a young man he had helped to fill in the quarry where there was now only a depression and a little wood.

We can be fairly certain that, along this road and in the dell, Dr Mantell pursued the studies that led in 1825 to his giving the name *Iguanodon* to the teeth and bones, discovered by his wife, which had spurred his interest and invention. He sent a tooth of *Iguanodon*, collected by himself, to New Zealand where his son became a member of the House of Representatives, declaring in writing that 'this is the first tooth ever discovered'.

In *The Geology of the South East of England*, published in 1833, Mantell wrote (on p. 268) that the teeth had been discovered 'by Mrs Mantell in the Spring of 1822', and he refers to the figure of the teeth on p. 54 of the earlier work. But it is curious that his diary, which he kept fairly regularly from January 1, 1819 until June 14, 1852, makes no mention of the momentous discovery in the spring of 1822, and there is no entry between January 1st and May 1st in that year. On May 1st he has completed the dedication of his *Illustrations of the Geology of Sussex* as he calls it, and presumably the earlier months were occupied by his labours as an author. The labours of Mantell to establish himself as a prominent geologist and discoverer of fossils will be recalled in the appropriate places in the text descriptive of *Iguanodon* but his claim to fame firmly rests upon the fact that in May 1822 he published and figured dinosaurian materials which can still be examined or referred to.

In the same year, but in July, James Parkinson published a

small book entitled *Outlines of Oryctology, An Introduction to the Study of Fossil Organic Remains especially of those found in the British Strata* (London, 1822). James Parkinson was a remarkable man. Born in 1755 he had studied under the great anatomist John Hunter and became a medical practitioner in London. He is remembered today as the identifier of Parkinson's disease or the shaking palsy (*paralysis agitans*), but he was also a keen geologist and one of the founders of the Geological Society of London. He published many medical, political and palaeontological papers but his book of 1822 is important because it contains the first mention of a dinosaur's generic name. On page 298 of that work, Parkinson writes 'Megalosaurus (*Megalos* great, saurus a lizard). An animal apparently approaching the *Monitor* in its mode of dentition, and not yet described. It is found in the calcareous slate of Stonefield, subordinate to the upper part of the lower or great oolite series, including the forest marble. Drawings have been made of the most essential parts of the animal, now in the Museum in Oxford; and it is hoped a description may be shortly given to the public. The animal must in some instances, have attained a length of forty feet, and stood eight feet high.'

This statement is important historically and some writers claim that it is the earliest indication of dinosaurian material that is still available to us. These bones were in the Ashmolean Museum, at that time in Broad Street. The University Museum, which now houses many important historical specimens including *Megalosaurus*, was not opened until 1860.

It is also maintained by some that Parkinson's use of the name *Megalosaurus* is the first dinosaurian generic name ever used. To establish a name for an animal adherence must be made to certain international rules. In earlier times these could be enumerated as a description, definition or indication.

Megalosaurus is not described in Parkinson's words, as he himself implies, and it is not defined. *The International Code of Zoological Nomenclature*, which also applies to fossil animals, specifically states (Article 16 b(i)), 'mention of a vernacular name, type locality, geological horizon, host or a label or specimen in a collection' does not constitute an indication. Since we also know from Platt's discovery that at least another large dinosaur existed in the Stonesfield slate, it does not appear that the name *Megalosaurus* can be claimed to be validly established on Parkinson's description, and it becomes therefore a *nomen nudum*.

We find that Parkinson's *Megalosaurus* as an indication, in the ordinary sense of the word, that there was a dinosaur represented in the Stonesfield Slate is predated by Mantell's mention and figure of specimens, though no name was given to them.

The bones in Oxford were described in detail under the name *Megalosaurus* by the Rev. William Buckland, F.R.S., Professor of Mineralogy and Geology in the University of Oxford, in 1824. It is said that the name itself, meaning 'large lizard', was the joint composition of Buckland and his friend, the Rev. W. D. Conybeare.

Following the establishment of this first dinosaurian genus, dinosaurian discovery proceeded with some speed. *Iguanodon*, as a name, was founded, as we have seen, in the following year, though teeth and bones had been known since 1822. Mantell was busier than ever uncovering the fossils of Sussex. It must have been a special pleasure for him to discover *Megalosaurus* in the Tilgate Forest and demonstrate his finds to Professor Buckland.

At the same time he began to develop an apparently strange conceit. It was that as his fame increased as a collector of fossils and as a geological author, so should his medical practice increase among the people of quality. He had been hard-working and successful in Lewes so perhaps a move to Brighton, a large and fashionable seaside resort, would result in fame and wealth. He made the move in the beginning of 1834 and on May 1st wrote in his diary: 'My reception in this town has certainly been very flattering so far as visitors and visitings have been concerned but my professional prospects are not encouraging.' His museum grew in quantity by collecting and donation and people came in considerable numbers to see the specimens.

Towards the end of 1835 there were several of Mantell's friends interested in forming a public museum or Scientific Institution, and by April 1836 the house, No. 20 the Steine, which is now a hotel, was given over to the purposes of a museum. However there was no success with the movement to found a permanent public museum around his own collection and though greatly disappointed, he sold his collection to the Government for £4000 (then $20,000) on March 4, 1839. The Government bought the collection for the British Museum and, in the following August, Mantell duly received the money from the Museum Trustees.

In 1832 Mantell had described his *Hylaeosaurus* ('wood-lizard') to the Geological Society and its name stems from the publication of that description. This was an armoured dinosaur and, with *Iguanodon*, was the first of his collection to be put on display in the British Museum, where we know Mantell saw them in July 1841. By that date, thanks to the enthusiasm and labours of Mantell, Buckland and others, three recognized 'dinosaurs' had been collected and described and thus had valid names. They were *Megalosaurus*, a carnivore (1824); *Iguanodon*, a herbivore (1825) and *Hylaeosaurus*, an armoured form (1832).

In 1841 Richard Owen, M.D., F.R.S., who was Professor of Comparative Anatomy at the Royal College of Surgeons in London, was engaged in a lengthy and detailed *Report on British Fossil Reptiles*. The first part was produced for the Annual Report of the British Association for the Advancement of Science and was published in 1840. The second part, ostensibly from a report to the Meeting of the Association at Plymouth in July 1841, was actually published in 1842 and it is in this, on page 102, that Owen first introduced the word Dinosaurians to the world. On page 103 he refers to 'a distinct tribe or sub-order of Saurian Reptiles, for which I would propose the name of Dinosauria', and in a footnote he defines this as '*deinos*, fearfully great; *sauros*, a lizard'. The tribe or sub-order included the three genera already mentioned. It is in this work that Owen establishes (p. 94) the genus *Cetiosaurus* for massive bones, particularly vertebrae, from the Isle of Wight, from the Tilgate Forest of Sussex, and from Buckingham and Oxford. There is no mention of bones such as we know were seen by Plot in 1677 or Platt in 1755 and 1758 and Owen concluded in this report that *Cetiosaurus* 'may be presumed to have been of strictly aquatic and most probably of marine habits'. He classified it in 1841 as a Crocodile, and, indeed this reference is still maintained in the second edition of Owen's *Palaeontology* (1861), p. 301.

The point is more than pedantic. We now know that *Cetiosaurus* is an amphibious herbivore or sauropod and thus, though he did not quite recognize it, Owen had in 1841 one representative of each of the four major groups of dinosaurs that we now recognize.

The dinosaurs, those fearfully great dinosaurs, were well and truly founded and the passage of the subsequent years has shown the richness of the contents of many a geological deposit in many a land. Lands and dinosaurs were reunited and given names that none of them had borne when the lands were being shaped and the dinosaurs were alive.

CHAPTER III

The Environment of Dinosaurs

So geographers, in Afric maps,
With savage pictures fill their gaps,
And over uninhabitable downs
Place dinosaurs for want of towns.

SWIFT *Poetry*, emended

The earliest dinosaurs that we know in the geological record are forms of carnivores, *Thecodontosaurus primus* von Huene and *Zanclodon silesiacus* Jaekel which, as listed in 1938 by Martin Schmidt, come from the Lower Wellenkalk of Germany. This early stage is to be equated with the Anisian Stage of the Lower Trias and thus precedes the Landinian that contains the Santa Maria Formation of Brazil. From this last have come the remains of the clumsy vegetarian *Spondylosoma absconditum*, that may not in fact be a dinosaur but was described as one by von Huene in 1942.

There are also the bones of *Saltopus elginensis*, a little carnivore, from the Middle Trias of Scotland and also described by von Huene as long ago as 1910. Not all of these names will remain after consideration of their systematic characters but they are thus rooted in the literature, as compared with the latest record (*The Fossil Record*, 1968) which classes the earliest dinosaurs as of Stübensandstone (i.e. late Triassic) age. However, the beginning can be dated as about 200 million years ago.

The very last dinosaurs are no more easily selected but by Lance times, or its equivalents in North America, Europe, India, Mongolia and Patagonia, the dinosaurs were on their last legs and making their last stands. This stage of the Cretaceous can also be dated approximately, as sixty-three million years ago. These dates are based on radioactive potassium–argon data.

Thus over most of the continents, with the exception so far of Antarctica, dinosaurs lived through some 140 million years.

35

This is an impressive span of time which, even if dated back from this very moment, still brings us to early dinosaur times in the Jurassic. Obviously an immense amount of animal and plant variation and development, of geological and climatic change, must have been accomplished in this great period of time. Given our very recently computerized data of continental drift and palaeomagnetic variations, there must have been a great deal of geographical change. It is possible now to consider the Mesozoic in ways which were quite impossible thirty years ago and to derive, from the latest advances of the physical sciences, data which shed a new light on the lifetime of dinosaurs, quite apart from the quantitative increase in our knowledge of dinosaurs gained by new discoveries and new studies in these same decades.

There is thus no question of bringing up to date the maps founded on the works of Arldt and of Gregory and Barrett that illustrated the Jurassic and Cretaceous worlds in the first edition of this book. A wholly new arrangement of the continents is to be explained, and this in turn makes easier the explanation of many of the difficulties of the surprising constancy in the world-wide distribution of the dinosaurs.

This geographical change is sometimes a difficulty for the young palaeontologist. He is prepared to find changes in fauna and flora in the world of the past, but it is apparently hard for him to accept the fact that the hills do not last for aye or the continents remain static. Some of this difficulty undoubtedly comes from our too frequent use of Mercator's projection on our maps. Flattering as this was to the British Empire, by stretching its more northerly and southerly parts, it confuses size (Greenland is slightly larger than South America on such maps although South America is twelve times the size of Greenland) and makes a realization of continental relationships more difficult, though for navigators at sea its maps (and charts) have advantages. A more conical projection, such as the Sanson-Flamsteed Sinusoidal, gives a more top-like appearance in which the equatorial line is more obvious.

It is at this line that the relationships between the Pernambuco region of eastern South America and the Gulf of Guinea region of West Africa seem to be so opposable and one can believe

36

more readily that the top-like rotation of the earth from west to east could produce drifting in a floating continental mass.

We know now that the continents are less dense than the heavier under-ocean rocks and that these continents on which we live float, like ice, upon the denser, underlying mantle. The cause of the drift is less well explained and has not yet gained complete acceptance. There is no doubt that there is now evidence in favour of it that is fairly general knowledge and must find scientific acceptance too.

Australia, for example, has a remarkable fauna of marsupials so diversified that the continental mass must have been separated off from adjoining continents at the time when marsupials were well distributed in other parts of the world. They have become extinct in nearly all these other parts but have been saved and diversified in Australia by its very isolation. But Australia also has large dinosaurs with possible African affinities. From these it can be suggested that Australian separation took place in late Jurassic or very early Cretaceous times. The relationship of Indian fossils also suggests that there were once closer associations with Africa than now appear possible.

We have the superficial resemblance between the South American and the West African coasts and recent studies show that in several parts of the world, including the Maritime region of Canada, continental movement can be verified and actually measured. It may be asked whether this continental movement has always been going on, or if there was aggregation of lands to form the more southerly continent before this drift began, and why, of course, so spectacular a fragmentation should have been inaugurated in the late Palaeozoic or early Mesozoic. Palaeomagnetic evidence, that is, evidence of the former directions of the magnetic pole which is 'fixed' or fossilized in some ancient minerals, seems to show great wandering of the magnetic pole. Unfortunately, although such magnetized materials give direction and can be made to suggest latitude, they do not give longitude, so that their influence is not wholly satisfactory for orientation and the establishment of what it was precisely that moved—the pole or the continent upon which the palaeomagnetic evidence is now located. Quite recent evidence clearly indicates that the problems are more easily solved if it is accepted that the continents moved.

This movement of continental masses is of great importance in understanding the environment in which dinosaurs developed and became widely distributed. Some such a movement could be anticipated if the geographical factors are considered. The oceans greatly exceed the combined lands in area and, if these lands were together in one continent, a marked degree of eccentricity might be introduced into the earth's orbit. If the earth were on a truly vertical axis this eccentricity could be part of the centrifugal force at the equator.

The earth's axis is not, however, vertical but is usually at an angle, often quite a considerable angle, and in 1968 this inclination is $23\frac{1}{2}°$. This tilt is the cause of the seasons in a world whose continents are distributed as now. If in the late Palaeozoic geological periods the continents were connected *en masse* on the southern side of the equator this would explain the distribution of ice-age deposits that we now find separately in South America, South Africa, India and Australia. This geographical condition can be seen in the 'reconstruction of the Continents for the Upper Palaeozoic', reproduced here, by permission, as Figure 2. For comparison there is also reproduced (Figure 3) Sir Edward Bullard's reconstruction for mid-Mesozoic time.

Perhaps it is possible that the forces inherent in the unequally balanced crust in early Mesozoic time caused a convection current of the underlying mantle rock and thus begin a movement in which the African and South American continents were gradually forced apart, the latter swinging to the westwards about a pivot in what is now the Canadian Shield. Two notable pieces of evidence support this: first the crumpling of the western side of North and South America along the ploughing front of these continents and the longer, dragged-out continental shelf of the eastern side of the more southerly parts of these continents; on the other hand, the reverse situation can be seen on the physical maps of Africa, India and Australia; that is, there is a ploughing that culminates in the great zone of mountain building and volcanic and earthquake activity that runs along north-west Africa, through Italy, into Turkey, across the Himalayas of India and on and down into Indonesia. In the Atlantic the Mid-Atlantic Ridge stands as witness to the movement, as does the Indian Ocean crest if contemporaneity of these structures can be proved.

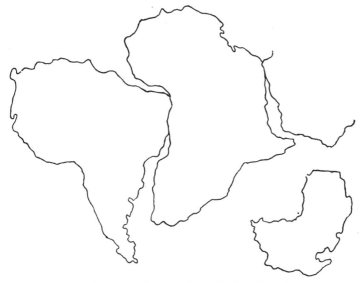

FIG. 2. The southern continents in the Mesozoic.

At any rate the age of the partition would appear to be before the end of the Lower Cretaceous, or Mid-Mesozoic time. This is exemplified by the Wealden in England and the rather earlier beds in Tanzania (Tendaguru beds). There are no Australian dinosaurs of later date and there is a reasonably good relationship of European and Asian dinosaurs at this time. However, the widest common representation of the dinosaurs of America (mainly North America), Europe and Africa occurs in Middle or Upper Jurassic times.

The evidence of South America does not, unfortunately, help us much in comparison with Africa for there are more Triassic and many more Cretaceous forms than Jurassic in each of these continents. It can be assumed that the number of Cretaceous forms is not too important, for they are the results

39

of independent evolution from earlier stocks. At any rate, the main argument for the shift is geological and the point has been made clear that there is no Cretaceous debris in the Atlantic, which tends to show that the division was in the late Jurassic.

The older palaeogeographic maps, with their west to east continents would seem, of course, to have afforded ample room for development. Subsidence, on the lines of the great rift valley formations that we know in Africa, could have explained the separation of areas once obviously joined but there appears now to be no evidence for this in the oceans. There are apparently no lost dinosaurian 'Atlantises'.

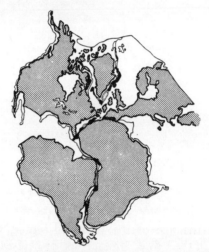

Fig. 3. The continents fitted along the continental shelves. Regions of overlap in black. (After Bullard, Everett and Smith.) Courtesy of *Scientific American*.

On the other hand, the new reconstructions do not wholly demolish the north and south continents that were considered essential to palaeontologists earlier in the century but shapes and names have been changed. Gondwanaland is not lost and its association of Africa, Madagascar, India, Australia and Antarctica explains very easily the distribution of plants, animals, sediments and ores.

On the northern hemisphere the tilt of North America introduced the coast of Labrador to southern Greenland and

40

brought the British Isles within reasonable range of the Canadian Maritimes. The south of Spain fits naturally into or onto Algeria and West Africa was applied to the eastern states of the USA. The northern continent is now known as Laurasia.

Though the exact timing of the break-up is not known, it seems to have started in the late Trias and probably was over by the early Cretaceous. While much of the evidence rests on the remains of fossil plants and fossil vertebrates, the dinosaurs are not very useful in the story, although the continental association of earlier days is useful in explaining their distribution, as we shall see.

Fig. 4. Continents arranged by tin ore belts. (After R. G. Schiuling.)

The life of dinosaurs was, however, affected by much smaller areas than continents. Indeed one can go much further than this and say that each kind of animal, being a biological complex, has its own environment, a set of circumstances that largely hedge, or contain, its development when young, its general viability, and the factors that will contribute to its length of days or years. Environment is a complex equation but an equation none the less and one that all living things must observe. Human beings tend to forget this because some human beings have the intelligence to test the margins of our limitations and the courage occasionally to break through into other and

41

wider conditions of life. This can happen to animals mainly by chance and there are no indications that dinosaurs were more than modestly successful in their bionomic, or ecological, excursions.

What is environment? What is ecology? and what were the relations of the dinosaurs as diversely modified reptiles to these limiting circumstances. Environment is the total world of an animal's life or the existence of a group of animals. It will include the nature of the ground (low-level, high-level, rocky, swampy, etc.), the soil, the vegetation, the temperature, the rainfall, the climate as a whole, and, of course, the other animals whose competition it must meet directly, as predator or prey, or as competitor for food. In other words, it is the external world of experience. In the course of time several of these factors may change so that the life of any group of animals or any individual must be one of adjustment if the living is to be successful. Change in environment can be a spur to new opportunity for success or it may introduce elements to which the animal can make no response. Thus the life of any animal (or plant or human being for that matter) must be a continual adjustment to the external environment. But living things have an environment themselves—their inner living processes, their physiology and metabolism that function in a physical framework that is itself subject to change, accident, injury, disease and decay. So we have the confrontation of two environments in every life. Factors may change in both, factors over which the individual animal can have no control but whose unhappy effects an animal society, if it is at all organized, can often alter or mitigate. Were dinosaurs a society in the zoological sense?

It is obviously difficult to reconstruct the threads of life lived many years ago but the attempt to do so is fascinating for it is nothing less than a great exercise in detection in which we may find criminals that we can never bring to justice and heroes we can never reward.

Although the dinosaurs were never seen alive by any men we have their bones, eggs, imprints of skin and footprints. We can, in many instances, open their skulls and estimate their brain capacities and the *relative* measure of their sense-organs. We can detect disease and, by analogy with modern reptiles, particularly crocodiles, alligators and large lizards, we can reconstruct or estimate their living processes, their anatomy and physiology, with some hope of accuracy. The geological circumstances of their finding, the rocky covering (or matrix) surrounding their bones will tell us something of the circumstances, at least of their burial, and perhaps of their basal environment. We get a clue to the geological landscape more satisfactory than that which Surveyor gave us of the moon. In other words we can get clues to the stratigraphic facies of the fossil. Surveyor is a very recently invented instrument of the space scientist but the geologists have their probes of modern invention too. Radioactive isotopes of oxygen can help to tell us bygone temperatures. We cannot quite put our fingers on the pulse of past ages but we can take their temperatures and we have more radioactive aids to give us the date of the events we are trying to probe or to reconstruct. Other fossils can tell us something of the animals or plants living in the same environment. Occasionally a fossil land surface will show us the marks of raindrops and may reveal the direction of long-vanished prevailing winds.

In very few cases do we ever get anything like a satisfactory statistical sample of the contemporary life. The chances of fossilization or preservation are too great for this, to say nothing of the chances of fossils being found by, or being brought to, someone who can make them meaningful. The medium is the message only in a highly educated society and, in this affluent age, there is little social or financial advantage in being a palaeontologist. But these facts are important. We shall come to see that by the very nature of their habitat certain forms and whole groups of vertebrates, such as the land-living pterosaurs and the birds, have been quite lost to the geological record and must remain blanks in the records of vertebrate evolution.

On the positive side, we can take the Age of Reptiles and divide it into the Triassic, the Jurassic and the Cretaceous geological periods that together we classify as the Mesozoic Era. We can date these periods and furnish them with a quite remarkable list of things on a fairly realistic and probably pretty accurate background, making in all a stage sufficiently broad and deep to provide for the dinosaurs' diversified play.

The Triassic period which saw, as we have said, the emergence of dinosaurs, began some 225 million years ago. It lasted for approximately 45 million years, a period of time that is easy to say but which includes a span far beyond our own comprehension. The same period of time, taken back from today, goes far beyond the remotest inkling of man's ancestry and includes climatic and geographic changes of profound importance.

When we think of the beginning of dinosaur life we are therefore dealing largely with imponderables, for we have no experience of the degree or of any quantity of the kind of animals that the dinosaurs represent. They have no descendants today and their nearest relatives, the crocodiles, are not very close in appearance or in habits to the remarkable creatures we are to consider in detail. In the circumstances it may be hard to combat the feeling that this is a dream world, composed by scientists for their own diversion. It is by no means so and, though there are many gaps in our knowledge, we have much knowledge too.

The Trias began almost imperceptibly in many parts of the world, succeeding the Permian geological period. Its name— Trias—comes from the three main divisions in which it is characteristically displayed in Germany, though they are not repeated wherever the Trias occurs. It is, however, generally divided into Lower Trias, Middle Trias and Upper Trias, each of which is now subdivided into standard names.

The period in general was one of emergence, continents being lately risen higher out of the ocean. Conditions on the continents were not quite uniform so that some variety of habitats was possible. The continents were not in their present position but showed something of the 'huddle' that had been characteristic of the later Palaeozoic geological periods.

Thus North and South America presented a concave front to Africa and Europe, the north-western part of Africa being closely applied to the Atlantic coast of the USA and making the Gulf of Mexico an inland sea. The 'feet' of both South America and Africa were applied to Antarctica and Australia, with India and Madagascar wedged between northern Australia and the south-east coast of Africa. This is no mere geographical speculation. We have, for example, freshwater amphibians of a

44

highly specialized kind from Triassic rocks of South Africa, Australia, India and Madagascar and there has recently been found a closely comparable lower jaw fragment from the Beardmore Glacier region of the Antarctic south of Tasmania and New Zealand.

However all this geographical arrangement may be, the Trias has left its mark on the various parts of the world in quite different ways. As has been said, it was named for the German occurrence which is far from typical of the rest of the world. In central Germany it consists of red marls and beds of gypsum and rock salt, sandstones overlying limestones and dolomites which, in turn, overlie coarse red sandstones with rock-salt and gypsum.

In England the middle member of the German series (Muschelkalk) is missing so that it becomes a double series mainly of Lower and Upper Trias but furnishing beds of more importance than is often thought. The English Trias extends in a strip from the coast of Devon north-eastwards to Durham, with a north-western branch across Cheshire to Morecambe Bay. In Cheshire the salt deposits and works at Middlewich, Nantwich and Northwich are well known and the reptilian footprints on the sandstones of Storeton Hill and Lymm have attracted attention and have been studied for over one hundred years.

In South Wales, fissures in older rocks were filled by debris in Triassic times and this includes remains of early mammals, probably referable to the monotremes which today are found only as *Echidna* and *Ornithorhynchus* (the platypus) in Australia. These fissure fillings are being most painstakingly and skilfully examined at the present time.

In Scotland, the Trias has proved rewarding to the vertebrate palaeontologist, for a number of important reptiles, including some dinosaurs and dinosaur ancestors, have been discovered in rocks of perhaps Middle Triassic and certainly Upper Triassic age near Lossiemouth, in Moray. They too have been examined and reconstructed with great skill in recent years to disclose a fauna quite different from that that had been envisaged, and one which sheds a new light on the origin of dinosaurs.

Elsewhere around the world Triassic rocks of marine kind are

45

known from Switzerland, Israel and Jordan, and of terrestrial kind (red beds) in India. In the Soviet Union, Triassic red beds and vertebrate fossils have been found in the Perm basin west of the Urals. In France, too, non-marine red beds occur. However, by far the most important series of deposits of this age are known from South Africa, Brazil and the United States.

The Karroo Beds of South Africa, whose Middle and Upper Beaufort Series and whose Stormberg Series are attributed to the Triassic, have yielded great quantities of fossils of great evolutionary significance. Hundreds of types have been described, yet Robert Broom, who did so much to discover and elucidate them, once estimated that the rocks of South Africa, which cover, of course, a wider range than the Trias, probably contained 800 thousand million fossils. While it is not possible to estimate the correctness of this supposition it forms one instance from which we can judge how incomplete is our knowledge of the evidence that fossils could furnish of the life of the past, and we must bear in mind how representative even this would be of the forms that lived and many of which were not fossilized by the chances of death and burial.

The South African beds suffered massive intrusion by volcanic products and it is interesting to note that the South American deposits in the Parana Basin of south Brazil, where the reptile faunas are somewhat different from those of South Africa, are also overlain by great flows of lava. Triassic deposits of about the same age occur in New South Wales in eastern Australia.

The Triassic deposits in the United States have received a great deal of attention because of their fossils but also because they provide some of the most colourful scenery in North America. They occur in two great series, the first of which is the eastern or Newark Series stretching from Nova Scotia on the north-east down to North Carolina. They run in a series of troughs, formed by faulting, which were filled up with debris while they sank or foundered. The greatest of the troughs, that of Connecticut, covers an area of 100 miles by 25 miles. The rocks consist of conglomerates, sandstones, silts and shales, either of a grey or a striking red colour. Such beds are those that would result from erosion and be spread out, in various degrees of coarseness, by rivers. There are no marine fossils in the

Newark Series so its products are entirely those of a continental area, with land plants and freshwater fishes and many dinosaur bones and footprints. The dinosaurs crossed the streams and their sands leaving the abundant footprints that are famous in Connecticut and at Turners Falls, Massachusetts.

The ripple marks of the water and the pits of the raindrops help to recreate a very understandable scene. But it is also one that helps to explain the colours. The grey or dark beds are those formed under water or vegetation whereas the red beds are due to oxidation and to seasonal changes. The bright red colour characteristic of so many Triassic rocks may therefore be due to seasonal climatic changes and not necessarily to aridity.

This great eastern series is matched by a western series that covers much of Arizona, New Mexico, Texas, Utah and Wyoming. The formations are not the same everywhere and some are more fossiliferous than others. Thus the Chinle of New Mexico, Arizona and Utah, though giving only occasional animal fossils, provides many fossil trees (as exemplified by the Petrified Forest) and gives the bright colours of the Painted Desert. In Texas the Dockum formation and in Wyoming the Popo Agie are the important fossil-bearing formations. The more westerly parts of the western Triassic show the effects of frequent invasions by the seas, but elsewhere, as indeed around the world, the principal scene is one of emerging continents with erosion of older structures.

There were rivers and streams of fresh water, small lakes and ponds. In these water-vegetation flourished and the occasional log was transported, sometimes as in the western USA, an *Araucaria*-like tree or a fern frond or parts of evergreens. In the waters were fishes and amphibians, or the crocodile-like phytosaurs, and the very first crocodiles too. Many of these were large, for the skulls alone of some Triassic amphibians were 3 feet long.

The size and number of these reptilian contemporaries is of great importance for it must be made clear that the dinosaurs, whatever their future, did not arise as a ruling race but emerged from groups of competitors as large as most Triassic dinosaurs and in most cases as well-adapted to their varied habitats. This helps to emphasize the well-established biotic zones in the

THE DINOSAURS

Trias, for although many parts of the continental Trias were undeniably arid as can be seen by the deposits and the salty remnants of atmospheric evaporation, there were many regions of lush vegetation and of considerable population.

Much of this land must have been similar to the Amazon river region with jungle or closely set vegetation, and with swamps. Higher up and away from the swamps would be more open regions with lesser vegetation. We have considerable evidence as to what this vegetation was. The western United States and the Petrified Forest have produced the remains of giant logs derived from conifers with trunks 10 feet in diameter and up to 200 feet high. There are also widespread remains of true cycads, cycadeoids and ferns. These, together with tree ferns, constituted the forests, and if the identification is correct (as it should be) there is some evidence, at least in Colorado, that the first angiosperm, a primitive palm, had already made its appearance. The swamp flora consisted essentially of ferns and 'scouring rushes' (horsetails or scrub grass) and, of course, of much plant debris borne into the swamps by streams or flood waters.

As a whole the flora is considered to be poor; probably some 400 species of plants have been identified throughout the world of the Trias, but some of its elements, particularly the cycads and the horsetails, were to have long associations with the dinosaurs.

Over the lands the temperature was warm from polar circle to polar circle, and high temperatures and sub-tropical vegetation were to be found in Spitsbergen and Greenland.

The seas were warm too, perhaps 18°F higher than now. There was no trace of melt water from the Permian ice ages and very little freshwater contamination during the Trias. Life was literally teeming. Ammonites were in profusion and have proved remarkably useful as index fossils to many geological levels, although they narrowly escaped extinction towards the close of the period. Reef-building corals were also active and a great reef belt extended along what is now the mountain and earthquake belt along the Mediterranean and eastwards. The reefs and associated deposits (dolomites and 'dolostones') can be seen today in the Alps, the Dolomites and the Himalayas.

48

In these warm waters the brachiopods (lamp-shells), the echinoderms and the first lobster-like crustaceans all flourished too, the ancestry of many modern forms being thus established. Vertebrates too began a mastery of the seas as the crocodiles, ichthyosaurs and plesiosaurs were born.

In the long warm days and nights of the Trias there is evidence of occasionally more humid spells and in Europe, at least, there was apparently more humidity at the close of the Trias and the beginning of the succeeding period, the Jurassic.

Towards the end of the Trias there was an outburst of volcanic activity along much of what we now call the Pacific Coast of North America and during the succeeding Jurassic period there was a gradual diminution of the continental conditions both territorially and climatically.

The result of this was that the lands were, on the whole, low-lying, with lakes, pools, meandering rivers and swamps, and all of these were liable to invasions by the sea. Vegetation was consequently more intense and luxuriant than in the Trias with the continuance of mild and even subtropical climates. Europe had these extensive low-lying lands but the great belt of rock movement and instability was that which gave rise to Tethys, the primal mediterranean sea in the then wider region of what is now both the Mediterranean and the Alpine heights. This belt has remained a line of crustal weakness, of earthquake activity and of mountain building.

South of this line the ancient Gondwanaland, or the southern complex of continents, began to break up and drift towards the positions we now know. This was, however, a slow process with profound effects upon the nature of the continental faunas.

In the general geographical conditions we have indicated it is not difficult to see the kind of deposits that would be laid down. The rivers and draining flood waters brought a good deal of material from the land so that the seas became muddy and clays and sands were deposited. These are seen in character and in name in the English Jurassic succession, for example the Oxford Clay and the Northampton Sands of the Middle Jurassic. In the seas there was an accumulation of minute globules of calcium carbonate, perhaps aided by very small algae, that resulted in the production of oolites, egg-like limestones that, as the Inferior Oolites and the Great Oolites Series, are especially characteristic of the Jurassic System of Central England.

In England the Jurassic is composed of a series of beds running from the Dorset Coast to the Yorkshire Coast and extending from East Anglia to the Welsh Border. As we shall see these Jurassic rocks have played an historic part in the British dinosaur story and have yielded many important, indeed unique, specimens.

In Scotland, a small but significant series of Jurassic rocks are to be seen in the Western Isles and in Northern Scotland, where workable coal seams occur. Jurassic rocks of importance occur in France, Germany (where the Lithographic Limestone of Upper Jurassic age must be noted) and in Spain. In the USSR and in South-east Asia, in North and Central Africa and in Australia, there are important series of rocks that may yet produce important dinosaur remains.

In the United States, marine faunas are found in the west, and in the Gulf of Mexico which made its entry into the south-eastern scene at this time. The land fauna is closely similar to the European fauna. The most notable fauna comes from the series of late Jurassic continental freshwater deposits called the Morrison, whose name is derived from the sequence of beds seen at Morrison, near Denver, in Colorado.

In Canada great inland seas laid down the rocks that underlie the prairies.

Over this vast area the temperature continued mild and often subtropical and there was sufficient rainfall to maintain a luxuriant vegetation. The low-lying lands had forests of cycads, ferns and abundant horsetails. Elsewhere there were conifers and many other evergreens. Yet the Jurassic world was not the sombre green that it was once thought to be. The cycads had coloured fruits or flower-like cones and thus something like a beginning of blossoms were on the land.

The waters of the oceans were in the 70°F range and there were calcareous (limy) seaweed or red algae in abundance. Corals and sponges formed reefs in the clear waters along the Mediterranean and all along Japan, and ammonites were very common and diversified so that their shells are especially used to identify layers or zones of the Jurassic sequence in all parts of the world.

Reptiles were widespread in the waters. Crocodiles and turtles, ichthyosaurs and plesiosaurs were all adapted in different ways for life in water and, in the air, the pterosaurs had already become proficient, the rather primitive *Dimorphodon* being found in the Lower Lias (at the base of the Jurassic) in Dorset, England.

On the land the reptiles were dominant. The old kind of amphibians were gone, though the first frogs and toads were in evidence. The profuse vegetation provided shelter and food for a host of insects, reptiles and mammals. Already there were struggles for dominance and for possession of niches in the environment. Almost every coign of vantage was occupied so that dinosaurs were far from being alone or having everything their own way in the so-called Age of Reptiles.

The Jurassic lasted for approximately 45 million years and was succeeded by the Cretaceous, whose name is derived from *creta*, the Latin word for chalk. Chalk is one of the characteristics of the period but there are many other kinds of deposits. The period saw widespread subsidence of the continents and transgressions of the sea, so that swamps and deltaic deposits are common. Of these the Wealden of England is a well-known example.

In England greensands were deposited in shallow waters, and bluish muds (such as the gault) where the water was deeper. Chalk was formed in the later part of the period by the slow accumulation of tiny shells, of pieces of large shells and of the remains of microscopic algae that have tiny plates of calcium carbonate (coccoliths). It is difficult to realize the immense time involved in the making of such deposits. The English Chalk is over a thousand feet thick and is estimated to have accumulated at a rate of 1 foot in 30,000 years.

There is evidence that in some parts of the world the Chalk Sea was not far distant from desert areas on land but on the land there were coal-forming swamps in the United States and glacial deposits in Australia. Elsewhere were the great swampy regions around which the dinosaurs lived. Broad valleys, with slow meandering streams, gave living room for other kinds of

51

dinosaurs and in the great delta regions there was a mingling of quite different kinds.

The early Cretaceous saw a continuation of the flora of Jurassic times, cycads and gingkos, conifers, ferns and horsetails. How far any angiosperm—or flowering plant—relieved this dominantly green countryside is hard to say, for, as has been said, there is some evidence that they began in the Trias. However, by the middle Cretaceous a remarkably rich and almost modern vegetation was widespread. The poplar, fig, beech, magnolia, plane, ivy, willow and laurel and forms nearly related to the elm and the oak have been recognized. Flowers gave colour to the scene and began that long and intimate connexion with insects that we see today.

The change of flora must have been of great importance because the cycads, which had for so long been the foodstuff of many land animals, gave way in competition with the new wave of more advanced plants. And yet the newcomers must have caused new problems too. We know the climate continued mild over most of the world but there is evidence of seasonal change and this must mean that the deciduous trees shed their leaves in the winter. The fall had literally come into the world and many vegetarians must have felt the pinch of hunger, perhaps for the first time, in the later Cretaceous years.

The period, which was of longer extent than its predecessors, lasting some 65 million years, saw many important changes in geography and inhabitants in its latter part. The great mountain-building movements, known as the Laramide revolution, began, which were to produce the Rocky Mountains in the north and the Andes in South America. These changes drained much of the old swamp and lake land that had sheltered and maintained dinosaurs but they were not alone in their discomfiture. The fauna in the sea changed abruptly too. Ichthyosaurs and plesiosaurs had gone by the close of the Cretaceous and the wide ranging mosasaurs, short-lived but highly successful lizards of the sea, died out too. In the air the pterosaurs died out leaving that medium to their rivals the birds.

The invertebrates also lost ground, for the ammonites became extinct. The ancestors of modern forms became prominent in that crabs and lobsters, shell fish, especially clams and oysters,

52

THE ENVIRONMENT OF DINOSAURS

flourished. Echinoderms were still numerous, sea-urchins, starfish, as well as free-swimming and stalked crinoids.

The mammals began to grow more numerous but their numbers were not such that they would have posed a new threat to the dinosaurs.

None the less, whatever the causes (and these will be considered in detail in a later chapter) many kinds of reptiles, which had long enjoyed success in various elements during the Trias, Jurassic and Cretaceous, became extinct towards the close of the last-named period. The supremacy of the air was given over to the birds; fishes gained dominance in the seas; and on the land the small and hitherto insignificant mammals, rarely found as fossils even in the latest Mesozoic strata, almost suddenly became the masters, to flourish widely and to possess the earth, while the reptiles, that had held sway for more than 200 million years, dwindled and gave up their reign. Some kinds of reptiles, it is true, lingered on and have descendants living at the present time, but their place in the modern fauna gives little indication of the great reptilian power that existed all through the long Mesozoic Era.

53

The Origin of Dinosaurs

Here are we, in a bright and breathing world:
Our origin, what matters it?
WORDSWORTH *Excursion*

One of the schemes of classification of the reptiles, past and present, is based on the characters of the roof of the skull above and to the side of the brain case. It depends on the absence or presence of openings, called fossae or fenestrae, in this cranial roof and especially in its temporal bone regions. Those reptiles, such as the primitive and ancient Cotylosauria and the Chelonia (turtles and tortoises), which have no perforations in the roof, are placed in the Sub-class Anapsida (Greek, *an* without; *apsis*, arch). The Sub-class that particularly concerns us is the Diapsida (Greek, *dis*, double; *apsis*, arch) the members of which have two openings on each side of the skull in the temporal region, the upper of them being known as the supratemporal fossae and the lower the infratemporal fossae. The two openings on each side are separated by the arch formed by the postorbital and the squamosal bones. (See p. 69)

If this sounds at all complicated or uncertain it should be made clear in Figure 5, p. 64. Looking at this diagram it will be seen that there is a series of openings on the side of the skull from back to front; the two temporal openings, the orbit, the preorbital foramen, just in front of the orbit, and the external naris, or nostril, towards the front of the skull. In some forms there is another small foramen in the maxillary bone between the nostril and the preorbital foramen (f ʺ).

These openings serve two anatomical functions: they make the skull lighter in weight and, at the back, they provide rims or ridges for the attachment of muscles for the lower jaws. The results of this arrangement obviously affected the diet, the habits

THE ORIGIN OF DINOSAURS

and therefore the life of the animals and as such they will be discussed later. Meantime, the persistence of these features helps the search for an ancestral group from which dinosaurs may have come.

One of the earliest and most primitive reptiles with a diapsid skull is *Youngina* from the Kistecephalus zone (Upper Permian) of South Africa. This was a small carnivore, with a skull 2½ inches long. The body characters were comparatively primitive and the body proportions are thought to have been like those of lizards. Indeed *Youngina*, which is clearly derivable from a primitive Cotylosaurian (anapsid) is what is now called a Lepidosaur and is thus associated with the ancestry of the modern lizards and snakes. It is more precisely a member of the Order Eosuchia, a name derived from the Greek words for 'early' and for one kind of crocodile. The word 'crocodile' itself comes from a Greek word that means 'lizard' and only in one dialect was used for its modern connotation, so there is etymological confusion in these scientific names. *Youngina* is early, in that it is Upper Permian in age, but it has no relationship with any crocodile past or present.

The small skull has many primitive features among which are the retention of the postparietal, supratemporal and tabular bones at the back and the presence of an otic notch, and there was also a pineal foramen. There were teeth in the margins of the jaws, small, sharp, and recurved, and obviously for the prehension of a small but active prey. There were also teeth on the palate. The skull is triangular, meeting in front in a 40° angle. with the greatest width equal to just over a half of the length and with the height equal to just over a third of the maximum length.

This skull has superficial resemblances to another diapsid, *Euparkeria*, from the Lower Trias (Cynognathus zone) of South Africa, which has a slightly larger skull at 3½ inches, also with a 40° angle in front. The greatest width is just over a half of the total length and the height just over a half of the length. In other words the *Euparkeria* skull is higher. If the skull of *Youngina* were heightened it would result in a heightening of the skull openings which would then present a close resemblance to those of *Euparkeria* but the latter has a preorbital foramen

55

in the upper jaw and a foramen in the lower jaw. The palate of
Euparkeria is, however, closely similar to that of *Youngina* and
the number of teeth around the jaws and the distribution of
palatal (holding) teeth is very similar in both forms. Though
Euparkeria has lost the pineal foramen (or opening for 'the
third eye'), primitive skull bones such as the postparietal and
the postfrontal (which are also found in *Youngina*) are retained.
In brief it is possible that the Upper Permian *Youngina*, an
Eosuchian, may be on an ancestral line leading to the Lower
Triassic *Euparkeria* or a similar form which is a member of the
Order Thecodontia and the Sub-order Pseudosuchia ('false
crocodiles'). The number of vertebrae in front of the sacrum is
the same in both forms but beyond this it is impossible to draw
comparisons for the skeleton of *Youngina* and other Eosuchids
is imperfectly known though they seem to have been small
crawling animals, adapted for life on dry land.

Most of them did not survive the passing of the Permian, a
boundary line that saw great changes in the vertebrates. Indeed
only 23 per cent of forms living in Permian times went on into
the Triassic. In periods in which there was much aridity, speed
of movement in chasing and capturing prey was of paramount
importance and it is not without significance that the small but
swiftly moving Eosuchians were succeeded by partially bipedal
carnivores in the Trias, small animals it is true, but with
potential for speed in the relative lengths and the structure of
their limbs. This was a circumstance that affected other groups
of reptiles as well, notably those ancestral to the mammals, but
it was of particular moment for the evolution and development
of several groups of great importance in the Mesozoic, among
which the dinosaurs were pre-eminent.

The exact relationship of the Eosuchia and the Pseudosuchia,
though shadowed by the examples given above, is difficult to
define, for while they have the same ordinal rank the descent of
the latter from the former, indicated by their relationship and
time, cannot be clearly defined. Broom (1930) in his diagram of
the evolution of amphibians, reptiles, birds and mammals,
shows the Pseudosuchia to be direct offspring of the Eosuchian
stem but in the years that have passed little more convincing
evidence has accumulated and both Colbert (1965) and Romer

(1966) indicate a vague connexion but nothing more. Nor can we be sure of the place, though a strong common geographical association of the two Orders in Africa would suggest that the conditions there and their selective effects may have been determinant.

For our present purpose the Pseudosuchia are by far the more important and among them *Euparkeria*, to which we have referred, is very typical of the Archosaurs, or ruling reptiles, in which the Pseudosuchians have a fundamental place. The skull of *Euparkeria* has been briefly described. The remainder of the skeleton shows that the animal could walk on all fours or run on the hind legs. These were about half as long again as the front, though the lower leg and the thigh were much the same length. In other words the bipedal powers existed but there is no evidence of the adaptation for speed that some of the later bipeds show. A paired series of overlapping armour plates was arranged down the back. *Euparkeria* had sclerotic plates in the eye but these are rare in other Pseudosuchia or in the related groups that constitute the Thecodontia.

It is hard to generalize about a Sub-order that contains five families when they are of somewhat dissimilar nature and rather unknown characters. In essence, however, the family Euparkeriidae is represented by *Euparkeria* and the other families in the Sub-order are different only in degree. Many of them also come from East or South Africa and thus continue the strong African element in this group.

From these there developed a series of small bipeds of more specialized characters. Although they were probably mainly running animals, some are thought to have been able to climb and even to live in trees. This is not being truly arboreal for many animals, especially goats, can walk up the trunks and the branches of trees. Few Pseudosuchia are completely known but the group is considered of great evolutionary potentiality. Small and agile reptiles in the more or less dry or even arid Triassic conditions had every incentive towards adaptation and from this there came a diverse group of highly adapted reptiles. Certainly from some such kind of reptile came the crocodiles, the birds, the pterosaurs or flying reptiles, and the two Orders, Saurischia and Ornithischia, that together constitute the group that is popularly known as dinosaurs and which, therefore, share a common point of origin.

It can thus be seen that the Pseudosuchia are of unusual importance, particularly with regard to the dinosaurs, for they are not only ancestors to dinosaurs but also to many of the reptiles that were consistently the contemporaries of dinosaurs.

The idea of the two-fold, or diphyletic, origin of the dinosaurs is far from new. It was first presented by Prof. H. G. Seeley in 1887, and was received with little comment and no noticeable support. In 1914, Freiherr F. von Huene advanced additional support for, and generally re-examined, the theory and the two-fold origin has long been accepted.

When we come to the next chapter we shall see that dinosaurs can be readily divided into two great groups according to the structure of the pelvis. Some, which are called Saurischia, have an ordinary reptilian arrangement of these bones, while the others, called Ornithischia, have a pelvis constructed superficially like that of a bird. There are many other features which distinguish the two Orders, but the pelvic characters are quite often preserved and are the more readily perceived. Yet in the long history of the whole group, and so far back as can be traced, there is no form known which is intermediate between the two, nor is there any merging of characters.

Associated with the differences in the pelvic structure are differences in the skull, and again these features are retained throughout the history of the respective groups and are not intermingled. We shall also see later that in nearly all the examples of bipedal ornithischian dinosaurs that we know at all well, and in the horned dinosaurs or Ceratopsia, there are remains of tendons on the backbone which have become ossified. These are particularly well seen in *Iguanodon*, but they are characteristic of all the bipedal, and are even to be found on the most primitive, forms. Among the bipedal Saurischia, however, even the most advanced members show no trace of them. This important distinction suggests a rather different manner of moving about and perhaps of feeding, and is directly due to the difference in the fixation of the pelvis and the sacral-pelvic relationships.

With regard to the ribs, abdominal ribs, or gastralia, are to be found in the Saurischia, even among the more advanced genera, but so far no ornithischian is known to have them, except *Stegoceras* (*Tröodon*) a highly specialized and aberrant bone-head.

It will be seen, therefore, that whatever relationship exists between the two Orders, and despite a near common ancestry in a relatively small Sub-order, profound differences exist between the two which suggest not only different developmental trends within the branches themselves, but that the Ornithischia budded off from the parent Pseudosuchian stem later than the Saurischia, and that the parent stock itself had become more highly developed in the interval.

The Pseudosuchia was a slowly progressive stock and the impetus it gave to its offshoots was practically the same, but the change in its own evolutionary position produced a different impetus in the two new Orders. Thus the Ornithischia may have started better equipped than their elder brothers.

Von Huene has suggested that the Saurischia came directly from the most primitive representatives of the Pseudosuchia, while the Ornithischia came from more specialized members of that Order, 'by a stage of bipedal hopping creatures, in which the pelvis became adapted to this new locomotion by retroversion of the pubis and the development of a praepubis' (von Huene, 1914). Discoveries made in Brazil by the same authority greatly strengthened these assumptions. During the years 1928 and 1929, Freiherr von Huene was working in the Triassic deposits of south Brazil and obtained a large number of fossil reptiles, among which are many new forms of Pseudosuchia, both large and small. Some of these approximate so closely to the primitive Saurischia that it is possible only to differentiate them by the proportions of the skull and neck vertebrae, and by the characters of the interclavicle, the acetabulum, and the calcaneum (von Huene, 1929).

The most primitive Saurischia are known as the Coelurosauria and the earliest forms of these are very close to such Pseudosuchia as are contained in the family Euparkeriidae. A detailed study of the genus *Euparkeria* has recently been made by Rosalie F. Ewer (1965) and from it emerges evidence for at least one line of dinosaurian evolution. There can be no doubt

59

of the close similarity in many essential features between, for example, *Euparkeria* and *Ornithosuchus*, which is now regarded as a basal member of a saurischian group. *Euparkeria* has features which could be ancestral to *Ornithosuchus* and the Carnosaurs, or large carnivores which we shall see were developed during the Jurassic and Cretaceous. On the other hand, it is clear that it is not ancestral to the smaller Megalosaurid line of carnivores that were contemporaneous with the Carnosaurs. The latest evidence would seem to suggest that this second line of carnivores was developed from another Pseudosuchian, related to the Euparkeriidae but originating in an East African genus of the Middle Trias (*Teleocrater*). However, the evidence for this is far from complete.

It is also made clear that the ponderous, amphibious dinosaurian giants known as the Sauropoda and their predecessors, the Prosauropoda, could have been developed from *Euparkeria*. So the evidence of ancestry is there for one-half of the dinosaurian (Saurischian) stock.

So far as the ornithischian half is concerned, the identification of their originator is more difficult. Various features in *Euparkeria*, especially the structure of its ankle bones, excludes it from the role of great-grandfather.

It is only relatively recently that Crompton and Charig discovered *Heterodontosaurus* from the Cave Sandstone of South Africa. This is probably of Upper Keuper, that is late Triassic, age. The description shows relationships that undoubtedly link it with well known Ornithopod (bipedal and herbivorous) dinosaurs of later times. On the other hand the evidence for its ancestry is obscure, for it has already advanced some way along the specialized ornithopod path. Its relationships with earlier forms such as *Lycorhinus*, of which a lower jaw with similar postcanine teeth have been described, must await further material of the latter, which has not previously been recognized as a dinosaur.

In 1964, Leonard Ginsburg published a brief description of part of a jaw and the teeth of *Fabrosaurus australis* that had been found in the Upper Red Beds of the Stormberg Series (i.e. Norian) of Lesotho (formerly Basutoland). This appears to have affinities with the early armoured dinosaur *Scelidosaurus* and seems at the moment to be the earliest ornithischian that we know. It is interesting that these African relicts have this apparent relationship: that *Heterodontosaurus* should foreshadow *Hypsilophodon* (from the English Wealden) and that *Fabrosaurus* seems to suggest a connexion with *Scelidosaurus* (from the English Lower Lias). I have tried to show elsewhere (p. 243) that there are striking similarities between these English genera in which some sort of ancestral relationship appears to exist. This does not mean that these African discoveries now neatly solve the ancestry and relationship of the later forms. What it does seem to show is that there must have been a very considerable evolution of higher Thecodont or early dinosaurian forms in the Middle and slightly later parts of the Trias. There is still much to be collected and much to be known, although the evidence seems to suggest that the ancestors of at least three lines of dinosaurian evolution will be found eventually in the Sub-order Pseudosuchia.

The discussion of the ancestry of dinosaurs as a group must not obscure the fact that this was only one part of a great series of vertebrate developments that were taking place in Triassic and later times. The geological periods of the Triassic, Jurassic and Cretaceous, are together grouped as the Mesozoic, and very commonly called the Age of Reptiles.

There were many kinds of amphibians and reptiles living in the world when the dinosaurs became part of it and throughout their reign there were great developments and increase of many forms of life both vertebrate and invertebrate. Dinosaurs never lived alone and the association of animals that lived then was just as important as that we see as part of the balance of nature now. Consequently it is interesting to pay some attention to the reptilian contemporaries of the new Orders. The dinosaurs entered a world in which there were already the early forms of swimming reptiles, ichthyosaurs and plesiosaurs, and such land-living kinds as Rhynchocephalia, the early forms of Chelonia-like creatures, and the great variety of Cynodont and Anomodont reptiles, now so well known from South African deposits, which were later to produce the mammals and so, ultimately, Man.

The Amphibia were, of course, also well represented, as

might be expected, but they were soon afterwards to decline considerably.

During the later part of the Mesozoic there was a much wider diversity of life; snakes, lizards (including the mosasaurs), pterosaurs (flying reptiles), crocodiles, chelonia, ichthyosaurs, plesiosaurs, birds, and multituberculate and marsupial mammals being widespread.

This, then, was the world in which the dinosaurs, sprung from the little Pseudosuchia, lived and moved and had their great development. In the preceding chapters we have seen something of the physical and biological characters of that world, we have now described something of the origin and relation of the dinosaurs, and in the next and succeeding chapters we must deal with the structure of these dinosaurs themselves and with the description of their varied modes of life.

CHAPTER V

The Anatomy of Dinosaurs

Thou hast clothed me with skin and flesh,
And hast fenced me with bones and sinews.
JOB 10:11

We have seen in the last chapter how the dinosaurs are thought
to have arisen and what their closest relatives were. We have
also tried to explain what the term 'diphyletic' means, and how
the two Orders, Saurischia and Ornithischia, were originally
evolved at different times, though probably from the one
ancestral stock, and how they were differentiated. Although,
as we have said, pronounced and persistent anatomical differences exist in these two Orders, there are also a number of
similarities but it should be emphasized that their grouping
together under the popular name of Dinosaur is a relic of an
old classification rather than a new concept. Modern classification takes little heed of the external appearance alone and,
unless the skeletal characters support the overlying resemblances, there is no real justification for assuming that there is
systematic relationship.

What then are the anatomical characters that distinguish the
dinosaurs as a whole? From what we know of their descent it
is not surprising that they share many features with the related
Orders of the Thecodontia (the Order which includes the
Pseudosuchia), the Crocodilia, the Pterosauria (flying reptiles),
and the birds. It is obvious also that in discussing the general
anatomy of the whole group we are not giving anatomical
guidelines for one and every dinosaur. If all were nearly alike
there would be few sub orders, families, genera and species. In
the succeeding chapters on the particular kinds of dinosaurs we
shall mention the more important variations in structure from
the conventional pattern. Meantime, the task is to describe the

63

principal and typical conditions of the skull, backbone, shoulder-girdle and fore limbs, and of the pelvic girdle and the hind limbs. In this chapter these characters will be described simply and generally and the student who desires a more

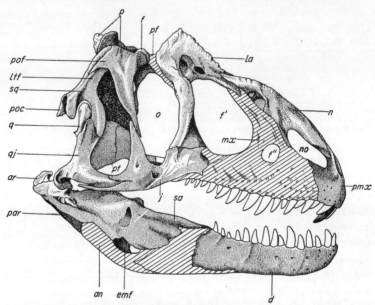

FIG. 5. Skull of *Antrodemus valens* (Saurischian). Right side. Approx. ⅛ nat. size.

KEY: *an.*, angular; *ar.*, articular; *d.*, dentary; *emf.*, external mandibular foramen; *f.*, frontal; *f′.*, first antorbital foramen; *f″.*, second antorbital foramen; *fm.*, foramen magnum; *j.*, jugal; *la.*, lachrymal; *ltf.*, lateral temporal fenestra or vacuity; *mx.*, maxilla; *n.*, nasal; *no.*, narial opening; *o.*, orbit; *oc.*, occipital condyle; *p.*, parietal; *par.*, prearticular; *pd.*, predentary; *pf.*, prefrontal; *pmx.*, premaxilla; *po.*, postorbital; *poc.*, paroccipital; *pof.*, postfrontal; *poso.*, postsupraorbital; *pso.*, pre-supraorbital; *pt.*, pterygoid; *q.*, quadrate; *qj.*, quadratojugal; *s.*, splenial; *sa.*, surangular; *so.*, supraorbital; *sq.*, squamosal; *stf.*, supratemporal fossa or upper temporal vacuity.

detailed or advanced statement on any particular group is referred to appropriate sources in the literature detailed in the Bibliography at the end of the book.

Dinosaurs are reptiles that were originally classified in the

Super-order DINOSAURIA, but as this is really diphyletic it cannot be regarded as a natural Super-order and for many years has been used merely for convenience. It is the intention here to discard it as a scientific term. Dinosaurs being reptiles are to

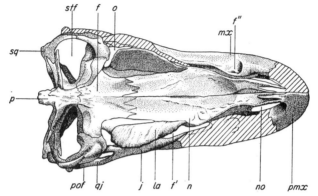

FIG. 6. Skull of *Antrodemus valens* (Saurischian). Top view. Approx. ⅛ nat. size.

See key for Fig. 5.

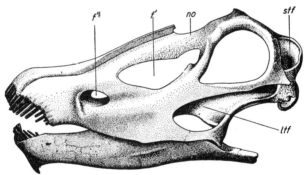

FIG. 7. Skull of *Diplodocus*. Left side. Approx. ⅛ nat. size.
See key for Fig. 5.

be regarded strictly as such and, in the absence of good evidence to the contrary, must not be invested with the mammal-like characters, anatomical, physiological and mental, that some published representations would seem to suggest.

The skull (Figs. 5 to 10) of most dinosaurs is striking in two

65

respects; those of size and apparent simplicity of structure. With regard to the first, it may be said that the skull is usually small in proportion to the size of the body, and, in some dinosaurs, smaller proportionately than in almost any other

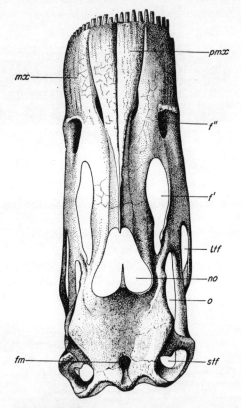

FIG. 8. Skull of *Diplodocus*. Top view. Approx. ¼ nat. size.
See key for Fig. 5.

reptiles known; and with regard to the second, the simplicity of structure is due to the reduction of the bones in the skull roof, particularly in the temporal region, resulting in the formation of an upper and a lower arch, and consequent upper and lateral temporal vacuities (see especially Fig. 5). This condition has already been described (see p. 54) as diapsid. Added to these, as seen from the side, are the antorbital (in front of the orbits) vacuities consisting of narial openings (nostrils) which are sometimes high on the face, but are always separate except in *Diplodocus*, openings in the maxillary bones, the preorbital

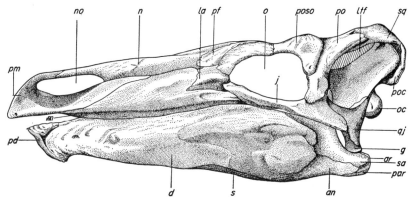

FIG. 9. Skull of *Stegosaurus stenops*. Approx. ¼ nat. size.
See key for Fig. 5.

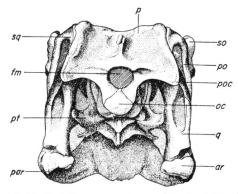

FIG. 10. Skull of *Stegosaurus stenops*. Approx. ¼ nat. size.
See key for Fig. 5.

foramina, one in front of each orbit, and the orbits themselves. Furthermore, there are occasionally foramina in the jugal bones (as in *Tyrannosaurus*) and occasionally small openings in the centre and back of the skull between the parietal and supra-

67

occipital bones (in ornithischians). There are foramina associated with the dentition on the outer rim of the maxilla and the dentary. There is no pineal foramen in the dinosaurs, although a rudiment of it was said to occur in *Plateosaurus* (von Huene, 1926).

From front to back on top of the skull (Fig. 6) the bones are the paired premaxillae, which may bear teeth, as in the Saurischia, or be toothless and beaked with a rostral bone in front, as in many of the Ornithischia; immediately behind them are the nasals; and, in the Saurischia, articulating with the premaxillae in front, the nasals towards the midline of the skull, and forming the side margins of the front half of the skull, the maxillae. In the Ornithischia the maxillae are separated from the nasals by the premaxillae. At the junction of the premaxillae and the nasals are the (usually) paired nostrils or narial openings. At the junction of the maxilla and the premaxilla in *Tyrannosaurus* there is a small opening and in each of the maxillae themselves there is another foramen. The nasal bones are usually narrow in front and expand posteriorly until they terminate against the frontal bones, but sometimes they expand and then contract to their frontal suture. In the hadrosaurs they are often raised to a keel in the midline. Behind the maxillae and on the outer sides of the nasals are the lachrymal bones which form at least part of the hinder border of the preorbital foramen. Posteriorly the maxillae meet the jugal bones which form the lower border or edge of the more backward part of the skull. On its inner side, and near its front, the jugal is met and joined by a sideward projection of the lachrymals, and the bar thus formed on each side separates the orbits from the preorbital vacuities if present. In *Diplodocus* the lachrymals are absent and the quadratojugal forms the lower margin of the orbit.

In the middle, behind the frontals (or frontal as it is often called since in many cases, and especially in old individuals, the two frontals are fused to form one bone), are the parietals. They too may fuse and they may be very short, as in *Diplodocus* and *Camarasaurus* or very long and expanded as in the Ceratopsia. At the outer and lower extremity of the skull, behind but sometimes below the jugal, is the quadratojugal which sends up an ascending process to meet the squamosal bone,

68

which, on each side, lies behind and just below the parietals. Further forward the jugal sends up a process to cover in the back and side of the orbit and on the upper part of the side it meets the postorbital or postfrontal bones, or both. In the dinosaurs the postfrontals may exist (as in *Camptosaurus* and *Iguanodon*) separately, but often they are fused with the postorbitals which take their place. The latter bones are generally small but may be large, as in the Ceratopsia in which they are responsible for the support of the supraorbital horns. Thus the orbits are mainly bounded by the lachrymal, postorbital (with or without the postfrontal) frontal and jugal bones, although other small bones—the prefrontal and the supraorbital—may take part. Behind the orbits, the lateral, or lower, temporal vacuity, on which we have laid some importance, has its borders formed from the postorbital (sometimes with the postfrontal), squamosal, quadratojugal, quadrate and jugal bones. The upper temporal vacuity, on the upper surface of the skull, is accordingly bounded by the postorbital, squamosal and parietal bones, with the addition of the postfrontal and part of the frontal.

On the lower, hinder and inner corner of the quadratojugal is the quadrate, usually in dinosaurs a large and prominent bone differing in strength and direction in the Saurischia and the Ornithischia. The quadrate in the Saurischia reaches up to the squamosal and has sutural junctions with the quadratojugal and the pterygoid of the palate and although these connexions lend stability to the whole structure in some forms, as we shall see, there is a certain measure of mobility. The quadrate is especially important in all reptiles as it furnishes the articulation for the articular bone of the lower jaw (indeed this association is one of the diagnostic characters of the Class Reptilia) and the point of fixation determines the gape (or width of the open mouth).

The back of the skull is furnished by relatively few bones, though the posterior aspect varies greatly according to the height or lowness of the skull, and this, in turn, depends on the kind of dinosaur (Fig. 10).

The roof of the occipital region is formed, of course, by the parietals and squamosals in varying degree. In some forms the parietals are scarcely visible, in some armoured forms the squamosals cannot be seen. But below these, with or without an intervening space, lies the supraoccipital with the wing-like opisthotics on each side and again below this, but connected with the supraoccipital and opisthotics are the comparatively small exoccipitals which form the lateral borders of the foramen magnum. The exoccipitals at their base articulate with the basioccipital which forms not only the floor of the foramen magnum but also provides the occipital condyle, with which the skull moves on the atlas and axis of the vertebral column. There is, however, much variation from this simple plan in the different families and genera: for example, in some Theropoda the exoccipitals form the floor of the foramen magnum. Beneath these, of course, can be seen the hinder view of the palatal bones.

FIG. 11. Stapes of *Corythosaurus*. (After Colbert and Ostrom.)

Both Saurischia and Ornithischia have an open otic notch between the squamosal and the quadrate, and in the latter the squamosal has a projection over it. The tympanum (ear drum) would seemingly face backwards and slightly outwards and the stapes, the long columnar bone that connects the fenestra ovalis of the brain case with the tympanum in its upper part, would run almost horizontally. The stapes has been found only a few times in the dinosaurs, so it is difficult to give any general account of it but it must usually have been long and was almost certainly made up of a thin bony part and a cartilaginous part (extra-stapedial cartilage) that was in touch with the tympanum (Fig. 11). It lies precisely between the quadrate and the paroccipital process of the opisthotic. Von Huene described the stapes in *Plateosaurus* and Colbert and Ostrom have found it in both a saurischian and an ornithischian. Lull and Wright have restored the probable appearance of the otic region for *Anatosaurus*. The function of an ear among dinosaurs is discussed later.

The palate is composed mainly of the following bones, from

front to back: premaxillae, maxillae, separated in their hinder half by a trowel-shaped vomer, the palatines, and the pterygoids. The last-named bones send out processes at their sides to the jugals (though this connexion is sometimes made by an ecto-pterygoid), and also processes behind to the quadrates. The latter processes are separated by the basisphenoid bone, which is in contact with the basioccipital, so that in this way the complicated structure surrounding the brain-case is intimately connected up and supported. One important feature of the palatal view is that the teeth are confined to the margins of the premaxillae and maxillae, and there are no teeth on the palate as is the case in some other reptiles, including some ancestral to the dinosaurs.

The lower jaw, or mandible, is composed, as in other animals, of two halves, the connexion in front, or symphysis, being cartilaginous. In the Ornithischia, a toothless predentary bone was present and this appears often to have been sheathed in horn to form a sharp beak. Each half, or mandibular ramus, consists largely of the dentary lined on part of its inner side by the splenial. The dentary is always present and always bears teeth except in a few specialized Theropoda, which are toothless. Along the upper and inner side of the dentary is, in some forms, a long thin bone which is partially covered by the splenial. This bone, well shown in some Theropoda, has been variously named the supradentary or presplenial. Behind, both the dentary and the splenial rest upon the angular, immediately above is what is often the largest bone in the back of the mandible, the prearticular. At the back of, or above, these bones are the surangular and the articular, the latter of which forms the greater part of the surface for the articulation with the quadrate. Arising behind, above the level of the tooth row is the coronoid, which may in some forms at least have a pre-coronoid or intercoronoid in front of it. There is no coronoid process in the Sauropoda but in the Ceratopsia it is double.

The openings in the mandible consist mainly of small for-amina for the passage of nutrient blood-vessels and nerves, as, for example, on the outer edge of the dentary for the supply to the lips. On the inner or lingual side a row of foramina is associated with the developing teeth. In the Theropoda an opening, the external mandibular foramen, occurs between the dentary, surangular and angular bones. This is small in some carnosaurs and is absent in sauropods, prosauropods and some ornithopods. The large opening seen in the posterior part of dinosaur and other reptilian mandibles is for the transmission of blood-vessels, nerves and muscles to the jaw-bones themselves.

In the lower jaw, as in the upper, the teeth are confined to the margin of the jaw, and are either in sockets or in a groove. The teeth vary considerably in pattern in the different kinds of dinosaurs, being pencil-like in *Diplodocus*, spatulate or leaf-like in some other giant sauropods, sabre-like in the carnivorous theropods, and expanded and almost flower-like in armoured forms like *Stegosaurus*. In most dinosaurs there is no differentiation among the teeth in an individual, as in mammals and some mammal-like reptiles, and all are alike except for size. However the dentition may be composed of single teeth or of a mass of compressed teeth as in the hadrosaurs.

Traces of the rod-like hyoid bones, usually highly ossified ceratobranchials, have been found in many genera and the length of the bones in some forms has given rise to the supposition that some dinosaurs had a protrusible tongue. The complete hyoid apparatus has been reconstructed by several authors (see Fig. 12).

One important feature in dealing with skulls is the angle formed by the main axis of the skull and that of the backbone. In the quadrupedal herbivorous dinosaurs and the Triassic bipedal carnivores the line of the skull is approximately a continuation of the line of the vertebral column, but in the later bipedal forms the two axes form more nearly a right angle.

The eyes were generally directed more sidewards than toward the front, and most often were of large size. In many dinosaurs the eyes were protected by a series of bony plates covering most of the cornea and arranged much like the diaphragm of a camera. It was reported that these sclerotic plates occurred in the Theropoda but this was in the days when the Prosauropoda, or at least *Plateosaurus*, shared that place in classification. They do not seem to have been seen in Theropoda, although there is always the possibility that they were sometimes developed in

72

cartilage and thus have not been preserved. But they are identifiable in Prosauropoda and can be seen in some Sauropoda and are well known in many ornithischians, especially hadrosaurs and ceratopsians.

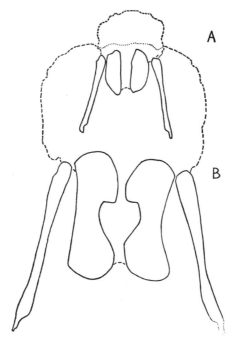

FIG. 12. Restoration of hyoid apparatus. A. *Psittacosaurus* B. *Protoceratops*. (After Colbert.) Approx. ½ nat. size.

Unlike the diaphragm of a camera they were not moveable or contractile. Their function was almost certainly resistant to pressure, a function that we shall see sustained in the Sauropoda and hadrosaurs but which is less easy to justify (except on hereditary grounds) in the horned dinosaurs. We shall refer to this aspect of dinosaurian life later.

The main stresses and strains of the body, and the greater part of the bulk, are borne by the vertebral column, and with the front end of this, of course, the skull is articulated. There are naturally differences of arrangement associated with the

73

manner of locomotion, whether partially upright, as in the case of the bipedal dinosaurs, or approaching the horizontal, as in the case of the quadrupedal forms. The disparity between the lengths of the fore limbs and hind limbs meant that most of the quadrupeds had a backbone that sloped forwards and backwards from the rump. The vertebral column is composed of vertebrae, differentiated into five regions, the number in each region varying considerably in different families and genera. In structure each vertebra is composed essentially of a more or less cylindrical centrum, or body, like a large bobbin in structure, the ends of this body articulating with the preceding and succeeding vertebrae. On the upper or 'back' surface of this centrum arises a more or less complex structure consisting of processes, projecting forwards, sideways, backwards and upwards, for the attachment of muscles and for articulation with other vertebrae and the ribs. The largest process, that directed upward, is known as the neural spine and varies greatly in size; in some megalosaurids it is enormous. The laterally directed process (diapophysis or transverse process) is for the attachment of one head of the rib (tuberculum), while the other head of the rib (capitulum) is attached to a somewhat similar process (parapophysis) which arises from the side of the centrum itself in cervical centra. In the dorsal centra the parapophysis rises on to the side of the neural arch. The complicated upper structure is known as the neural arch, and really arches over the neural canal in which the spinal cord lies on the upper surface of the centrum. The centrum and arch are connected usually by a suture.

Now, in the dinosaurs, the structure of this neural arch and the shape and character of the centrum supporting it may vary considerably. The articular ends of the latter may be flat (when the condition is known as amphiplatyan) or cupped (amphicoelous) or only the hinder one may be cupped (opisthocoelous condition).

The regions into which the vertebrae are divided are as follows:

(1) The two vertebrae, in structure unlike the rest, known as atlas and axis, which are articulated closely together and with

the occipital condyle. Together they form the surface upon which the skull is able to move. In those dinosaurs in which they are known they appear to resemble closely the corresponding bones of the crocodiles.

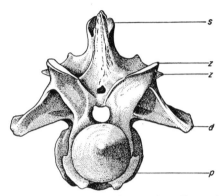

FIG. 13. Cervical vertebra of *Antrodemus valens*. Front view. Approx. ⅓ nat. size.

KEY: *d.*, diapophysis or transverse process; *p.*, parapophysis; *s.*, neural spine or spinous process; *z.*, anterior zygapophysis; *z'.*, posterior zygapophysis.

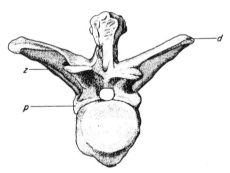

FIG. 14. Dorsal (thoracic) vertebra of *Antrodemus valens*. Front view. Approx. ⅙ nat. size.

See key for Fig. 13.

(2) The cervical vertebrae (Fig. 13), which may be anything from six to seventeen in number, the former number being recorded in the bipedal Mongolian dinosaur, *Psittacosaurus*, and

75

the latter in one of the long-necked sauropods. All the cervicals bear double-headed ribs, the lower articular head being attached to a process on the centrum (the parapophysis) and the upper to the transverse process of the neural arch. In the horned dinosaurs (Ceratopsia) some of the cervicals are commonly fused together for better support of the massive skull.

(3) The succeeding dorsal vertebrae vary in number from ten to eighteen or so in various families, the smaller number being found in the great sauropod *Diplodocus* and the larger in the bipedal herbivore *Iguanodon*. The dorsals (Fig. 14) also bear ribs, but there is no articular facet on the centrum and the complete rib attachment is on the neural arch, upon the sides of which the parapophyses are now also set.

In Theropoda and Sauropoda there are additional surfaces on at least the hinder dorsal vertebrae for articulation with the adjacent vertebrae. The additional facet on the back of the vertebrae is called the hyposphene and fits into a groove, called the hypantrum, on the front of the vertebra behind. A somewhat similar arrangement exists in the vertebrae of snakes. In the Sauropoda the cervical and anterior dorsal vertebrae are often much hollowed, combining lightness of weight with considerable strength.

(4) The next series of vertebrae is the sacrals, which are intimately associated with the attachment and support of the pelvic girdle. The centra concerned are always fused. The primitive number of sacral vertebrae, as seen in the Triassic bipedal forms known from Germany, was three, but it gradually increased in later forms, the increase being generally at the expense of the preceding dorsals, though sometimes the caudals are included in the sacrum. The maximum number known is eleven, found in the horned dinosaurs (Ceratopsia) of the Upper Cretaceous of North America.

Before leaving the sacrum it should be mentioned that in the armoured and quadrupedal forms known as stegosaurs, and in the unarmoured quadrupedal but amphibious Sauropoda, the neural canal was here enlarged to form a cavity so much as twenty times the size of the brain. The function of this important nerve centre, or 'sacral brain' as it has been called, was as a booster nerve control of the movements of the large and heavy hind limbs, and particularly the heavy tail which was sometimes a means of attack and defence.

(5) The last of the vertebral series is that of the caudals, or tail vertebrae, which are usually very numerous in the dinosaurs (Fig. 15). Some of the bipedal forms and the large sauropods have long tails often containing fifty to seventy vertebrae. On the undersurface of the caudals, and articulated at their junctions, are pieces of bone forming a Y-shaped structure and known as chevron-bones or chevrons. The function of these was to protect the vessels immediately below the vertebrae from injury when the tail was dragged upon the ground. In the large sauropods the last of the caudal vertebrae are frequently long and rod-like with conical articular ends so that during the life of the animal they formed a sort of whip lash.

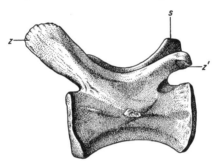

FIG. 15. Mid-caudal vertebra of *Antrodemus valens*. Left side. Approx. ¼ nat. size.

See key for Fig. 13.

These, then, are the principal series of the vertebrae, but the more important varieties and their peculiarities will be described in the following systematic chapters.

The pectoral girdle, for the support of the fore limbs and the associated musculature, is a comparatively simple structure in the dinosaurs because in nearly all of them the clavicles and interclavicle are wanting. Von Huene (1926) described what he took to be traces of these structures in early Triassic dinosaurs, and Osborn (1923, 1924) reported an interclavicle in the Mongolian ornithopod, *Psittacosaurus*, and slender clavicles

77

occur in the Mongolian *Protoceratops*. The bones that remain may be very shortly described; for with the sternum seldom ossified, they are the coracoid and the scapula (Fig. 16), which together form a rather narrow but elongated bar of bone, somewhat thickened and irregular in shape at its lower end. Of the two the scapula is the larger, the coracoid being a small and irregularly rounded to subcircular bone; each bears a facet so

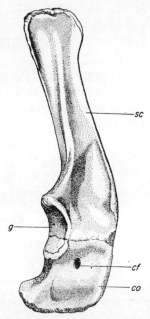

FIG. 16. Shoulder girdle of *Triceratops*. Approx. $\frac{1}{10}$ nat. size.
KEY: *co*., coracoid; *cf*., coracoid foramen; *g*., glenoid; *sc*., scapula.

that when the bones are normally articulated the facets are adjacent and form a notch, called the glenoid notch, in which the articular head of the upper arm bone, or humerus, is placed. The coracoid usually has a foramen near the articular margin, and the bone in many forms (e.g. *Trachodon* and *Stegosaurus*) is brought rather in front of the chest, while the scapula is a long, slender, flat, unpierced bone stretching upwards and backwards and slightly bent to conform to the shape of the body. In the Saurischia the scapula has often a prominent projection

78

at its lower end. It covers, of course, part of the outer surface of some of the dorsal ribs. Often the coracoid and scapula are fused together.

The sternal bones are two imperfectly ossified, rather obliquely T-shaped or sometimes oval-shaped elements which lie in the front of the chest in Sauropoda and in the Ornithischia. The bones may be fused in the latter and they had connexion with cartilaginous ribs (Fig. 17).

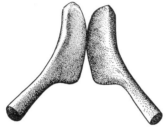

FIG. 17. Sternal bones of *Iguanodon atherfieldensis*. (From Hooley.) Approx. ½ nat. size.

The bones of the fore limb (Fig. 18), and of the limbs in general, vary considerably in character. Some are solid and massive, while those in other forms are hollow and light. There is sometimes great disparity in the size of the limbs as the femur is often much longer than the humerus. This is the case not only in most of the bipedal forms, where it might be expected to occur, but also in many of the quadrupedal, more especially the armoured, types.

In many cases the humerus is shorter than the scapula. It may be of somewhat indefinite shape, or it may have a distinct head (as in the sauropod dinosaurs) and be reminiscent of the crocodilian humerus in appearance. Usually both the upper surface (for articulation with the coracoid and scapula) and the lower surface (for articulation with the radius and ulna) are rough and irregular and must have been covered with an articular surface of cartilage during life.

The radius and ulna are often massive also and are never fused together, but remain separate bones, and must also have had cartilaginous articular.surfaces. The latter bone frequently has a greatly developed olecranon process ('elbow-bone' or

79

'funny bone') which is sometimes much roughened for the insertion of the muscles for straightening the limb. The development of the olecranon reaches its maximum in the three-horned dinosaur, *Triceratops*. The carpus or wrist is difficult to describe in most forms of dinosaurs because it is seldom found

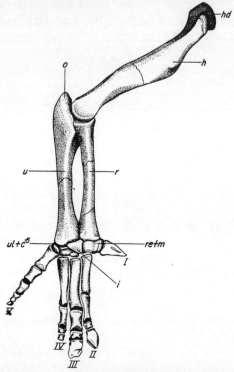

FIG. 18. Right fore limb of *Iguanodon atherfieldensis*. (From Hooley.) Approx. ⅛ nat. size.

KEY: *h.*, humerus; *hd.*, head; *i.*, intermedium; *o*, olecranon; *r*, radius; *re + m*, radiale + 1st metacarpal; *u.*, ulna; *ul + c⁵.*, ulnare + carpale 5.

with its constituents in position and because in many forms (e.g. hadrosaurs) it was largely cartilaginous and seldom preserved. However, the carpus and the tarsus (ankle) are so complex and difficult even for palaeontologists that it will be wise to give a diagram of their relationships to other bones and to explain their significance (Fig. 18).

It may seem that in anatomy generally the terms have been made as confusing as possible. In most cases the names used in comparative anatomy have come from human anatomy and, are relatively old, dating from the days when the language of both the humanities and the sciences (such as they were) was Latin. The main structures in the human body, and their counterparts in animals, are well known. The terms humerus and femur, or arm bone and thigh bone, are generally understood. Why complicate the issue? The answer, as every engineer knows, is that power generated by main levers or engines often requires small but intricate means for its transmission. It will not help, however powerful our thighs, however graceful our lower limbs, if their effects cannot be transmitted to our feet which, as we all know, lie in a different plane from that of our legs. There has therefore to be a joint that can transmit the impulses of our vertical limbs to our relatively flat feet.

It will help and save time and space if we contrast the arms and legs in this joint enterprise, remembering that in most animals the two limbs have a somewhat similar role which we, as human beings, have lost. The table shows the relative parts:

ARM				LEG
Humerus (upper arm bone)		=	Femur (thigh bone)	
Radius		=	Tibia (shin bone)	
Ulna (with funny bone)		=	Fibula	

WRIST				ANKLE
Three upper bones	Radiale	=	Tibiale–Astragulus	
	Intermedium	=	Intermedium	
	Ulnare	=	Fibulare–Calcaneum	

Two median bones	Centrale 1	=	Centrale 1
	Centrale 2	=	Centrale 2

	Carpale 1	=	Tarsale 1	
Five lower bones	Carpale 2	=	Tarsale 2	Five lower bones
to match the	Carpale 3	=	Tarsale 3	to match the
fingers	Carpale 4	=	Tarsale 4	toes
	Carpale 5	=	Tarsale 5	

Then come the five metacarpals in the palm and the five fingers.

Then come the five metatarsals in the instep and sole and the five toes.

81

In most of the theropods there are pieces of bone that can be identified with some difficulty; in sauropods there is a single flat plate of bone; and in the Ornithischia as a whole (except the hadrosaurs and the ankylosaurs) there is better representation of carpal elements and more understanding of the complex. In many dinosaurs, especially the bipedal forms, there was a tendency to reduction of the number of digits (fingers and toes) so that a reduction of carpal and tarsal elements is only to be expected. In *Iguanodon*, which has become one of the best-known dinosaurs, the elements became fused and they can therefore be well seen, especially in younger specimens (see Fig. 18).

As for the fingers themselves, they vary in number from five in early theropods and in such ornithischians as *Iguanodon* and *Camptosaurus*, down to two in the great flesh-eaters *Gorgosaurus* and *Tyrannosaurus*. There can, too, be considerable variation in the length of the fingers, such a form as *Coelurus* (*Ornitholestes*) showing a remarkably long hand. The end of the fingers (terminal phalanges) may have claws (as in most theropods) or hoofs as in the hadrosaurs. In other words, they may be compressed sideways or they may be broad. And all of this is, of course, in accordance with the habit, whether bipedal or quadrupedal.

The pelvic girdle may be, as we have seen, one of two distinct kinds, a truly reptilian form, or a so-called bird-like form. Both of these are illustrated (Figs. 19 and 20). The pelves are structures of a three-fold purpose, viz. for the attachment and support of the limb musculature, to provide the articular surface and opening, the acetabulum, for the head of the femur or thigh bone and for the support of the abdomen especially in bipedal forms. Each pelvis is attached to the sacral vertebrae by means of the uppermost of its bones—the ilium. The pelvis consists essentially of three bones; the ilium above, the pubis below and in front, and the ischium below and behind. The three bones articulate along a more or less horizontal line which is intercepted by a semicircular opening in the ilium and two quadrants, one on each of the other elements. The resulting circular opening, for the head of the femur or thigh bone, is known as the acetabulum (*a* in the figures). This opening has, however,

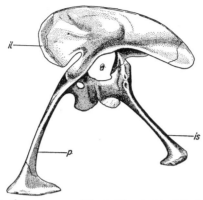

FIG. 19. Pelvis of *Ceratosaurus* (bipedal Saurischian). Left side. Approx.
$\frac{1}{16}$ nat. size.

KEY: *a.*, acetabulum; *il.*, ilium; *is.*, ischium; *p.*, pubis; *p'.*, post-pubis.

become closed again and the bones fused in some armoured dinosaurs.

The ilium varies very considerably in different kinds of dinosaurs. It is generally rather triangular in theropods, almost semicircular in sauropods, and elongated and sharp-pointed, rather like the head of an ice axe, in Ornithischia. In hadrosaurs and some armoured dinosaurs, there is a thickened process

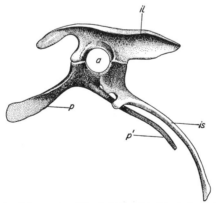

FIG. 20. Pelvis of *Iguanodon* (bipedal Ornithischian). Left side. Approx.
$\frac{1}{30}$ nat. size.

See key for Fig. 19.

83

above the acetabulum for the origin of a muscle to the tail and there are understandable thickenings on the upper border in those armoured forms that bear heavy bone plates.

The pubis, as we have already said, provides one of the main diagnostic characters for distinguishing the two main groups of dinosaurs. In theropods it is a relatively slender rod much expanded at its upper and lower ends, the whole bone being pendant at an angle of approximately 70° from the horizontal. The distal (lower) end is joined by cartilage to the distal end of the pubis of the other side and this region is greatly expanded in the large carnosaurs, *Gorgosaurus* and *Tyrannosaurus*, when it forms a keel that has left its imprint on ground where these dinosaurs have rested or have fed. In theropods the ischium is a shorter subcircular rod much expanded at its upper end but less thickened at the lower. It too is in contact with its opposite fellow.

In sauropods the pelvis is relatively simple and triradiate also, the rounded ilium being almost as extensive, fore and aft, as the lower bones. The pubis is short and flattish, more vertically directed than that of the theropods and contains a foramen near its junction with the ischium. The ischium is flattish, slightly expanded at its lower end and projects backwards at about 60° from the horizontal. These conditions are greatly different from the variations of the pelvis in the Ornithischia, even bearing in mind that the latter have bipedal and quadrupedal forms also.

In the ornithischians the pubis becomes a backward-facing rod that runs down alongside the long and rod-like ischium, sometimes this pubis is long and sometimes it is short, its function having been taken over largely by the ischium. The pubis has, however, a rod-like or an expanded, sometimes wing-like, anterior process that sticks out prominently in front and is mainly for the support of the abdomen. This dual role suggested that this was a close parallel with the condition in birds, but the dinosaur condition is that the anterior part is a prepubis, the true pubis being the hinder part. The dinosaur pubis is therefore an 'imitation' of the avian condition and not the same condition. This tetraradiate condition, in which the long and pointed ilium is underlain by a rifle-like structure obtains in most of the ornithopods but there are variations in the quadrupeds. In

Ankylosaurus the ilium develops a great overlapping flange above the acetabulum which is closed, and the pubis has virtually disappeared. In the Ceratopsia the prepubis may be very much reduced so that a triradiate condition seems to exist in *Monoclonius* and *Triceratops*. While the base of the pubis is never expanded in the Ornithischia the lower end of the ischium is dilated in the hooded hadrosaurs, no doubt in association with a strengthening of the origin of an iliocaudal muscle for moving the tail in aquatic forms.

But it was not only in the hadrosaurs that the dinosaur tail played an important part, most bipedal forms used the tail as a balance. When the animal moved with speed, it was bent forward, the weight of the skull, neck and body being counterbalanced by the tail which was lifted off the ground. This placed the centre of balance in and around the rump and thus demonstrates the need for a strong and efficiently arranged musculature between the pelvic girdle and the tail. As has been said, ossified tendons, running along the back of the vertebrae and the sides of the neural spines, are constant features of many Ornithischia.

The femur in dinosaurs is usually larger than the humerus (Fig. 21) and is generally vertical to the body, whereas the humerus may be almost at right angles horizontally to it. The femur, as a rule, is built on a bird-like plan, and one of its prominent features is a process arising on the middle of its length, known as the fourth trochanter, and associated with the highly developed musculature of the limbs and the tail. The head of the femur articulates in the acetabulum by a more or less convex and distinct head. The distal end of the bone is differentiated into two prominences, or condyles, separated by a groove, for articulation with the lower leg bones, the tibia and fibula.

The tibia is the more prominent of the two, is generally stout, and is distinguishable by the rather unusual angulation of the upper articular surface. On the front of this is an expansion, known as the cnemial crest, for the attachment of the extensor muscles since there is no knee cap, or patella (Fig. 22).

The proportionate lengths of the tibia and the femur are important for in most swiftly moving vertebrates on land, the tibia is longer than the thigh bone. The relationship is, therefore, some indication of speed. The fibula is a much more slender, and usually a straighter, bone. At their lower ends the tibia and fibula are in intimate contact with the first two tarsal (ankle) bones. These have already been enumerated with those of the wrist. The tibia articulates with the astragalus, with which it is sometimes fused, and which has a prominent ascending process in some of the early theropod dinosaurs, while the

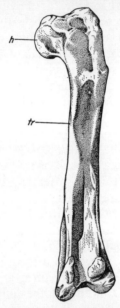

FIG. 21. Right femur of *Ceratosaurus nasicornis*. Back view. Approx. ⅛ nat. size.

KEY: *h.*, head; *tr.*, fourth or inner trochanter.

fibula rests upon the small calcaneum, and is sometimes (but less frequently in Ornithischia) also fused to it; while not infrequently, especially in the Stegosaurian armoured dinosaurs, the astragulus and calcaneum are fused together as well, forming a smooth convex ankle joint. The other tarsal bones are usually fused into one element, but they may be distinct, reduced in number, as appears the case in the hadrosaurs, or absent altogether.

The hind foot, like the fore foot, is variable in character and may be three-toed or five-toed, clawed or hoofed. Where the number of digits is reduced there is still some trace, as a rule, of the original number. Three functional digits are present in most of the bipedal forms (Fig. 23), while five are present in the large sauropods. The feet may be plantigrade (as in sauropods and armoured forms) or digitigrade, as in theropods and

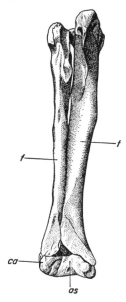

FIG. 22. Right tibia and fibula of *Ceratosaurus nasicornis*. Front view. Approx. ⅓ nat. size.

KEY: *cc.*, cnemial crest; *t.*, tibia; *f.*, fibula; *a.*, astragalus; *ca.*, calcaneum.

ornithopods, where it attains a bird-like form. The toes may be of moderate size or greatly elongated, and the ends of the toes may carry hoofs.

Such then are the bony internal elements which served as the foundation for the attachment of the muscles and the other fleshy portions of the creature. But in the dinosaurs, as in some other reptiles, notably the crocodiles among present-day forms, there were often bony elements of a more external nature that are grouped under the name of the exoskeleton. The most

87

obvious and remarkable bony structures to be noticed under this heading are the various armour devices. These are found in the Theropoda and Ornithopoda to some extent, but they are characteristic of the Stegosauria, Ankylosauria and Ceratopsia. This armour may take the form of upstanding bony spines or plates (as in *Stegosaurus* itself), as polygonal plates or bosses of varying size lying on or in the skin, as interlocking scutes

FIG. 23. Right hind foot of *Iguanodon atherfieldensis*. (From Hooley.)
II–IV metatarsals and phalanges. Approx. ⅛ nat. size.

forming shields or bars, or merely as tiny peas of bone (ossicles) in the folds of skin between the shields and bars. Considerable variety exists in the nature and arrangement of this dermal armour which will be dealt with in the various families affected. A less important, and in life certainly a less conspicuous, kind of exoskeleton is that composed by the abdominal ribs (Fig. 24). These are a series of ribs covering the abdomen, much less

FIG. 24. Double abdominal rib of *Antrodemus valens*. Approx. ⅓ nat. size.

robustly developed than the ordinary vertebral ribs, but more numerous with two sometimes occurring to each one of the ordinary ribs in the length of the body concerned.

Their development in dinosaurs is restricted, with only one exception, to the bipedal and carnivorous Theropoda, and the Prosauropoda, and they are found well developed not only in the early Triassic forms such as *Plateosaurus*, but in such late Cretaceous genera as *Ornithomimus* (Sternberg, 1933). In these, however, they never reached the stage of development attained in some other Orders, as for example, the plesiosaurs in which the abdominal ribs came to form a sort of plastron.

FIG. 25. Restoration of musculature of *Chasmosaurus*. SEE FIG. 1. (From L. S. Russell 1935.)

The skin of the unarmoured kinds of dinosaurs is very imperfectly known. It was probably smooth in some forms, scaly in others, while in *Anatosaurus* we know it to have been thin and flexible with a mosaic pattern of little polygonal plates. *Iguanodon* apparently had a thin tuberculated skin, in which the tubercles even occurred on the skin between the fingers.

Dinosaurs, being reptiles, had, of course, no hair or feathers. The muscles or fleshy structures are almost entirely unknown, though bony indications allow a certain amount of imaginative reconstruction. Associated with sauropod skeletons there have been found gastroliths or stomach-stones used, presumably, for the attrition of the food. Many dinosaur eggs have also been found but these will be dealt with more fully in the description of the particular dinosaurs.

89

The Physiology of Dinosaurs

From far, from eve and morning,
And yon twelve-winded sky,
The stuff of life to knit me,
Blew hither: here am I.
A. E. HOUSMAN *A Shropshire Lad*

The stuff of life is by no means all bone and muscle. For those who are justifiably wearied with the names of bones and their connexions there is hope that a happier and more exciting tale can be made of the things that make bone and muscle work, the story of eye and ear, of voice and heart and the very breath of life itself.

Dinosaur life as seen in many restoration pictures appears to have been cunning, swift and merciless. These were indeed, dragons of the prime. But we may dare to ask for confirmation, to wonder if dinosaurs were not as other reptiles or even as other vertebrates and we know enough specimens now to be able to reconstruct much of the story of their living processes and evaluate them in a modern world.

In the world today we can still examine the nearest living relatives, the crocodiles. It is true that crocodiles and alligators would seem to have little relevance to swiftly moving bipeds on land but the underlying animal mechanism—the physiology—must be closely similar.

No man has seen a living dinosaur. We are wholly dependent on specimens of bones, eggs, skin impressions, footprints and a whole series of physical investigations that can now be made into the world of dinosaur times.

Oxygen isotopes help us to recapture the temperature of the oceans, palaeoclimatic studies, rock chemistry and the study of fossil plants can make clear the general conditions and even local variations of the environment. We have already mentioned several of these as contributors to our knowledge of the

90

Mesozoic scene but that also have their direct evidence for the dinosaurs themselves.

Were dinosaurs warm-blooded? A question not infrequently asked can be answered by such studies. Did dinosaurs have colour vision? That is another that may also be answered but by a very different series of investigations and assumptions.

No soft parts have ever been discovered in any find of dinosaur remains and even attempts to determine the nature of such parts by chemical (trace elements) means have so far failed. The so-called dinosaur mummy is not a mummy in any popular sense and shows a fairly complete skeleton with the imprint of the skin pattern upon it. There are many finds that given us a clue as to the nature of the skin covering, and this is valuable from the physiological point of view.

We can reasonably assume that the nature (though not the size) of heart and lungs and the space to be devoted to other body contents will have their modern counterparts that are reliable evidence. We can discuss the effects of body size and their physiological advantages to large or small dinosaurs.

The brain has never been recovered but the brain cavity is accessible to us in a number of skulls. We can make casts from this to disclose *relative* size of brain regions and glands and the number and position of the cranial nerves. This is no substitute for working on a real brain but, with other evidence of sensory organs, it can help.

All dinosaurs were reptiles so we may profitably turn to an up-to-date definition of reptiles, remembering of course that modern lizards, snakes, tortoises and turtles as well as crocodiles are a poor remnant of a once rich world. However, a comprehensive description that looks at both present and past forms, tells us that reptiles are poikilothermic tetrapods, mostly living and reproducing on land, though several have become water living.

Further, reptiles are distinguished from amphibians (of past and present) by having a horny skin, metanephric kidney, and by having the embryo in an egg shell with suitable protection (cleidoic condition). Reptiles are separated from higher groups, such as birds and mammals, by the nature of their covering and by the absence of hair and feathers, as well as by their temperature control mechanisms.

Actually we are not on very sound ground in that last sentence, for there is good evidence that the reptilian ancestors of the mammals may have had hair and that the reptilian ancestors of the birds may have had feathers and consequently that both these ancestors had something (namely blood) to keep warm. But neither of these ancient kinds of reptiles were dinosaurs, so we can safely rephrase the definition to cover our present needs.

Reptiles as defined are thus in a median state of development. Their organization is more advanced than that of fishes and amphibians. Their eggs no longer need be laid in water or moist conditions and this 'cleidoic' condition means a closed state in which the embryo is shut up with all that it needs for development in a more or less impermeable shell. In most cases this egg was left to develop in some simple nest such as dinosaurs made and the sea turtles still dig.

Crocodiles dig a nest and lay eggs; these are covered with sand and further eggs are laid. The nest is then covered up and would be invisible were it not that the mother crocodile usually sleeps on top of it. The eggs are very susceptible to moisture and will be spoiled by it. Dinosaurs may have had the same sort of nesting habits.

While reptiles produce eggs, not all of them are laid, and several modern lizards and snakes and the ancient, swimming ichthyosaurs hatched the eggs within the mother's body so that the young were born alive. This is not at all the same process as the birth of mammals. There is no evidence of this process (ovo-viviparity) in dinosaurs.

Crocodiles, as we have said, because of their ancestral relationship, may be taken as some anatomical and physiological indication of conditions in dinosaurs. The crocodilian tongue cannot be protruded and it is possible from the known development of the hyoid bones in dinosaurs that a tongue did exist in them too, and it has already been suggested that it might be protrusible. This could have been of some advantage to the herbivorous forms. The gullet in crocodiles, and perhaps in dinosaurs, is large and used for the storage of meat until it can be digested in the stomach. Crocodiles have a very powerful digestion that will effectively dissolve bones. This ability would account for the absence of any really solid materials in dinosaur coprolites.

The stomach is relatively small and this may be suspected in dinosaurs too, even in the sauropods, and the crocodilian lungs, well developed and separate, hang freely in the chest cavity, though with attachments to other structures. It is important to note that an effective diaphragm exists though it is formed by a different muscle from that in mammals.

The vascular system—heart and blood circulation—of crocodiles is among the best developed in all reptiles, for the heart is four-chambered, although a small aperture (the foramen Panizzae) connects the two aortae as they leave their separate ventricles. It means that arterial blood is distributed to the head, neck, gut, trunk and tail, while the other (right) aorta with its slightly mixed blood (arterial blood having come through the foramen Panizzae) gives the venous supply to most of the abdominal organs. This is a kind of circulation that could satisfactorily supply dinosaur activity, for the limitations of that were imposed by other factors.

A poikilothermic animal (as most reptiles have been) is in plain language a cold-blooded one, but this does not mean that they are necessarily cold. In water-living, cold-blooded animals the temperature is close to that of the water but on land things may be very different. As reptiles the dinosaurs absorbed heat from the sun, from the surrounding air, or from the ground. They also developed body heat through food or by activity. Most present-day reptiles avoid the direct heat of strong sun which could result in overheating and dehydration. In places like Texas or Central Africa one does not find snakes in the open but rather in shady places, in the undergrowth or around trees. Overheating leads to congestion of blood supply, over-heating of body organs, and the loss of body fluids. This soon leads to death, for reptiles have no inbuilt temperature regulation like that of mammals. Eating in reptiles produces heat and torpor and leads to comparatively long periods of non-activity. It should also be pointed out that the food demands of cold-blooded animals cannot be estimated on a warm-blooded basis.

Theropods needed less food than tigers and sauropods did not consume the amount of vegetation needed by an elephant.

When exercise is involved a problem clearly arises. Heat is generated in accordance with the bulk of a body which can be represented as the cube. Heat is lost in accordance with the area of the body surface and can thus be represented as the square. Thus a large dinosaur would build up an amount that would take time to be dispersed—for the animal to cool. A smaller dinosaur, whose bulk and body surface would be less unequal, could therefore be fairly active without distress, particularly in shady glades. One must not forget, however, that while large dinosaurs take time to cool they would also take time to heat up, so that all in all the dinosaur mode of life is not too difficult to reconstruct. Carnivores need flesh, but one doubts if dinosaurs were particular as to whether it was very fresh. Large carnivores could use sheer bulk against their prey and could no doubt wade into water of some depth. Little flesh-eaters could run in and out of shady lanes and snatch the busy, cropping herbivores or other reptiles. Little dinosaurs could afford an alternation of speed and rest. Large dinosaurs almost certainly ambled leisurely on their terrifying way.

Faced with somewhat similar problems, the bipedal plant-eaters no doubt formed small herds to feed, to rest and to drowse in the leafy groves, their bursts of speed being reserved for flight from enemies.

Since the general climate of the Mesozoic was equally warm, almost from pole to pole, the dinosaurs were bathed in warmth and their external atmosphere largely compensated for, if it did not actually equal, the absence of an internal heat system such as mammals have. Shade, coolish waters and luxuriant vegetation formed the background to a very stable kind of life that is not difficult to imagine. One can picture warm sunshine and drowsy groves where a small herd of modest herbivores rests on hind limbs and tail, their jaws champing away on the contents of their cheek pouches. Around the margins of the group a wary little carnivore steals among the trees, looking for a slothful victim and principally wary lest he disturb a larger animal of his own kind, for we have some proof of cannibalism. The odd reptile of a different kind scuttled in the undergrowth, while

94

THE PHYSIOLOGY OF DINOSAURS

beyond the trees the splash of water told of an invasion of the sauropods' swamp or of a sauropod stirring itself. What was lacking was speed, and almost certainly cunning, in the daily round. Elsewhere in the open, an armoured dinosaur moved unhurriedly from grove to grove, or a biped stretched itself facing the sun or letting its less warm rays slant upon its back.

A life, with no yesterdays to remember and no tomorrow to fear, for nearly 150 million years. Dinosaurs came and went, vegetation changed, the colour of flowers came and was followed swiftly by a new sound, that of the bees. The drowsy days of the dinosaurs went on and on.

It is hard to speculate on dinosaurs' thoughts. The brain cannot be completely known for none of its substance exists. We can explore the brain cavity that once held the tissue, we can see the pit in its floor that held, among other things, the pituitary gland that controlled the animal's growth and the functions of other endocrine glands, including those of sex. We can estimate something of the length of the brain by the foramina for the cranial nerves whose position is fairly stable among lower vertebrates.

The swell of optic lobes can be assessed, the otic region can be reconstructed and the olfactory region can be defined; these are shown in Figures 26–32. But what do they mean? Obviously there can be no accurate description, we can write no prescription for dinosaurs' eyes, or estimate the capacity and range of dinosaur ears. The senses have, however, had their place in scientific literature.

Let us first consider what we can know of the brain. We certainly do not know it as an actual organ but it has been studied, and it is available for study, in a number of different kinds of dinosaurs in the form of a cast of the so-called brain cavity. This is more accurately to be called the endocranial cavity, the space enclosed by the cranial bones.

This cavity has not been examined in reptiles as often as might have been expected and for many years the classic study of the brain of *Sphenodon* by Arthur Dendy, made in 1911, was the principal account. This showed that the brain of that living reptile of very ancient lineage only occupied half of its brain case and was surrounded by threads of connective

95

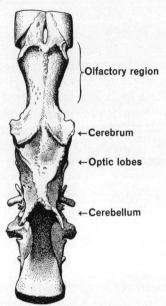

Olfactory region

←Cerebrum

←Optic lobes

←Cerebellum

FIG. 26. Brain of *Tyrannosaurus*. Top view. × ¼ nat. size.

tissue. Observations made on crocodile skulls have shown that crocodiles too have much smaller brains than their brain cavities would otherwise lead one to expect.

Now *Sphenodon* and the crocodiles are of ancient ancestry and warn us that in dinosaurs the size of the braincase could exaggerate the size of its contents. Casts of dinosaur endocranial cavities have been made. They are known from the theropods *Ceratosaurus* and *Tyrannosaurus*, from the prosauropod *Plateosaurus*, the sauropods *Barosaurus* and *Camarasaurus*, the

FIG. 27. Brain of *Tyrannosaurus*. Right side. × ¼

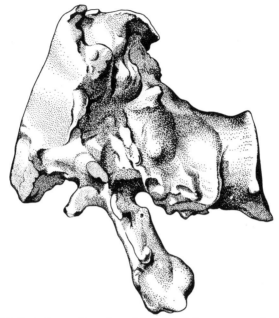

FIG. 28. Posterior portion of cranial cavity of *Camarasaurus*. Left side, showing cast of pituitary cavity below.

ornithopods, *Iguanodon, Anatosaurus* and *Pachycephalosaurus*, and from such armoured dinosaurs as *Stegosaurus, Kentrosaurus, Ankylosaurus, Protoceratops, Anchiceratops and Triceratops*.

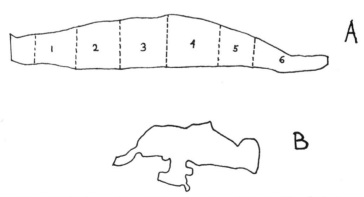

FIG. 29. Endosacral cast (A) and endocranial cast (B) of *Anatosaurus.* × ⅙. From the left.

97

From this evidence several things are clear: the dinosaur brain is relatively small, sometimes ridiculously small, compared with the size of the body; and it shows little advance in structure over the crocodile brain.

FIG. 30. Reconstruction of brain of *Anatosaurus*. (From Lull and Wright.) × ¼.

The first thing to observe is that both brains are low and elongate as compared with the rounded and compact brains of higher (i.e. more advanced) animals, such as birds and mammals. The surface of the brain, which is known in crocodiles and postulated in dinosaurs, is smooth and not convoluted.

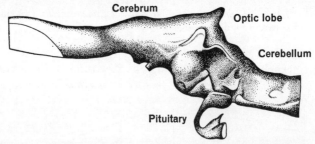

Cerebrum

Optic lobe

Cerebellum

Pituitary

FIG. 31. Brain of *Stegosaurus*. Left side, showing pituitary (below).

Both brains start, at the front, with the slightly expanded olfactory bulbs (the seat of the sense of smell) which are connected by a thin tube, the olfactory tract, with the cerebrum, which is expanded laterally and vertically and is the fore brain or the part of the brain containing the co-ordinating and largely instinctive mechanisms. Behind the cerebral lobes or hemispheres (for these are paired structures) are the small, egg-shaped optic lobes, side by side but leaning back on the front surface of the united cerebellum, or hind brain, which controls the complicated movements of the reptiles and deals with balance and pose.

Immediately below the optic lobes, in the centre of the lower brain surface, is the pituitary gland which is of great importance, as we shall see. Behind and below the cerebellum is the medulla oblongata, containing the vital centres for respiration and heart control.

FIG. 32. Brain cast of *Stegosaurus*. Top view. × ½.

Along the side of the brain, but mainly in the region behind and below the cerebral hemispheres and the medulla, are the ten important cranial nerves, remembered by countless students through various (and sometimes unprintable) mnemonics. However remembered, they are the olfactory (for smell) and at front, optic (of the eye), oculomotor (for eye muscles), trochlear (for an eye muscle), trigeminal (mainly sensory), abducens (for an eye muscle), facial (face muscle), auditory (for hearing),

99

glosso-pharyngeal (swallowing) and the vagus (going to heart and lungs).

The functions of these nerves are best known in mammals but their importance in reptiles must have been as great. It is interesting to note in looking at the Figures how much importance was placed on the sense of smell (with an invariably large olfactory bulb) and on the eye, with its special lobes and four associated nerves. A great deal had to be accomplished over the vital functions and in the body by the vagus nerve. Of course the body and limbs had their own nerve supplies carried through the spinal cord.

It is unfortunate that hardly any dinosaurian brain cast has anything like a complete brain. In *Tyrannosaurus, Plateosaurus, Pachycephalosaurus*, and *Anchiceratops*, the long olfactory tract can be seen, and the rise of the cerebral hemispheres is clear in nearly all of them. In *Plateosaurus, Barosaurus, Anchiceratops*, and *Tyrannosaurus* the drawn-out upper parts of the optic lobes can be seen; thereafter, in all the casts the observable features are less defined until the marked cut-off of the foramen magnum at the back.

The pendent, trigger-like pituitary body can clearly be seen directed slightly backwards in some of them. It is known to be large in *Tyrannosaurus* which is, however, a large brain, and in *Pachycephalosaurus*. The pituitary gland (or hypophysis) is an endocrine gland; that is, its chemical products are hormones which are passed directly into the blood stream. There is a chain of endocrine glands that includes the adrenal and the sex glands, but the pituitary appears to be the regulator of the series. It is the gland that controls growth, and interference with its function can cause dwarfism or forms of overgrowth.

Various workers in recent years have shown that the pituitary in reptiles has an influence on the ovaries, on the regulation of water metabolism and on part at least of the mechanism of skin colouring. That these were equally under pituitary control in dinosaurs is probably also true, though skin pigmentation in dinosaurs and modern reptiles probably differed considerably.

An estimate of brain structure would seem to show that thinking in dinosaurs was almost impossible. Response to nervous stimuli occurred and must have accounted for most of their action, for it seems that reptiles in general do not have the high degree of instinctive behaviour that is characteristic of modern birds, and modern reptiles certainly have little aptitude for learning.

Among reptiles of today, for example, tortoises seem to have some little social organization but once again we must carefully exclude the dinosaurs from the sort of social behaviour that is developed by living birds (e.g. penguins) and the mammals. It would appear to be certain that dinosaurian life was at a different tempo, the result of stimuli, including of course those of the nose, eye and ear.

The olfactory, or smelling, region of the brain appears to have been well developed in all dinosaurs whose brain casts we know and the nasal openings in all dinosaurs are large, sometimes very large. The extraordinary development of the nasal passages in the hadrosaurs will be described later but these passages are exceptional and presumably for a very special purpose. It is, of course, probable that the sense of smell was important as an aid to the recognition of food, of enemies and of friends.

It can be assumed that the sense of smell was good but it should be remembered that not all the nasal chamber is devoted to smelling, for in reptiles the chamber is well supplied with blood vessels and could therefore be of use in heat control. This area could be one of the very few areas, if not the only area, open to reptiles for this purpose.

There is no evidence of the place for or the presence of Jacobson's organ in dinosaurs.

The eye is well developed in dinosaurs and in some of them it is very large. In many forms the eye was strengthened in front of a ring of sclerotic plates which differed in pattern in groups of similar dinosaurs (hadrosaurs, for example). In modern reptiles there is sometimes a small ring of overlapping plates between the sclera and the cornea. These often number fourteen, and this number occurs in hadrosaurs.

Various purposes have been ascribed to these plates. It has been thought that they were protective, or that they moved and could compress the eye thus giving some measure of 'accommodation', or it has been suggested that the eye could be pressed against the plates thus varying the focus (power of accommodation). However this function in modern reptiles is achieved by muscular power and crocodiles, the ancient relatives of dinosaurs, seem to manage the safety of their eyes on land and water and their shift of focus without the aid of sclerotic plates.

The eyes of dinosaurs undoubtedly functioned as well as their nervous system and brain reception permitted and it would seem that their visual perception was adequate but it is interesting to speculate if, like so many modern reptiles, they had a measure of binocular vision. Some almost certainly did.

Many modern reptiles have reddish or yellowish eyes and who can say what glinted from the long-lost eyes of dinosaurs or if the eyes shared in a general colour scheme for the animals' concealment and protection?

One intriguing question is whether dinosaurs had colour vision. According to Angus Bellairs (1957), lizards, tortoises and perhaps snakes see colours but he doubts that crocodiles share this power. The question is not so fatuous as might appear at first sight for although among mammals only men, the great apes and monkeys enjoy colour, we know that birds have a wider range of colour vision than we have and turtles have satisfied Dr Ida Mann (1950) as to their gifts in this direction. If turtles and lizards do see colour, as is agreed, and crocodiles *may*, then there is an ancestral evolutionary possibility that dinosaurs wandered around in a world of colour. After all, the flowers and the bees came into the world in the Mesozoic and the bees saw the colours.

The structure of the ear has already been described and it was undoubtedly similar to that of the crocodile. The sense of hearing was therefore fairly well developed and it may be presumed to have served to give warning of peril of one kind or another and to have aided the recognition of members of its own kind. Presumably this presence of an efficient ear implies some ability of voice. Once again there can be no proof of this but the occurrence in many forms of hyoid bones, and rather massive ones in the ceratopsians, suggests that dinosaurs had a good voice. In this they may well have equalled the crocodiles, all of which have a short and loud croak or bark by means of

102

which they identify one another in the dark or which they use when they are angry (Fig. 33).

We may therefore hear, in our imagination, the full-throated croak of a *Tyrannosaurus* disturbed over its food or the bark of a lonely *Triceratops* on a warm, dark Cretaceous night.

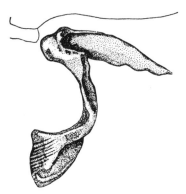

FIG. 33. Hyoid of *Triceratops serratus*. (After Lull.) × ¼.

The otic region, which is partially reconstructed in Fig. 34, shows that the three semi-circular canals, that are associated with the balancing function, are often observable. We could hardly doubt that equilibration would be satisfactory in dinosaurs but the direction, that is the plane in which the

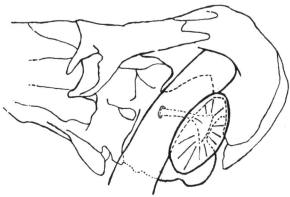

FIG. 34. Tympanum and stapes of *Anatosaurus*. (From Lull and Wright.)

103

external semicircular canal lies, is an accurate guide to the angle at which the head was carried when the animal was resting. This is very important in reconstructing the poise of the animal in general.

The nature of the jaws and teeth is another important aspect in the reconstruction of the animal's life but their characters are so much part of the identification and classification of the individual dinosaur that the description and discussion are best left to the systematic chapters of this book.

However, post-cranial physiology is important, and although we have no evidence at all of the size of heart and lungs, some questions may be answered. It is not possible to conjecture realistically the heart or respiration rates of dinosaurs. Among living reptiles both rates vary considerably according to temperature and activity. Respiration can be either astonishingly low (1 respiration an hour) or as high as 200 a minute depending on species and conditions, though neither is likely to have been a dinosaurian state. A resting dinosaur with a temperature of 80°F (=27°C) might have a heart beat of 35 per minute if living reptiles are any guide but what the heart beat and respiration would be after exercise it is impossible to say.

The spinal cord of dinosaurs is notable in that a sacral enlargement is found (or rather its cavity is found) in many dinosaurs and this is unusually large in sauropods and in *Stegosaurus*. In fact, many animals have enlargements of the cord in both shoulder (brachial) and sacral regions. In man there is a cervical enlargement (about 38 mm. in circumference) and a lumbar enlargement (about 33 mm. in circumference) compared with a circumference of about 22 mm. in the intervening region. In turtles the two enlargements are marked and in all cases the enlargement is to provide a more extensive innervation to the adjacent limbs.

The unusually large size of the sacral nerve centre is due to the unusually large size of the hind limbs (as compared with the front legs) and the tail.

Perhaps a few words should be said here about eggs. We shall see in due course that eggs are known of sauropods, ornithopods and armoured dinosaurs. These vary a great deal in size and it would be interesting to calculate the growth rate from a known embryo to a known adult but this can only be done in the case of *Protoceratops*. The eggs are about 8 inches long with a wrinkled shell, and the adult dinosaur is all of 6 feet long. This growth of approximately twelve times is not very remarkable. Eggs of large pythons which may be 15 feet or more in length and of considerable girth, are often only 5 inches by 2, and here obviously much growth takes place. A crocodile egg of about 3¼ inches length and 2 inches width brings forth a little crocodile 11 inches long. The largest tortoises lay an egg about the size of a tennis ball.

These observations may be of some interest but they can help us little in the dinosaurs, for the number of discoveries of eggs are few and good grounds for attribution to parentage are fewer. But dinosaurs laid eggs and, as has been said before, we know of no instance of baby dinosaurs being developed in the body of the mother.

However, growth rates depend upon size and the length of life. The former is well known to us but we can only speculate on the latter. It is most unlikely that dinosaurs shared the longevity attributed to crocodiles and tortoises and we have little with which to compare them.

Ages of large mammals are usually known from zoological gardens but the normal age of elephants in the wild is not known.

Perhaps a fifty-year-old dinosaur was not only old but fortunate, fortunate that is to have escaped many natural hazards, such as broken neck or broken limbs, quite apart from the unkind attentions of its fellows.

CHAPTER VII

Classification

Where order in variety we see
And where, though all things differ, all agree.
POPE *Windsor Forest*

The first English dinosaur remains ever discovered which are still available to us were collected from Jurassic and Wealden (Cretaceous) deposits in the southern half of England early in the nineteenth century. They were first described by Professor W. Buckland in 1824 and by Dr Gideon Mantell in 1825. These reptiles were, respectively, *Megalosaurus*, a flesh-eating animal, and *Iguanodon*, a herbivore, both bipedal. To this number of unusually large reptiles there were soon added *Hylaeosaurus*, an armoured herbivore (1832), and a very large amphibious animal, *Cetiosaurus* in 1841.

It was in 1841 that Richard Owen, then Hunterian Professor of Comparative Anatomy and Physiology in the Royal College of Surgeons in London, an enthusiastic worker on animals of all kinds but especially on fossil vertebrates, continued a study on fossil reptiles that he had begun in 1839. This famous 'Report on British Fossil Reptiles' is in two parts in the *Report of the British Association for the Advancement of Science* 1839 (published 1840) and for 1840 and for 1841 (published together in 1842).

It was in this second (1841) report that Owen discussed these new kinds of reptiles and proposed (p. 103) the name Dinosauria. This volume is something of a rarity even in England and no excuse is given therefore for the reproduction word by word of what is the foundation document of the dinosaurs.

DINOSAURIANS

'This group, which includes at least three well-established genera

of Saurians, is characterized by a large sacrum composed of five
anchylosed vertebrae of unusual construction, by the height and
breadth and outward sculpturing of the neural arch of the dorsal
vertebrae, by the twofold articulation of the ribs to the vertebrae,
viz. at the anterior part of the spine by a head and tubercle, and
along the rest of the trunk by a tubercle attached to the transverse process only; by broad and sometimes complicated
coracoids and long and slender clavicles, whereby Crocodilian
characters of the vertebral column are combined with a
Lacertilian type of the pectoral arch; the dental organs also
exhibit the same transitional or annectent characters in a greater
or less degree. The bones of the extremities are of large propor-
tional size, for Saurians; they are provided with large medullary
cavities, and with well-developed and unusual processes, and
are terminated by metacarpal, metatarsal and phalangeal bones,
which, with the exception of the ungual phalanges, more or less
resemble those of the heavy pachydermal Mammals, and attest,
with the hollow long-bones, the terrestrial habits of the species.

The combination of such characters, some, as the sacral ones,
altogether peculiar among Reptiles, others borrowed, as it were,
from groups now distinct from each other, and all manifested by
creatures far surpassing in size the largest of existing reptiles,
will, it is presumed, be deemed sufficient ground for establishing
a distinct tribe or sub order of Saurian Reptiles, for which I
would propose the name of *Dinosauria*.[1]

Of this tribe the principal and best established genera are the
Megalosaurus, the Hylaeosaurus, and the Iguanodon; the
gigantic Crocodile-lizards of the dry land, the peculiarities of the
osteological structure of which distinguish them as clearly
from the modern terrestrial and amphibious Sauria, as the
opposite modifications for an aquatic life characterize the
extinct *Enaliosauria*, or Marine Lizards.' (Quotation from
pp. 102–3.)

[1] Gr. Deinos fearfully great: Sauros a lizard. In the tabular arrangement of
extinct Saurians founded by M. Herm. v. Meyer on the development of their
organs of motion, the *Megalosaurus* and *Iguanodon* are grouped together in
Section B, with the following character:—Saurians with locomotive extremities
like those of the bulky terrestrial Mammals: '(Saurier mit Gliedmassen ähnlich
denen der schweren Landsaugethiere).' *Palaeologica*, p. 201. No other grounds
are assigned for their separation from other Saurians.

It will be seen from the last paragraph that Owen did not include his own genus *Cetiosaurus* in the new 'tribe or sub order' for the reason that to him it seemed 'to have been of strictly aquatic and most probably of marine habits' and he included the genus in his organization of the crocodiles. He still maintained this position in the second edition of his *Palaeontology* in 1861. The point is, that if Owen had recognized his genus of *Cetiosaurus* ('whale reptile') as a part of his Sub-order Dinosauria, as it now is recognized, he would have had each of the four main kinds of dinosaurs represented in the new classification.

The diagnosis elaborated by Owen has, of course, become greatly modified as subsequent discoveries have extended widely the knowledge of dinosaurs, their history, distribution and nature.

The long list of those who have contributed to this knowledge and the unravelling of the complicated story of dinosaur development and evolution contains the names of the most famous of vertebrate palaeontologists and comparative anatomists, of whom mention will be made many times in succeeding pages.

Among British contributors the chief have been W. Buckland, J. W. Hulke, T. H. Huxley, G. Mantell, R. Owen and H. G. Seeley in the past, and more recently Robert Broom, Sir Arthur Smith Woodward and D. M. S. Watson. Their American counterparts have been E. D. Cope, O. C. Marsh, W. D. Matthew, J. B. Hatcher, S. W. Williston, C. W. Gilmore, H. F. Osborn, Barnum Brown and R. S. Lull, and in recent times E. H. Colbert, A. S. Romer and J. Ostrom in the USA. In Canada the names of the Sternbergs, W. A. Parks, L. M. Lambe and L. S. Russell must be noticed.

The principal European authorities have been L. Dollo, O. Abel, E. Fraas, Baron F. Nopcsa, W. Janensch, A. Wiman and Freiherr F. von Huene, while O. Kuhn and A. F. de Lapparent are happily still with us. In China, C. C. Young has performed a remarkable task in overseeing the important results of Chinese investigation.

A large number of young, enthusiastic and critical students are now at work in many parts of the world and it is only natural that so many assiduous workers should have created several different schemes of classification, though a pattern of general agreement can now be seen and is interpreted in that used in the current edition of A. S. Romer's *Vertebrate Paleontology* (1966).

We have seen that the name Dinosauria is not now regarded as that of a natural Order and that the animals that have long been included in it are more correctly divided among two natural Orders. The first of these was named the Saurischia ('reptile hips') by H. G. Seeley and included the bipedal, flesh-eating theropods and the giant, aquatic sauropods. Seeley also named the other Order as the Ornithischia ('bird-hips') that also contains bipeds and quadrupeds, but all were vegetarians and the quadrupeds were armoured in one way or another.

Seeley's classification was not, however, the first and it only appeared in 1887. It was preceded by E. D. Cope (1866), by T. H. Huxley in 1870 and by O. C. Marsh in 1878 and subsequent years. These papers nicely divide interest in classification between the two founding countries of the dinosaurs, England and the USA, and it is historically interesting to look at these views today.

The very first attempt to put some order into, and name to, what we now know to be dinosaurs actually took place before the name Dinosauria had been coined. It was by Hermann von Meyer who classified fossil reptiles according to their locomotion and one of his divisions was 'Saurians, with limbs like those of the heavy terrestrial Mammalia'. This was in 1830–32, but he later gave the name Pachypodes, or Pachypoda, to this group mentioned in the footnote to Owen's definition reproduced above.

Owen himself made modifications as the number of recognized dinosaurs grew. In the second edition of his *Palaeontology*, already mentioned and published in 1861, he added *Scelidosaurus*, the lower Jurassic armoured dinosaur, to *Megalosaurus* and *Iguanodon*, and he reduced the characteristics of the Order Dinosauria (incidentally a promotion from the Sub-order of 1842) to the following: 'cervical and anterior dorsal vertebrae with par- and di-apophyses, articulating with bifurcate ribs; dorsal vertebrae with a neural platform, sacral vertebrae

109

exceeding two in number; body supported on four strong unguiculate limbs.'

This definition obviously suggests that the three dinosaurs comprising the Order were quadrupedal and this was certainly in Owen's mind, for the full-scale models made under his supervision and erected on the geological island in the Crystal Palace Grounds, Sydenham, London, in 1854, were on all fours as shown in Plate I.

This classification relied upon the characters of the feet and with several more genera upon which to build, E. D. Cope, the Pennsylvanian professor, proposed a very different classification based upon the tarsus (ankle bones) and the ilium of the hip-girdle. Briefly this divided dinosaurs into three groups as follows: (Cope 1866)

Orthopoda ('Straight-feet')	Ilium narrow with anterior prolongation. Proximal tarsals distinct from each other and the tibia. (*Scelidosaurus*, *Hyaleosaurus*, *Iguanodon*, *Hadrosaurus*.)
Goniopoda ('Angle-feet')	Plantigrade. Astragalus distinct from tibia but embraces distal end. Anterior part of ilium dilated and plate-like. (*Megalosaurus*, *Laelaps*, *Coelurosaurus*.)
Symphopoda ('Grown-together-feet')	First series of tarsal bones confluent with each other and with tibia. Anterior part of ilium dilated and plate-like. (*Ornithotarsus*, *Compsognathus*.)

There are obvious disadvantages in this table: the first group, the Orthopoda, which is a name still quoted as a synonym of the Ornithischia, contains both quadrupedal armoured forms and unarmoured bipeds. The Goniopoda contains three bipedal carnivores and the Symphopoda contains a hadrosaur and a carnivore. Thus there is a hadrosaur in the Orthopoda and the Symphopoda, and there are carnivores in both the Goniopoda and the Symphopoda.

Thomas Huxley (1870) rejected this classification on the grounds that the relations of the tarsal bones to the tibia and fibula were not determinant and he went on to say: 'The Dinosauria about which we have sufficient information appear to me to fall into three natural groups: I. The Megalosauridae,

110

II. The Scelidosauridae, and III. the Iguanodontidae.' The characters on which he based this classification were much wider than those of von Meyer, Owen or Cope and included the teeth, the mandibular rami (lower jaw halves), the ilium, the femur and the presence or absence of dermal armour. Huxley also had more specimens on which to base his views.

I. The Megalosauridae: Maxillary teeth sharp pointed, serrated; mandibular rami deep and thick, anterior part of ilium as large as posterior, proximal end of femur more or less crocodilian: no dermal armour (*Teratosaurus*, *Palaeosaurus*, *Megalosaurus*, *Poikilopleuron*, *Laelaps*, and probably *Euskelosaurus*).

[It may be noted at the time of writing that of these genera *Teratosaurus* and ?*Euskelosaurus* are prosauropods, *Laelaps* is a synonym of another carnivorous genus and *Palaeosaurus* is very doubtful as to provenance.]

II. The Scelidosauridae: Maxillary and mandibular teeth sharp-edged triangular crowns, serrated; mandibular rami slender and tapering; anterior part of ilium more slender than posterior; proximal end of femur with subglobular head on a neck at right angles to axis but parallel to plane of condyles: armour of bony plates or scales. (*Thecodontosaurus*; *Hylaeosaurus*; *Polacanthus* (?); and *Acanthopholis*. [At the time of writing *Thecodontosaurus* is regarded as an unarmoured prosauropod.]

III. The Iguanodontidae: Teeth above and below with obtuse subtriangular crowns: enamel is ridged and crowns worn by mastication; mandibular rami unite in toothless symphysis: anterior part of ilium more slender than posterior: head of femur as in Scelidosauridae: no dermal armour: (*Cetiosaurus*, *Iguanodon*, *Hypsilophodon*, *Hadrosaurus* and probably *Stenopelyx*).

[At the time of writing *Cetiosaurus* has long been regarded as a sauropod: *Hypsilophodon*, though close to *Iguanodon* has slight body armour, and *Stenopelix* may be a hypsilophodont.]

However, this was not all. Professor Huxley had trouble with *Compsognathus* which agreed with all three groups in 'the ornithic modification' especially of the hind limbs. He therefore added it to the other groups to make the Order Ornithoscelida

111

which was divided into (I) Dinosauria, with relatively short cervical vertebrae, and with the femur as long as, or longer than the tibia, (II) The Compsognatha, with relatively long cervical vertebrae and the femur shorter than the tibia.

In 1887 Professor H. G. Seeley, who had publicly differed with Huxley on the latter's presentation of his classification before the Geological Society of London, published his paper 'On the Classification of the Fossil Animals commonly named Dinosauria' (Seeley, 1887).

Here he drew attention to the memoirs of Professor O. C. Marsh of Yale (Marsh 1878–84)[1] which divided dinosaurs into four Orders and three Sub-orders, using all parts of the skeleton. These Orders were the Sauropoda, comprising the allies of *Cetiosaurus*; the Stegosauria, which included the allies of *Scelidosaurus*; the Ornithopoda, formed for the allies of *Iguanodon*; and the Theropoda, that included genera related to *Megalosaurus*. The Theropoda has Sub-orders for Coeluria and Compsognatha.

Marsh's classification was as follows:

Sub-Class DINOSAURIA

Premaxillary bones separate; upper and lower temporal arches; rami of lower jaw united in front by cartilage only; no teeth on palate. Neural arches of vertebrae united to centra by suture; cervical vertebrae numerous; sacral vertebrae co-ossified. Cervical ribs united to vertebrae by suture or ankylosis; thoracic ribs double-headed. Pelvic bones separate from each other, and from sacrum; ilium prolonged in front of acetabulum; acetabulum formed in part by pubis; ischia meet distally on median line. Fore and hind limbs present, the latter ambulatory and larger than those in front; head of femur at right angles to condyles; tibia with procnemial crest; fibula complete. First row of tarsals composed of astragalus and calcaneum only, which together form the upper portion of ankle joint.

(1) Order Sauropoda (Lizard foot.)   Herbivorous.

Feet plantigrade, ungulate; five digits in manus and pes; second row of carpals and tarsals unossified. Pubes projecting in front, and united distally by cartilage; no post-pubis. Precaudal vertebrae hollow. Fore and

[1] Principal characters of American Jurassic dinosaurs I 1878; II 1879; III 1880; IV 1881; V 1881; VI 1883; VII 1884; VIII 1884; IX 1887; Classification of Dinosauria 1882, 1884, 1885, 1896. All in *American Journal of Science*.

hind limbs nearly equal; limb bones solid. Sternal bones parial. Premaxillaries with teeth.

(i) Family Atlantosauridae. Anterior vertebrae opisthocoelian. Ischia directed downward, with extremities meeting on median line.

Genera *Atlantosaurus, Apatosaurus, Brontosaurus, Diplodocus,* ?*Camarasaurus (Amphicoelias),* ?*Dystrophoeus.*

(ii) Family Morosauridae. Anterior vertebrae opisthocoelian. Ischia directed backward, with sides meeting on median line.

Genus *Morosaurus.*

European forms of this order: *Bothriospondylus, Cetiosaurus, Chondrosteosaurus, Eucamerotus, Ornithopsis, Pelorosaurus.*

(2) Order Stegosauria (Plated lizard). Herbivorous.

Feet plantigrade, ungulate; five digits in manus and pes; second row of carpals unossified. Pubes projecting free in front; post-pubis present. Fore limbs very small; locomotion mainly on hind limbs. Vertebrae and limb bones solid. Osseous dermal armor.

(i) Family Stegosauridae. Vertebrae biconcave. Neural canal in sacrum expanded into large chamber; ischia directed backward, with sides meeting on median line. Astragalus co-ossified with tibia; metapodials very short.

Genera *Stegosaurus (Hypsirhophus), Diracodon,* and in Europe *Omosaurus,* Owen.

(ii) Family Scelidosauridae. Astragalus not co-ossified with tibia; metatarsals elongated; four functional digits in pes. Known forms all European.

Genera *Scelidosaurus, Acanthopholis, Crataeomus, Hylaeosaurus, Polacanthus.*

(3) Order Ornithopoda (Bird foot). Herbivorous.

Feet digitigrade, five functional digits in manus and three in pes. Pubes projecting free in front; post-pubis present. Vertebrae solid. Fore limbs small; limb bones hollow. Premaxillaries edentulous in front.

(i) Family Camptonotidae. Clavicles wanting; post-pubis complete.

Genera *Camptonotus, Laosaurus, Nanosaurus,* and in Europe *Hypsilophodon.*

(ii) Family Iguanodontidae. Clavicles present; post-pubis incomplete. Premaxillaries edentulous. Known forms all European.

Genera *Iguanodon, Vectisaurus.*

(iii) Family Hadrosauridae. Teeth in several rows, forming with use a tesselated grinding surface. Anterior vertebrae opisthocoelian.

Genera *Hadrosaurus,* ?*Agathaumas, Cionodon.*

(4) Order Theropoda (Beast foot). Carnivorous.

Feet digitigrade; digits with prehensile claws. Pubes projecting downward, and co-ossified distally. Vertebrae more or less cavernous. Fore limbs very small; limb bones hollow. Premaxillaries with teeth.

(i) Family Megalosauridae. Vertebrae biconcave. Pubes slender, and united distally. Astragalus with ascending process. Five digits in manus and four in pes.

Genera *Megalosaurus* (*Poikilopleuron*), from Europe. *Allosaurus*, *Coelosaurus*, *Creosaurus*, *Dryptosaurus* (*Laelaps*).

(ii) Family Zanclodontidae. Vertebrae biconcave. Pubes broad elongate plates, with anterior margins united. Astragalus without ascending process; five digits in manus and pes. Known forms European.

Genera *Zanclodon*, ?*Teratosaurus*.

(iii) Family Amphisauridae. Vertebrae biconcave. Pubes rod-like; five digits in manus and three in pes.

Genera *Amphisaurus* (*Megalodactylus*), ?*Bathygnathus*, ?*Clepsysaurus*; and in Europe, *Palaeosaurus*, *Thecodontosaurus*.

(iv) Family Labrosauridae. Anterior vertebrae strongly opisthocoelian, and cavernous. Metatarsals much elongated. Pubes slender, with anterior margins united.

Genus *Labrosaurus*.

Sub-order Coeluria (Hollow tail.)

(v) Family Coeluridae. Bones of skeleton pneumatic or hollow. Anterior cervical vertebrae opisthocoelian, remainder bi-concave. Metatarsals very long and slender.

Genus *Coelurus*.

Sub-order Compsognatha.

(vi) Family Compsognathidae. Anterior vertebrae opisthocoelian. Three functional digits in manus and pes. Ischia with long symphysis on median line. Only known specimen European.

Genus *Compsognathus*.

DINOSAURIA?

(5) Order Hallopoda (Leaping foot.)   Carnivorous?

Feet digitigrade, unguiculate; three digits in pes; metatarsals greatly elongated; calcaneum much produced backward. Fore limbs very small. Vertebrae and limb bones hollow. Vertebrae biconcave.

Family Hallopodidae.

Genus *Hallopus*.

This very familiar classification is, however, close to that of Huxley. As Seeley pointed out, the Theropoda of Marsh is identical with the Megalosauridae; the Ornithopoda is the Iguanodontidae renamed; 'while the Stegosauria is the Scelido-

114

sauridae of Huxley, enlarged like the other groups by Professor Marsh's admirable discoveries and renamed'.

Seeley went on to point out the importance of the pelvis in classification and the lesser importance of armour: the presence or absence of pneumatic conditions of the vertebrae and the characters of the base of the skull were also important. He figured the pelvic conditions of Stegosauria, Ornithopoda, Theropoda and Sauropoda that are reproduced here and argued that lesser characters of the limbs, ankles and feet were associated with the method of walking which, in turn, was shown by the main types of the pelvis.

After discussing vertebral and skull characters and rightly pointing out the need for the description of the materials being collected in some numbers he went on: 'The considerations adduced appear, however, to show that the Dinosauria has no existence as a natural group of animals, but includes two distinct types of animal structure with technical characters in common which show their descent from a common ancestry rather than their close affinity. These two orders of animals may be conveniently named the Ornithischia and the Saurischia, and defined by the following characters' (loc. cit., p. 170). A footnote points out that 'Ischia' is used by Aristotle for the pelvis, though as must have been widely known in the 1880s, the Greek word *ischion* means hip-joint and was commonly used in ancient Greek for the hips or loins.

We need not now repeat the characters of the two separate orders, for they will appear in their appropriate place in the succeeding chapters. However Seeley ended his paper with a tabular statement of dinosaurian classification carrying the picture up to 1887 (p. 116).

Since that date many new classifications have been made by Lydekker, Nopcsa, von Huene, O. Kuhn and others. These have varied the details and re-arranged some of the characters but have left the major groupings as they were. We have seen that the little Jurassic carnivore *Compsognathus* gave the earlier classifiers some trouble and it may be that it still has a significant place in one of the theropod evolutionary lines.

It has also been clear that the increase of discovery and the advancement of knowledge have demanded new classifications.

115

Cope, 1866	Huxley, 1870	Seeley, 1874	Marsh, 1878–84	Cope, 1883	Seeley, 1887
Orders.	Families.	Orders.	Orders.	Orders.	Orders.
Orthopoda....	{ Scelidosauridae { Iguanodontidae	... ...	Stegosauria.... Ornithopoda....	} Orthopoda.....	Ornithischia
Goniopoda...	Megalosauridae	Cetiosauria...	Sauropoda...	Opisthocoela[1] ..	} Saurischia
Symphopoda	Compsognatha	...	} Theropoda....	Goniopoda.....	
				Hallopoda	

[1] Sir Richard Owen grouped *Cetiosaurus* and *Streptospondylus* in an extinct Sub-order of Crocodilia named Opisthocoela in 1859; while *Megalosaurus* and *Iguanodon* were united to form the Dinosauria in 1841. This is the earliest and most definite reference of these animals to separate ordinal groups.

CLASSIFICATION

Dinosaur discovery, like other things, has had its ups and downs, its waxing and waning, but these last few years have seen a notable increase in re-classification. E. H. Colbert and A. S. Romer have been distinguished in these studies. More recently J. Ostrom, A. W. Crompton and A. J. Charig have made important suggestions. These will be considered in their appropriate places in the following pages when we deal with the main groups of the dinosaurs. From all this we shall see, as Seeley forecast, that the two great Orders of what we loosely and popularly call The Dinosaurs are indeed separate and the members of the respective Orders are the bearers of a long heritage which, at this moment, is not fully known.

Many of the characters that were chosen as criteria for classification are based essentially on the life that the creatures led. Their feeding habits, with their effect on the teeth and jaws, the pose of the body with its effects on the pelvis, and the structure of limbs and feet that dictated the mode of progression or were imposed on the animals by their way of life; all these may be useful in making order out of seeming bony chaos, but they are all important parts of the revealing story of the life of the various groups, a series of fascinating pieces of detective work to which we must now address ourselves.

The present classification (1969) of dinosaurs is:

Saurischia	Sub-order Theropoda.	Bipedal carnivores
	Infra-order Coelurosauria	Lightly built carnivores
	Infra-order Carnosauria	Large carnivores
	Sub-order Sauropodomorpha	Vegetarians
	Infra-order Prosauropoda	Pro-sauropod herbivores
	Infra-order Sauropoda	Quadrupedal herbivores
Ornithischia	Sub-order Ornithopoda	Bipedal herbivores
	Sub-order Stegosauria	Plated quadrupedal herbivores
	Sub-order Ankylosauria	Armoured quadrupedal herbivores
	Sub-order Ceratopsia	Horned quadrupedal herbivores

117

CHAPTER VIII

The Carnivorous Dinosaurs: Theropoda

Hunting their sport, and plundering was their trade.
DRYDEN *Translation of Virgil*

The carnivorous dinosaurs first appeared in the Trias and persisted until the close of the Cretaceous, their distribution during that great period of time being almost world-wide. Their remains have been found in both North and South America, in Britain, Germany, Asia, Africa, and Australia, and amongst them were the earliest to be found, examined, and described by scientific men. On glancing over the members of the Sub-order as a whole, there is definitely to be seen an evolution of more efficient kinds as the successive geological ages pass, and further, there are two distinct kinds, those of large size whose descendants became larger and more formidable, and those of smaller and apparently more graceful build whose representatives go on, in one genus or another, right through the history of the group. Usually, as we have seen, these two kinds are grouped into definite Infra-orders. It may be sufficient to say here that there is a great disparity in size among these carnivores, and that the largest known forms were produced towards the end of their history and were very formidable creatures indeed, and that the early Triassic forms were smaller and more awkward in their movements.

Unlike many chapters of the history of life, there is no profound mystery about these earliest dinosaurs; satisfactory positive evidence in the shape of numerous well-preserved and more or less complete skeletons has been obtained, and, for more than a century, there has also been available circumstantial evidence, in the form of footprints in shale and sandstone in the Connecticut Valley of Connecticut and Massachusetts, and

118

similar deposits in Pennsylvania, in New Jersey and New York State, USA. If there is lacking a concrete example of the transitional form between the Pseudosuchian ancestors and the first of these dinosaur lines, at least we seem to have some idea as to the process or processes that may have aided the transition; for most of these earliest remains are found embedded in reddish shales and sandstones that testify in some instances to the aridity of the climate, while in others, especially in American deposits, the colour seems due to alternate wetting and drying in a temperate climate.

Now aridity, whatever disadvantages it may produce, has some merit in a physiological way. It places a premium on all forms that can travel in search of food and water and is a great encouragement to agility. There seems no doubt, therefore, that the conditions obtaining when many of the dinosaurs found themselves introduced to the world were precisely those that would tend to promote a bipedal method of progression, just as they may do temporarily in the lizards of today. There is often greater possibility of developing a speedy cursorial power in the bipedal than in the quadrupedal. The dinosaurs appear to have taken full advantage of these opportunities, and, as we shall see, the bipedal forms were well-adapted for their life and times, and the carnivorous kinds were, at the least, formidable and, in some cases, terrible creatures of attack.

As has been said there are two main lines of flesh-eating dinosaurs that run from the Trias to the Upper Cretaceous. It is most unlikely that both are developed from the same Pseudo-suchian ancestor and it is intriguing to think that the poorly exposed outcrops of the 'Elgin Sandstones' of north-east Scotland may hold the key. For these light-coloured Lossie-mouth Beds have produced a remarkable fauna that is enumer-ated in *The Grampian Highlands* (1948, p. 69) published for the Geological Survey and Museum.

Here it states that the *Lossiemouth Beds* are terrestrial deposits. They have yielded *Ornithosuchus woodwardi* (and its synonym *Dasygnathus longidens*); *Scleromochlus taylori*; *Salt-opus elginensis*; which are all dinosaurs. Also found there are *Erpetosuchus*, a Pseudosuchian; *Stagonolepis*, an Aetosaurian thecodont; *Hyperadopedon* (*Stenometopon*) and *Brachy-*

119

rhinodon, which are Rhynchocephalian reptiles and *Telerpeton* one of the basal (Cotylosaurian) reptiles. All of them are given a Middle Triassic age by the distinguished palaeontologist D. M. S. Watson, but since that time a Middle Upper Triassic (*The Fossil Record*, 1968) age has been assigned to these beds and even an Upper Triassic (Rayner, 1968).

This means, of course, that an earlier date must be given to an ancestor for these early dinosaurs. *Ornithosuchus*, which was claimed to have Megalosaurian dinosaur affinities over seventy years ago but was widely regarded in the intervening years as the ideal ancestor to carnivorous dinosaurs, has now been abundantly proved (Walker, 1964) to be dinosaurian and close to the megalosaur stem. Walker suggests that the pseudo-suchian ancestor was *Euparkeria* and this, as we have already said, is a Lower Triassic South African form. There are now many interesting South and East African pseudosuchians of Middle Triassic age but the ancestry in the millions of inter-vening years and the waste of geographical miles must be hard to trace. Footprints, of which an abundance is known in the North American and European Trias, are hard to associate with names based on bones.

At any rate, in the later days of the Trias, there were probably three small carnivorous dinosaurs in the north-east of Scotland, which now, as fossils, are isolated from their kind which have been lost or undiscovered elsewhere. *Scleromochlus* which crosses the border between pseudosuchians and dinosaurs in various editions of textbooks, is considered a lightly built carnivore in these pages. And there are *Saltopus* and *Ornitho-suchus* each with a different potential. *Scleromochlus* was a small, apparently agile creature which was probably able to leap about, and the appearance of the restored skeleton is closely similar to that of some of the desert-living lizards of the present day. Several portions of skeletons are known and the animal appears to have been about a foot long from the tip of its pointed skull to the tip of its tail. The most remarkable feature about it is the small, almost triangular skull with its very small teeth; the whole skull measures only about $1\frac{1}{2}$ inches in length and a little less than 1 inch across at its widest points. The neck was short, the body slender, and the long lizard-like tail was

120

perhaps half as long again as the skull and body together. The sacrum was a comparatively stout little structure of four vertebrae. The front limb had the humerus and the forearm bones of about equal length, and a five-fingered hand, but the whole limb was only about half the size of the hind leg, which measured 4 or 5 inches. In it the femur, or thigh bone, was not quite so long as the lower leg bones, and the foot, with four long metatarsals, was four-toed. It is easy to imagine the little animal squatting on its hind legs with its fingers on the ground, ready to leap upwards and forwards in its search for food. So far as is known there was no armour of any kind in the skin and it may well have been very similar in appearance to the little lizards of today which are insectivorous. This does not mean that *Scleromochlus* was insectivorous, for its small, sharp teeth are suitable for a fleshy diet, quite apart from the fact that we have no evidence of Triassic insects here; but undoubtedly this dinosaur was active, and it is likely to have darted about the sandy places where it lived seeking its food dead or alive. The question as to whether the carnivorous dinosaurs actually killed their food or merely fed upon carrion is a vexed one for which there is little hope of a complete answer. Very probably they did both. It is difficult to imagine the food of *Scleromochlus* in particular. Many of its contemporaries were of much larger size, so possibly it lived on its smaller fellow archosaurs and the dinosaurs were probably not too particular about making a meal even of their own kinds.

Much of our picturing of these creatures is conjectural since we know so little of them and the number of individuals that have been recovered is small, but *Scleromochlus* is of great interest through its close association with the supposed ancestral stock.

The only species known is *S. taylori*, described and named by (Sir) A. Smith Woodward in 1907, and the type, or originally described specimen, is in the Department of Palaeontology of the British Museum.

Saltopus elginensis, described and figured by von Huene in 1910, is based on part of a skeleton without a skull. Its body vertebrae and the four sacral vertebrae are much the same in number as those of *Scleromochlus* and the general build of the

121

animal was similar. The femur, however, was shorter than the tibia and the metatarsals were long; two indications that this little dinosaur may have been even more active than its neighbour *Scleromochlus*.

The remains of similar, though often larger, reptiles have been obtained from Upper Triassic rocks of Colorado, Massachusetts, and New Mexico, in the United States, and Würtemberg in Germany. One of these German forms is *Procompsognathus* which was about 4 feet long. It came from Upper Triassic rocks at Pfaffenhofen, between Ingolstadt and Munich, and may represent an even more active member of this group, for the hind leg was three times as long as the forelimb and this may be taken as an indication of speed. These little creatures, lightly built and with hollow bones, may seem far from the popular idea of great and cumbrous dinosaurs. A far more satisfactory picture of them can be gained by a study of *Coelophysis*, an American example long known, at least in the literature but only reconstructed satisfactorily in recent years by E. H. Colbert of the American Museum of Natural History.

The original fossils were collected in New Mexico by a local collector, David Baldwin, in 1881, literally as a bagful of bones. They came from about fifty miles north-west of Santa Fe. The bones were duly despatched to Professor E. D. Cope in Philadelphia and, in due course, in 1887 that distinguished authority named three species of a genus *Coelurus*. In 1889 he changed the name for these particular species to *Coelophysis* ('hollow nature').

Nearly sixty years later in 1947 a party from the American Museum of Natural History happened to be in this neighbourhood and spent a few days at Ghost Ranch, a charming private home at that time. Here by chance they saw a few bones and this led to the discovery of what was virtually a graveyard of these little dinosaurs with many growth stages.

In consequence *Coelophysis* has become one of the best-known Triassic carnivores and life-size models of it are in several museums as well as the fine collection in New York.

This lightly built creature, up to 10 feet long, had some of its long bones hollow and this, with the long hind legs, twice as long as the front, all tells the story that it was a very fast mover,

122

as dinosaurs went. The neck and tail were long and would be stretched out as the animal sped on its way looking for lizards to eat. But some of the skeletons show small bones inside them and this suggests not that these were viviparous animals but that they were cannibals. Certainly the sharp little knives that were the teeth could have made short work of the victim.

There were other little dinosaurs living at the same time, such as *Podokesaurus*, 'the swift-footed reptile', from the Trias of Holyoke, Massachusetts. Unfortunately, very little is known about this little animal which was only about 3 feet long. The original specimen was lost in a fire and only casts of some of its bones and vertebrae are now available. From a study of these Dr Colbert has concluded that *Podokesaurus* was a form of *Coelophysis*, *C. holyokensis* (Talbot). The author's name, Talbot, is here in parentheses because his species has been moved to a different genus.

There exists therefore a group of contemporaneous but widely spread Upper Triassic dinosaurs that were light in weight, rapacious of appetite and swift of foot. Their number can be amplified by considering such forms as are represented by the numerous well-marked footprints that for many years have been found along the Connecticut River valley between Turner's Falls, near Greenfield, and South Hadley, near Holyoke, Massachusetts. The bird-like tracks in shaly sandstone which were first attributed to Noah's raven are now assigned to carnivorous dinosaurs, and throw much light on their method of movement. The tracks go in narrow series indicating a narrow tread, and the steps may be long or short. The tracks show clearly that these dinosaurs, even though they were early members of the group, ran with their legs well under the body and with one foot in front of the other. In other words, they ran much as the large running birds do rather than as modern lizards or crocodiles, and the reason they could do so was because they had much longer hind limbs. Sometimes the impression of a pelvic bone or of the tail is preserved showing where, so long ago, a tired little dinosaur sat down to rest for a moment or two.

If they are typical of the Triassic assemblage known or unknown, these little forms were more or less ancestral, for

123

there is no definite line that connects them, to a line of specialized and still comparatively small carnivores in the succeeding
Jurassic Age.

Two such dinosaurs, from different families but both Jurassic
in age, are of particular interest. One is known as *Compsognathus*
and the other as *Coelurus* (*Ornitholestes*). The former is European and the latter genera, now regarded as synonymous, are
from the United States.

Compsognathus is a member of a group of somewhat similar
small dinosaurs, with lightly constructed skeletons, called the
Coelurosauria ('hollow hinder-part lizards'). In this latter group
is the family Coeluridae. Typically they are small to medium-
sized and slender dinosaurs, which are, of course, carnivorous
and bipedal. The bones are usually hollow, the skull small, the
neck long and flexible, and the tail long, sometimes very long.
The fore and hind limbs are slender and long, the fore limb being
shorter than the hind limb but not so markedly so as in many
other Theropoda. Both the hands and the feet have three
functional digits, the others when present being vestigial. The
teeth are of the carnivorous type, but, as we shall see, in later,
Cretaceous, forms, some are toothless.

C. longipes Wagner, the type species, is the sole example of its
kind. It is well known from a unique and almost perfect skeleton
from the Solenhofen Limestone (Upper Jurassic) of Kelheim,
Bavaria. This locality is some thirty miles east of the famous
lithographic limestone area around Eichstätt. The specimen
is now in the museum of the Bavarian Academy of Sciences in
Munich. Many museums, including the British Museum
(Natural History), have plaster casts of this skeleton, so that it
may be useful to consider some of its many interesting features.
The skeleton was first described by Wagner in 1864, but has
since been re-examined and in part re-described by various
authorities, particularly by the late Freiherr von Huene and
Baron Franz Nopcsa.

The skeleton is preserved in a strange position, the head and
neck being drawn back and the backbone arched on account, it
is claimed, of the desiccation of the muscles after death, but
there are other possible meanings which are dealt with in
Chapter XII (p. 271). The skeleton measures about 2½ feet in

124

length. It was obviously a slender, delicately constructed animal, probably quite graceful and agile in life. The skull is small, delicate and little more than 3 inches long and the jaws have numerous sharp little teeth. The line of the long axis of the skull according to some writers was continuous with that of the long neck, but others consider it to have been at right angles to it. The fore limbs were approximately half as long as the hind ones, and in the latter the tibia was longer than the femur, and the metatarsals were long and slender, forming a structure much like that of a bird (tibiotarsus). The whole structure of the hind limb is decidedly bird-like in many respects. There were three functional fingers and toes and they were clawed. Apart from the interest of the skeleton itself, and the interest of the backward (opisthotonic) attitude in which it is preserved, there is an interesting inclusion in the body cavity. This is the remains of a small skeleton which was interpreted on the one hand, by Marsh, as an embryo (though he changed his mind later), and on the other, by Nopcsa, as an ingested reptile. It is now generally regarded as the remains of a meal. So far as is known the skin was not armoured, but traces of epidermal scales are supposed to exist, though these are probably only inorganic structures.

Von Huene in 1925 gave a new reconstruction of the living appearance and briefly described the habits. There is no doubt that *Compsognathus* was an agile little biped, able to run with some turn of speed and perhaps also capable of hopping and jumping. The nature of the teeth and the presence of the claws clearly indicate a carnivorous habit, but the length of the jaws or snout, the small size of the teeth, and the structure of the fingers, show that the prey could only have consisted of small animals. Some of the Theropoda are supposed to have been egg-stealers, but there is no justification for such an assumption in the case of *Compsognathus*. Most probably it lived upon small mammals and reptiles, including dinosaurs and pterodactyls, and birds whose first remains are known from the nearby Solenhofen and other similarly aged deposits.

Another interesting small dinosaur of Jurassic age is *Ornitholestes*, or 'bird-robber' as the name means. Its characters are well known from the finding of an almost complete skeleton of *O. hermanni* Osborn in the Bone Cabin Quarry (Upper Jurassic) of Wyoming. It also was a small and slender dinosaur, about 7 feet long, with a small but longish skull, a long flexible neck, and a long tail. The fore limbs were relatively large, with specialized hands ending in long and slender fingers, but the first finger was short and divergent. The feet were long and slender and each had three functional digits. Slightly curved claws were present on the hands and feet, those of the hand being a little more strongly curved than those of the feet. The long, slim and strong-clawed fingers are thought to have been suited for the capture of an active and elusive prey, and the generic name *Ornitholestes* indicates that this prey was thought, at least by Professor Osborn, to have been birds. Such a supposition, coupled with a skeleton so well preserved, form an excellent ground for the artists of restoration-pictures, and the drawing by C. R. Knight of *Ornitholestes* running with an *Archaeopteryx*-like bird in its hands has been reproduced in many books. However true or untrue this assumption may be the association of these two forms is of particular interest, because *Archaeopteryx* and *Ornitholestes* have hands of very closely similar structure. The same digits are involved except that the fourth metacarpal is missing in *Archaeopteryx*, and the arrangement, but not the length, of the other metacarpals is closely alike, while the claws are of the same curvature, as figured by G. Heilmann (1926), though much thicker at their base. We merely make this point in passing, realizing that Osborn and Knight had probably no intention of particularizing the 'bird in the hand' as *Archaeopteryx*, which is a Solenhofen bird, but only as a typical Jurassic member of that Class of animals that had so lately come into being.

Our knowledge of the earliest birds is so scanty, and their remains so rare, that it is idle to attempt the specification of the forms that *Ornitholestes* may have devoured, though it was very likely that lizards and small mammals were the main prey. The principal point of interest of this genus is that it was a specialized member of the group of small and agile dinosaurs, the specialization being most evident in the structure of the hand. *Ornitholestes* was established by H. F. Osborn as a name in 1903 with the type species *O. hermanni* which came from the

Morrison Formation (Upper Jurassic) of Wyoming. This famous formation is typically seen at Morrison near Denver, Colorado, and consists of deposits laid down by streams or in shallow waters. Many of the fine skeletons it contains are closely similar to those found in the similar continental uppermost Jurassic beds in England. But the nearest relations to *Ornitholestes* (incidentally Dr Percy Lowe thought *Archaeopteryx* to be a reptile and closely related to *Ornitholestes* [Lowe, 1935]) were not from Colorado or from England but from Maryland and Wyoming.

Many years before Osborn had described *Ornitholestes* (1903) or had redescribed it (1917), O. C. Marsh had given the name *Coelurus* ('hollow tail') to some incomplete remains of small dinosaurs. Three species in all were described: *Coelurus fragilis* (1879), *C. agilis* (1884) and *C. gracilis* (1888). The first two species came from Quarry 13 at Como Bluff, Wyoming, and other bones came from different quarries of the same region (see the splendid volume by Ostrom and McIntosh [1966]). The third species came from the Arundel (Cretaceous) of Maryland. These names sufficiently reflect Professor Marsh's conclusions as to the build and activity of the little creatures but the material at his disposal was fragmentary and there were no skulls. The vertebrae were hollow and the canal for the spinal cord was much dilated. Altogether what evidence there was suggested very active bird-like running creatures but there was no doubt as to their affinities. They had reptilian pelves.

The picture of *Coelurus* is amplified and overlapped by the information that *Ornitholestes* was able to give at a later date and it has become clear that the two names cover the same animal which, because of the prior naming by Marsh, must now be *Coelurus*. *Ornitholestes* thus disappears from use as a separate name but remains as a synonym of the former.

These were small active carnivores, running with head and neck outstretched, the body being balanced by the outstretched tail. Seldom more than 7 feet or so overall, they were ancient examples of an animal role now taken over by smaller mammals. That their role was successful can be judged from the fact that somewhat similar, though larger, forms occurred in most parts of the Jurassic and Lower Cretaceous world.

Indeed it is from another part of the world, from East Africa, that the next member of this light-footed brigade of dinosaurs comes. *Elaphrosaurus* is a name not common in the lists of popular dinosaurs but in age and development it seems to be a form developed from the *Coelurus* pattern and is very definitely a coelurosaur.

A German expedition working in what was then German East Africa in the years just before the first world war, unearthed a large number of remarkable bones of remarkable dinosaurs. The site was Tendaguru, a hill overlooking a village from which, and the surrounding area, came the hundreds of willing natives who did the digging. The bones, when given field treatment and first aid, for many were badly fractured, were packed and carried to Lindi, the port on the Indian Ocean some forty miles south-east of the diggings. From there the bones went to Berlin and they can be seen in much more understandable condition in the Geological and Palaeontological Institute and Museum.

Among these finds were parts of the skeleton of a coelurosaur that was named *Elaphrosaurus bambergi* in 1925 by W. Janensch, the leader of the expedition. The name, for what it is worth, means 'light (in weight) reptile'. It came not from Tendaguru but from Kindope, two miles to the north (see Fig. 35).

As restored in the Museum the whole skeleton is strongly reminiscent of *Ornitholestes*. The skull is modelled but the small, sharp and recurved teeth are known. The neck is about as long as the trunk, the former having rather elongated vertebrae and the latter with low square neural spines. The long tail exceeds the length of skull (modelled on the exhibit), neck and body. The sacrum, with certainly four sacral vertebrae, has a longish ilium and it is notable that both pubis and ischium have been given expanded distal (lower) ends; the latter, though unusual, appears to be natural and is like that of *Ceratosaurus*, which we shall discuss later.

The short fore limb, shorter than that of *Coelurus* (*Ornitholestes*), has a long three-fingered hand, with only slightly curved claws. The hind leg is very bird-like, is long, about twice that of the whole fore limb, and has the femur shorter than the long tibia and fibula. The tail has more than forty vertebrae.

128

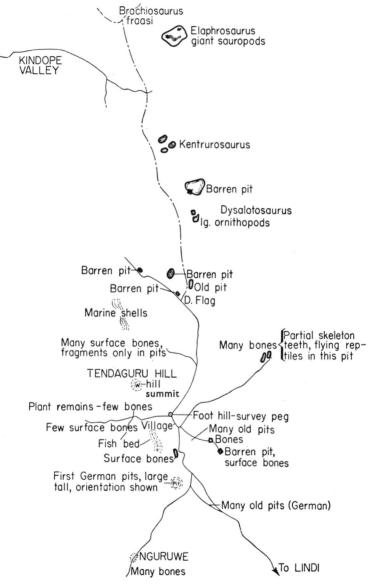

FIG. 35. Map of the Tendaguru district, Tanzania, East Africa.

All in all, this 19-feet-long dinosaur of the Upper Jurassic of what is now Tanzania seems to be somewhere between *Coelurus* and another very bird-like North American form, *Ornithomimus*. Like *Coelurus*, however, the hand was adapted for a special purpose which is also found, but to a less obvious extent, in *Ornithomimus*. It must be remembered that much of the evidence here is modelled, elements of one side being copied from the other, but much is also copied from allied forms (see Janensch, 1929).

Since that time A. F. de Lapparent has described two species of *Elaphrosaurus* (*E. gauthieri* and *E. riguidiensis*) on scattered remains from the Cretaceous of the Sahara. M. A. Arnimelech has figured so-called *Elaphrosaurus* tracks from the Judean Hills of Israel.

The Cretaceous coelurosaurs, or perhaps we should say the Cretaceous descendants of the forms we have described, were also very specialized, but in other directions, and it should be recognized that these advanced features introduce complications in our attempt to elucidate their habits of life. Of the main features, of bipedal habit, strength of limbs and purpose of teeth, where present, we may, and do, have positive evidence, but the finer valuations of hand and claw, although they may stimulate the imagination, trend towards a decided reduction of certainty in visualizing the habits. The most interesting of the Cretaceous forms are *Ornithomimus* (*Struthiomimus*) of Canada and the USA, *Oviraptor* of the Upper Cretaceous of Mongolia and *Caenagnathus*, based on a bird-like jaw from Canada.

It is unfortunate that the last two are represented by incomplete, almost insufficient, material so that their systematic position and place in the ecology of the late Cretaceous must remain somewhat in doubt. Of the remains definitely attributable to *Ornithomimus* ('bird-mimic') there have now been many discoveries of quite satisfactory material. In the early days, when Professor Marsh described the original material, only foot bones, parts of the vertebral column, and sacrum and pelvic bones were known. Marsh proposed the generic name *Ornithomimus* for *O. velox* in 1890, on material that came from Green Mountain near Denver, Colorado. *O. tenuis* and *O. grandis* were also named at that time. In 1892 the same author described two further species, *O. sedens* and *O. minutus.*

Marsh at first referred these species to the Ornithopoda, or vegetarian bipedal group, as he was impressed by the bird-like structure of the hind feet and the co-ossification of the pelvic bones. But none of these species had any skull remains.

In 1914 a nearly complete skeleton of an ornithomimid dinosaur was obtained by an American Museum of Natural History expedition to Alberta, and this, originally considered to belong also to the genus *Ornithomimus*, was described under the name of *O. altus* by Lawrence Lambe. Professor Osborn of the American Museum made it, in 1917, the type of a new genus which he called *Struthiomimus* ('Ostrich-mimic'). This is today considered to be a synonym of *Ornithomimus*, though the term has gained wide currency in the last fifty years.

One of the chief objections raised to the identity of the two genera was the occurrence of *Ornithomimus* in the Lance Formation (Denver) while *Struthiomimus* is found in the older Old Man (former Belly River) Series and Judith River Series. On these and on some slight osteological grounds, including the presence or absence of the fifth metatarsal as a diagnostic character, Osborn felt that he was justified in making the generic distinction.

Since that time many discoveries of importance have been made. It is true that the ornithomimid discoveries, in the strict sense, were of isolated bones and incomplete assemblages, but excellent specimens have since been obtained.

In 1935 W. A. Parks wrote on the 'Dinosaurs in the Royal Ontario Museum', which was then a part of the University of Toronto. He said: 'A peculiar family of bird-like dinosaurs, *Ornithomimidae*, regarded as *Theropoda*, is well represented in both the Belly River and the Edmonton formations, but usually by isolated bones only. These animals have no teeth and the head is light and delicate like that of a bird. The front limbs are short and the hind limbs are powerful; both carry clawed digits. The bones of the head are of paper thinness in places, making the preservation rare and the preparation difficult. The museum has the finest collection of these bird-like dinosaurs hitherto obtained, including two heads in a much better state of preservation than any others known. The mounted specimens are as follows *Struthiomimus samueli*—type specimen with head, Belly River formation 1926; *Struthiomimus ingens*—type specimen without head, Edmonton formation, 1931; *Struthiomimus currelli*—type specimen with head, the best skeleton yet discovered, Edmonton formation, 1931.'

The two specimens with heads are now mounted in the museum, in wall cases. As for the stratigraphical range of the species it is interesting to know that despite the alleged rarity of remains a very considerable number of finds is recorded.

Dale Russell (1967) has recorded that from the Old Man Formation (Belly River) in the vicinity of Steveville, Alberta, nineteen specimens of Ornithomimidae or 5·9 per cent of the fauna were collected. From the Edmonton Formation (Member A) five specimens or 9·1 per cent of the fauna were collected along the Red Deer River, Alberta. And from the Edmonton Formation (Member B), along the Red Deer River, there were twelve Ornithomimidae or 14 per cent of the fauna. When, however, it comes to specimens of Lancian age (Upper Edmonton Formation) along the Red Deer River, there was only one doubtful specimen, which none the less would amount to 5·6 per cent of the fauna.

The history of the collection of some of these specimens is recounted in L. S. Russell (1966) and in Dale A. Russell (1967). When all this is said and done there remains the fact that these dinosaurs are not after all so inadequately known and that there are these two splendid specimens on public exhibition in the Royal Ontario Museum, Toronto.

Yet the dinosaurs have suffered from their name. Lightly built, hollow-boned, long-legged and long-necked, they were bird- and ostrich-mimics. Nothing is easier than to imagine them high stepping their way across the Cretaceous meadows like an ostrich, the head moving in unison with the movements of the legs, and a fine turn of speed was there when the moment arrived for chase or for elusion.

Heilmann's artistry did much to perpetuate this picture (see Heilmann, 1926). Part of this is achieved by portraying a bird-like skull whereas the skulls in Toronto give no justification for the preorbital concavity, and the metatarsals are too long in the

132

drawing. Thus, a restoration like a bird has made it like a bird, and the restoration by Christman in Colbert (1961), Ostrom in 1964 and Kurtén in 1968, all manage to convey different aspects of reptilian probability. What then of the animal itself, illuminated by the various aspects of the Canadian finds?

The Ornithomimidae were very slender coelurosaurs with the relatively small skull set at right angles to the axis of the long and slender neck. The body was comparatively short and the tail very long. The fore limbs were shorter than the hind, but both pairs were long and slender. The skull has a large orbit in which, as in many Theropoda, sclerotic plates are present. There are no teeth in the jaws. The slender fore limbs were secondarily elongated and have specialized hands with three digits whose elongated claws are only slightly curved. In the pelvis the pubic bones have a foot-like symphysis, and the ilia are long, low and curved down in front, while the ischia are also curved, and have a smaller foot-like process. The pelvis, like that of some Theropoda and birds, shows a degree of fusion in its elements. The femur is shorter than the tibia, the feet have three long metatarsals rather crowded together, although the other portions are of moderate size, and the unguals are rather straight and short. There is said to be a trace of the fifth metatarsal. (A right foot, with digit 1, was described by C. M. Sternberg as *Macrophalangia canarensis* in 1932. It comes from the Old Man Formation of Alberta.) Abdominal ribs have been prominent, so that these structures persist from the earliest to the latest Coelurosauria.

The specimen that is the type of *Struthiomimus altus* (Lambe) is known from the very fine skeleton, mounted in a panel, in the American Museum of Natural History. This has been figured frequently for various purposes and has some points worth a passing mention; the figures are reproduced in Osborn (1917), Gilmore (1920), and Moodie (1923). Striking features are the small and lightly constructed skull, the comparatively long fore limbs, and the long tail with its closely articulated terminal portion. The position of the elements is of interest for here again there is strong recurvature of the spine, with associated uplift of the tail, and the retracted limbs. It is true that the hind limbs are out of position, so that the whole arrangement may be due to post-mortem influences such as the decay of muscles, but there is a strong suggestion of opisthotonos, to which we referred on page 124, and with which we deal on page 271. This position, in the medical sense, is due to tetanic convulsion brought on by the effect on the central nervous system of toxins such as those produced in tetanus (lock-jaw) or strychnine poisoning. It may be simulated mechanically by the drying up of the dorsal muscles, though the degree of retraction seems too large for that. The suggestion here of a mechanical post-mortem cause is hardly tenable and the medical cause will be discussed later.

From Osborn's descriptions and the Toronto evidence we can see that the skeleton is 13 feet long, so that the living dinosaur was a delicate and graceful creature, whose habits are somewhat doubtfully envisaged and whose appearance, as we have said, can stimulate the imaginative powers of the artist to the full. The generic name means ostrich-mimic, and unquestionably the structure of the skeleton in many ways is closely like that of the struthious birds we know so well in life today. These bird-like attributes, and especially the edentulous jaws, have made the exact determination of the habits rather difficult. Undoubtedly *Ornithomimus* was slightly bird-like in appearance (Plate VII), and able perhaps to run with some speed when pursued, as it often may have been. Some authors have suggested that the clawed and specialized fingers were used for pulling down branches and fruits, and this seems an admirable explanation if the arms were long and the neck unsuitable, but a moment's reflexion will show that in this case the head was better able to reach the fruit or branch than the hand, though it does not preclude the possibility that branches or fruits were pulled off by hand and eaten when on or near the ground. Osborn has suggested that the long claws were used to break into ant hills where the ants would be devoured by means of a prehensile tongue; or, alternatively, that they were used to gather molluscs which were crushed between horny pads on the jaws; that the animal was herbivorous and the claws used to pull vegetation towards the mouth; or that like the ostrich it was omnivorous. The first two of these suggestions depend on structures for which we have no evidence, though the last two are distinct possibilities.

134

Nopcsa (1922) has drawn attention to the admirable adaptation of the hand for uncovering or digging out eggs, the soft but tough covering of which would be easily pierced by, and would require, a sharp beak and movable neck such as *Ornithomimus* had. Heilmann thought that 'the contemporary small mammals would be better adapted to burrowing of that kind'. Some of the present-day small mammals are still better adapted to living on eggs, but some reptiles still manage to live thereby also. So *Ornithomimus* may also have found his food despite the competition of his little rivals. Gregory (see Osborn, 1917) suggested that the claws would be useful in tearing off the husks of fruit, and this idea fits in with the pulling off of fruit and the consumption of it on the ground. *Ornithomimus*, as we know from impressions and the tracks of similar dinosaurs, occasionally dropped the fore limbs on the ground, and when it rested, did so by sitting on the tail and the ends of the pubic bones. Thus, we may suggest, there is no impossibility and some probability that *Ornithomimus* tore off the fruit or fruit-laden branches from trees with the hands and strong claws, and, sitting down much like a squirrel, removed the husks or skins and managed easily with the long, movable neck to consume the food. One such individual may thus have consumed at the same time the scattered seeds of *Strychnos nux-vomica* and died in tetanic convulsion to leave remains that were not discovered until long afterwards. This is, however, sheer speculation and it is unlikely that we shall ever know the truth of this instance.

A smaller but essentially similar Cretaceous dinosaur of this kind is *Oviraptor philoceratops* ('egg-stealer fond of *Ceratops*') whose incomplete remains were found by the American Museum expedition working in Mongolia. Its skull was short, light and toothless. An interclavicle of T-shape is said to have been present, which would be an unusual feature in so late a dinosaur. *Oviraptor* was small, only about half the size of *Ornithomimus*, and its remains were discovered in close association with a nest of *Protoceratops* eggs. Once again we have stimulating circumstantial evidence. Was it a robber, about to suck the eggs or make off with new hatched embryos? Was it here by chance, for as we shall see, young dinosaurs seem to have lived, at least

135

for a time, apart from the hurly-burly of adult life and the presence of a small dinosaur beside or near a nest might not be too difficult to explain? Was it sheltering, during that fatal sand storm that overwhelmed it, in the slight crater-like lee of the nest? All these are possibilities as relevant as any more direct assumption.

Oviraptor had long hands too, like *Ornithomimus* and the predecessor, *Elaphrosaurus bambergi*. Quite recently two more ornithomimids were discovered by the Polish Mongolian Expedition and are under study in Warsaw. Similar forms as yet little known may be forthcoming from India and South America. At any rate we seem to see a widespread race of these long-fingered dinosaurs and we may be carried away by the adjective. Light-fingered gentlemen are robbers. Need the long-fingered dinosaurs have been robbers too?

Ornithomimus is a version of *Elaphrosaurus* with rather longer arms. All sorts of explanations for their toothless life have already been given. One very respectable authority says of *Ornithomimus* and *Oviraptor*: 'What kind of food could these strange reptiles have eaten? They certainly did not eat meat without teeth.' Why not? Vultures have no teeth and they certainly dispose of meat.

The long fingers with their sharp (but not sickle-shaped) claws could rip up meat more effectively than a vulture's beak and the portion could then be swallowed, gulped in fact as must have been habitual in theropods generally. Like vultures, the ornithomimids that we know have large eyes with sclerotic plates, and *Oviraptor* with a shortened face may even have had a measure of overlapping vision. Perhaps, if they were carrion eaters, they were blessed with a diminished sense of smell, like the vultures that find their food by sight and not by smell, as Darwin set himself to prove.

No doubt further discoveries will tell the fuller, if not the truer, story. At one time *Ornithomimus*, or its synonym *Struthiomimus*, was held to be the end of this particular line. In 1940, R. M. Sternberg, the son of the famous dinosaur writer and collector, C. M. Sternberg, discovered an almost complete lower jaw with toothless mandibles and a scoop-like symphysis that he described as *Caenagnathus collinsi*. The jaw came from the Upper Cretaceous of Alberta and was considered to be that of a bird, and since the whole jaw was about 8 inches long, its owner was thought to be a running bird of upland habit 'where it would be both companion and competitor to many well known dinosaurs'. It may however be an ornithomimid dinosaur and Alexander Wetmore has already withdrawn it from his avian classification.

Maybe it was the last of the meat-snatchers. The little coelurosaurs have been likened to jackals; their successors may have been ground-living vultures in reptile shape, and, as we shall shortly see, in their times there was an abundance of massive prey.

These small-skulled and lightly built coelurosaurs were not the mainstream of carnivorous development. The megalosaurs, gorgosaurs and tyrannosaurs, with their relations and offshoots, represent a main line that not so long ago was considered almost the only section of the Theropods worthy of notice. Now this has changed for a variety of reasons. The critical investigation of somewhat similar dinosaurs, often represented by scattered and unsatisfactory material, the analysis of the names and relationships of these various genera, species and groups, and the description of new material have produced a remarkable story with very satisfactory explanation.

This starts with the development and restudy of the Elgin material containing *Ornithosuchus*. This small skeleton has been known in a general way for nearly a century and has been alleged dinosaur, dinosaur ancestor and dinosaur again. The publication of his results by A. D. Walker has not only clarified this particular issue and presented a satisfactory picture of *Ornithosuchus*, but has cleared up other issues as well and has shown a surprising unanimity of structures persisting from the Trias to the Cretaceous in those large predators that have achieved such pictorial fame and are among the most interesting and historic of dinosaurs.

Ornithosuchus comes from the Upper Trias of Moray, the specimens being mainly from Spynie Quarry, near Elgin; the East Quarry, Lossiemouth, the West Quarry, Lossiemouth and from Findrassie Quarry.

The materials in several English and Scottish Museums have

been collated and it is now considered that only one species *O. longidens* (Huxley) is represented, though there are indications of a fairly wide range in size of the individuals.

As now described and figured by Walker, *Ornithosuchus* is represented as a sizeable carnivore up to 12 feet long. The large, deep skull with its very large preorbital foramen is followed by a short neck of substantial vertebrae, a body little longer than the neck and a long tail. The triradiate pelvis has a short ilium and there were only three sacral vertebrae. The shoulder and pelvic girdles retain some primitive features including a double row of bony plates above the vertebrae down the length of the back.

The hind legs were stout compared with those of the coelurosaurs, though some of the bones were hollow, and the femur was slightly longer than the tibia and fibula. The fore limb was about two-thirds as long as the hind and less strong. The hind foot had all five toes but the outermost were short.

Abdominal ribs were well represented. The presumption must be that this dinosaur was able to move well as a biped and with a turn of speed but, with an arching of the body, a measure of use of the fore limbs could be obtained.

That it played an important role as a carnivore cannot be doubted; there were other smaller forms on which to prey and part of the purpose of its armour must have been to protect it against the depredations of its own kind, for cannibalism was at least characteristic of early dinosaurs as we have already seen. All these dinosaurs had, of course, their size in an environment of generally smaller creatures and the use of the tail which could be a weapon of some value.

The latest classifications associate two other Triassic dinosaurs with *Ornithosuchus*: these are *Teratosaurus* and *Sinosaurus*. The former is known only by a right maxilla which is the type of *Teratosaurus suevicus* von Meyer (1861) from the Stubensandstein (Upper Trias) of Stuttgart, Germany. The maxilla bears several serrated teeth, characteristic of the carnivorous dinosaurs, but a good deal of confusion has been caused by the attribution of this specimen and species to the genus *Zanclodon* by Lydekker and others.

Sinosaurus is a genus founded in 1940 by C. C. Young, the

type species being *S. triassicus*. It has generally been accepted as a carnosaur, a term which we shall have to define now, since *Ornithosuchus*, and these other restricted genera, are the foundations or, at least, the beginnings, of a whole line of what are called carnosaurs.

The carnosaurs or the Infra-order Carnosauria are typically large-headed bipeds with a short neck (because of the large head) a longish back and a long, powerful balancing tail. The skull has large recurved knife-like teeth and orbits with the vertical diameter larger than the horizontal. The end of the pubis is enlarged with a rocker-like expansion. The hind foot is bird-like but with the big toe (hallux) rotated backwards. Astragalus (with a dorsal process) and calcaneum form a functional union with the tibia and the fibula. Both tibia and fibula are shorter than the femur (which is the reverse of the coelurosaur condition). The animals are medium-sized, like the Jurassic *Megalosaurus* and *Antrodemus* to very large, like the Cretaceous *Gorgosaurus* and *Tyrannosaurus*.

The word Carnosaur means 'flesh-lizards' or 'flesh-reptiles' and can be interpreted in one of two ways, either as fleshy reptiles, for these dinosaurs were large and muscular, or alternatively as being reptiles fond of flesh, for they were undoubtedly among the greatest carnivores that we know.

It can now be regarded as reasonable that the carnosaurian line or lines started in the Upper Triassic and went on by, with or through several dinosaurs, well known by name but less well known by material. In the group there are many of the most familiar dinosaurs in America and in Europe, of which many restoration pictures in books and journals have appeared. How far they can be fitted into a reasonable evolutionary picture remains to be seen but meantime the most important dinosaurs must be discussed both systematically and historically for some of these are amongst the dinosaurs longest known to us.

The first group must be those medium- to large-sized carnivores of the Jurassic, the English *Megalosaurus* and its relatives or alleged relatives and *Antrodemus* (or *Allosaurus*) of the United States and we shall have to discuss the three so-called Megalosaurids that also bore horns—*Ceratosaurus nasicornis* of Colorado, USA, *Megalosaurus* (*Proceratosaurus*) *bradleyi*

139

A. S. Woodward, and '*Megalosaurus wetherilli*' Welles, from Arizona, USA.

To begin with we must say something of *Megalosaurus*, the first dinosaur ever to be scientifically described. This name was first published without reference to species in J. Parkinson, 1822, ('Introduction to the Study of British Organic Remains' etc.) but this is not regarded here as founding the genus for the reasons already given. Professor Buckland did, however, establish the name in 1824 in his paper in the *Transactions of the Geological Society of London*, though the name itself was apparently thought up by Buckland and Conybeare. The basis for the name was a lower jaw, some vertebrae and rib fragments, bones of the pelvis and the right femur. These came from the Stonesfield Slate at Stonesfield, near Oxford.

These original materials, which can still be seen in the University Museum at Oxford, were soon amplified by other specimens and the name *M. bucklandi* was established by Hermann von Meyer in 1832.

Since that time there has been continuous discovery of material, often fragmentary, that can rightly be attributed to *Megalosaurus* and many other species have been added to the genus, not all of which can be sustained, as we shall see.

All the material available up to 1926, which was considerable and included ninety-six separate finds of European material and fifteen from beyond the European frontiers, were included in a detailed study, *The Carnivorous Saurischia in the Jura and Cretaceous formations mainly in Europe* by Freiherr von Huene and published in English and Spanish in Buenos Aires.

The name *Megalosaurus* means 'large lizard or reptile', and was the joint composition of Buckland and Conybeare, though Buckland is usually given the credit. In saying that the genus is ill-defined we mean that, although it has been known for so long, the remains discovered have been rather fragmentary and there have been many specimens from England and elsewhere referred to it that undoubtedly will prove to belong to other genera when a fuller knowledge of *Megalosaurus* is possible. None the less, as the historical genus and the one which is perhaps the best represented of all the Theropoda in Europe it deserves some description. In England remains have been obtained from the Jurassic of Oxfordshire, Dorset, Gloucestershire, Wiltshire and Yorkshire and from the Wealden of Kent, Sussex and the Isle of Wight and the so-called Neocomian of Potton, Bedfordshire. Bones attributed to the genus have been recorded from Australia, East Africa, France, Portugal, Greenland, India, Madagascar and the USA. From such well-distributed, if fragmentary, material it is possible to give some idea of, at least, the main characters.

The megalosaurs were carnivorous dinosaurs of heavy build and large size, the skull being a foot or more long. The orbit was large, with the vertical diameter the longer. There was a single large preorbital foramen. The teeth, four of which were on each premaxilla, were deep, 1–2 inches long, and compressed laterally so that the front and back edges are definitely sharp and are usually serrated with fine small 'teeth' like a very fine saw. The teeth are recurved when full grown, but at first project as little flattened cones, sharp at the point and with saw-like edges at front and back. On growth and on becoming curved backwards it is not unusual for the front serrations to become less distinct or even obliterated. Such sharp, recurved and posteriorly serrated teeth are somewhat like short bread- or steak-knives and must have been formidable weapons. The victim would have but a slender chance when gripped in the powerful jaws. The neck was stout, with short vertebrae, the body long and somewhat bulky, and the tail moderately long and flattened a little from side to side. The fore limbs were small, and the hand, though it had five digits, had the two outer ones reduced. The front limbs could not have been used for walking. The hind legs were long and stout, with the femur sometimes over 3 feet in length and longer than either tibia or fibula. The metatarsal bones were not united and the feet were definitely three-toed and digitigrade. There was an ascending process to the astragalus. In the foot the central (third) digit was the strongest and the other two functional ones were about equal. The fifth digit was missing and the first only vestigial and non-functional. The hands and feet bore strong curved claws. When first discovered, Cuvier estimated a length exceeding 40 feet and a bulk equal to that of an elephant 7 feet high for an individual whose femur measured 2 feet 9 inches. Buckland himself thought that some specimens might be 70 feet long.

Megalosaurs varied considerably in size, but probably more modestly from 10 to 25 feet from the snout to the tip of the tail though many of the remains are so fragmentary that an estimate of the complete dimensions is difficult. They must have been creatures of some importance in the Jurassic world, where, under rather more humid conditions than existed in the Trias, they would find luxuriant vegetation and a plenitude of animal life, both reptilian and mammalian, to satisfy their carnivorous wants. There have been many other species attributed to the genus, though few can be strictly accepted. The older specific names *M. insignis* Eudes Deslongchamps (1870) and *M. oweni* Lydekker (1889) are doubtful but A. F. de Lapparent recognizes *M. insignis* in the Jurassic of Damparis (Jura) France and *M. pannoniensis* Seeley (1881) in the Danian of the South of France. He (with Professor Zbyszewski) has also identified a form close to it in the Mastrichtian of Portugal. A. F. de Lapparent created a new species, *M. mersensis* in 1955 on teeth and vertebrae from the Jurassic of El Mers, Morocco and in 1957 (with G. Zbyszewski) instituted *M. pombali* from the Upper Jurassic of Portugal.

In all thirty species are listed in Kuhn (1965) and although most of these are to be referred elsewhere any useful review of *Megalosaurus* must deal in detail with the materials and with the author's views.

Footprints too have been added to the evidence. A. F. de Lapparent and Georges Zbyszewski have figured tracks and prints from Cape Mondego in Portugal and footprints are said to be in north-east Greenland.

Some of the forms listed and accepted by von Huene must now be reconsidered in the light of new discoveries of the last forty years.

Two specimens referred to *Megalosaurus* are of special interest because of the indications they give of, or perhaps more properly the resemblances they bear to, later forms. One of these, *M. parkeri* von Huene, from the Oxford Clay near Weymouth, Dorset, is remarkable for the size of the neural spines which are nearly 10 inches long, that is twice the length

142

of the vertebrae themselves. This unusual length is a foretaste of what we shall see later in an Egyptian form, *Spinosaurus*.

Von Huene pointed out that the general characters of the spines and the pubis removed '*M. parkeri* from the very typical representatives of the genus *Megalosaurus*. But for the present there are no reasons to give a new generic name.' Since then Walker (1964) taking the neural spines, the shape of the ilium and ischium and characters of the hind limb as diagnostic, separated it from *M. bucklandi* and the so-called *Streptospondylus cuvieri* and made it—the Oxford specimen of *Megalosaurus parkeri*— the type of a new genus *Metricanthosaurus*. The name means 'moderately spined lizard'. It is perhaps no more than an aberrant megalosaur but its spinous characters reminded von Huene of *Megalosaurus dunkeri* for which he named the new genus *Altispinax*. Here some of the vertebrae have spines four times the length of the vertebrae.

The spines of *Megalosaurus parkeri* reminded A. D. Walker of *Acrocanthosaurus* but without any sign of relationship between the forms. This genus was founded in 1950 by Stovall and Langston for a skull, vertebrae and limb bones from the Lower Cretaceous of Oklahoma. The name of the species is *A. atokensis* Stovall and Langston. Here the length of the dorsal neural spines is up to 300 mm. and this recalls the remarkable theropod described over fifty years ago. *Spinosaurus aegyptiacus* E. von Stromer, was a large flesh-eater in which the neural spines are recorded as having been 1·9 metres (6¼ feet) long. It lived in North Africa.

The purpose of neural spines is normally to form places of attachment for muscles, as can be seen beautifully on a horse's skeleton. But it would be a monstrous burden on any animal that required muscles of a thickness that needed neural spines several feet long. There are no comparable structures in any other dinosaurs, even the largest, but there is the remarkable group of Permian reptiles, the pelycosaurs, which had exaggerated and complicated neural spines. It has been assumed (and especially argued by A. S. Romer) that these upstanding bones were covered by a web of skin and that the function of this fin was associated with temperature control for the absorption, or the loss, of heat; and it is difficult to account for

143

a similar function in bipedal carnivores from England, Continental Europe, Egypt and Oklahoma, since in those days there was little of the inequality of climate that now marks these regions, to say nothing of the fact that this device, for whatever purpose it was, seems to have done little for so peculiar a group. We may regard them as a line, not necessarily a family line, coming off the more moderate megalosaurs.

Another interesting megalosaur is the portion of a skull, *Megalosaurus (Proceratosaurus) bradleyi* A. S. Woodward, from the Great Oolite of Minchinhampton, Gloucestershire, now preserved in the Department of Palaeontology of the British Museum. The skull was about a foot long, and on the upper surface above the narial opening there is preserved the indication of a small horn. In other features the skull is markedly different from that of *Megalosaurus* in the strict generic sense, and this incomplete skull appears to indicate a form intermediate between *Megalosaurus* and a much better known American form, *Ceratosaurus*. *Megalosaurus*, according to von Huene, had four premaxillary teeth, and loosely articulated pelvic bones and metatarsals. *M. (Proceratosaurus) bradleyi* had four premaxillary teeth, and a horn on the nose, but the pelvic and metatarsal bones are unknown. *Ceratosaurus*, however, had only three teeth on the premaxilla, a well-defined horn-core on the nose, and the pelvic bones are united as are three of the metatarsals. Thus, in those limited characters that are known, *Megalosaurus bradleyi* would appear to be somewhat intermediate to the two genera.

The type specimen came from Minchinhampton quarry, near Burleigh, Gloucester, which was closed for many years. It was recently reopened for stone for Gloucester cathedral and one hopes more satisfactory evidence of this dinosaur may yet be found.

Ceratosaurus was first described and named by O. C. Marsh in 1884, and since that time many examinations have been made of the remains, and numerous restorations of its appearance have been attempted. The best material is preserved in the United States National Museum, Washington, D.C., and was fully dealt with by C. W. Gilmore in his invaluable monograph on the 'Osteology of the Carnivorous Dinosaurs' (1920).

144

THE CARNIVOROUS DINOSAURS: THEROPODA

The most striking feature of this animal, at first sight at any rate, is undoubtedly the prominent horn-core over the nasals, and in Professor Marsh's descriptions it appeared to form the chief difference between the ceratosaurs and the then known megalosaurs. There are, however, numerous other differences which not only serve adequately to distinguish the genera, but even to suggest that *Ceratosaurus* belongs to a distinct family. Marsh, indeed, recognized this and actually created a new family called the Ceratosauridae for the reception of the genus, but few palaeontologists, with the important exception of Gilmore, have followed him and the genus is usually found today in the Megalosauridae.

The original material, upon which the genus was founded, was collected from the Morrison (Upper Jurassic) Formation, at Garden Park, near Canyon City, Colorado, by M. P. Felch between 1883 and 1884, and consists of the major portion of the skeleton. The whole skeleton, in the bipedal position, measures about 17½ feet long, and its most striking features are the unusually open skull with the single large preorbital foramen, the short neck, longish body and long tail, while the fore legs are markedly shorter than the hind legs. The skull is about 20 inches long and tapers to a sharply rounded end, so that its appearance when seen from above is a little like that of a crocodile, but there is no notch between the premaxilla and the maxilla. In addition to the horn-core on the nasal bones there are protuberances on the lachrymals just in front of the orbits and above the preorbital foramen. As has already been said, there are only three teeth on each premaxilla, compared with the four in *Megalosaurus*, *Gorgosaurus* and *Tyrannosaurus*. The bones of the pelvis are co-ossified as in *Ornithomimus*, as are also the three metatarsals. The latter condition, which occurs in the birds, is rare in the dinosaurs, and here affects the medial metatarsals as the first and fifth are missing, though there is evidence that the first was present in the living animal, though much reduced. The metatarsals, though shorter than usual, are robust and the fused structure formed the basis of a very strong hind foot. In Gilmore's illustration this coalescence looks pathological, but Gilmore has found no evidence of the bony outgrowths that might reasonably be expected if such were the

145

case, and advanced age, which can also produce coalescence, might have been the cause, but the ossification may be natural.

Among the most interesting features of the skeletal remains are the dermal ossifications also preserved in the matrix in what must have been their position in life, that is, just above the neural spines. These ossicles are irregularly shaped but elongate, and apparently lay in a continuous row along the centre of the back from neck to tail. There are indications also of other dermal ossifications, but their exact position is indeterminable. It is interesting to note that the row of median plates was preserved in the matrix about an inch to an inch and a half above the spinous processes of the vertebrae, and that therefore the intervening space represents the thickness of muscle and skin. It is but seldom that such positive evidence is present to help us in restoring the living appearance.

Attempts at such restorations have been many and that done under Professor Marsh's supervision, in 1892, merely endeavoured to show the complete skeleton in the walking position. This attempt has been proved to be inaccurate, but none the less has been extensively copied in all sorts of textbooks. Even so, an earlier restoration of the living appearance was done in 1889 by Frank Bond. Gilmore modelled a life restoration, copies of which are in many museums, including one on exhibition in the Department of Palaeontology of the British Museum, in which *Ceratosaurus* is depicted in the act of killing a young herbivorous dinosaur, *Camptosaurus*.

These restorations convey admirably the carnivorous propensities of this dinosaur. The lithe body, strong hind limbs and sharp, grasping, fore limbs, each with its set of stout claws, and the jaws with the set of cruel teeth, together suggest a habit that was cunning and rapacious, and meant death to the smaller of the contemporary reptiles or mammals. It is improbable, none the less, that the mental powers were so advanced as to justify the word 'cunning', but *Ceratosaurus* had a brain definitely much larger than that of the herbivorous types on which it must have lived. The brain-cast available for examination is not a particularly complete or satisfactory one, but there is no doubt that the cerebral, olfactory and pituitary regions are better developed.

146

The type species of *Ceratosaurus* is *C. nasicornis* Marsh, so called, of course, from the horn on the nose. It is important to remember that this horn is by no means the principal diagnostic feature of the genus, as we have already pointed out other more important characters, and it may well have been that the occurrence of this nasal prominence was a secondary sexual character, like the cock's comb and the peacock's tail, though these are not skeletal features.

Our knowledge and appreciation of the skeleton and habits of both *Megalosaurus* and *Ceratosaurus* have been greatly increased by, and are largely due to, work upon the remains of another American carnivorous dinosaur, namely *Allosaurus*. Before dealing with this dinosaur in any detail it may be well to point out a nomenclatural practice.

The name given to any fossil is applied when the first description of that fossil is published in such a way that further finds of the same nature would be recognizable from that first description. The concise list of distinguishing characters of the genus or species is called the diagnosis, and the specimen thus described and the basis of the name is called the type-specimen, and its name dates from the date of publication of the paper, book or memoir containing the description. Thus, should two persons work independently on what proves to be the same fossil genus or species, and each describes his material as new and applies a name to it, the name given by the writer who publishes it first, whether the priority is a day or a year or a century, is the valid one and subsequent names are called synonyms of the first. The generic name is the first word of the two (or three) in the specific name as *Allosaurus*, the specific name is the first and second, and not just the second as is frequently imagined, such as *Allosaurus fragilis* Marsh. If at a later date some other worker decides that the species has been put in the wrong genus and should be referred to another, the name of the original author is placed in brackets. Thus, to take a purely hypothetical case, if it were decided to place *A. fragilis* Marsh in the genus *Ceratosaurus*, the name would be changed to *Ceratosaurus fragilis* (Marsh). If two genera and species are made upon two different specimens which subsequently prove to belong to the same thing, then the law of priority prevails

147

and the earlier name of both genus and species is used. The recital of these facts will be superfluous to the initiated, but the explanation of the nomenclatural system may be of some interest to the ordinary reader. It is not an arbitrary system and is controlled, and cases adjudged, by an International Commission. The rules of zoological nomenclature are published and separate rules exist for botanical nomenclature.

The purpose of introducing this matter at this point is on account of the divergence of opinion on the generic name *Allosaurus*. In 1870 and later Professor Leidy described some fragmentary remains under the name of *Poicilopleuron (Antrodemus) valens*. The name was put in this way in case subsequent material would show that it was not really *Poicilopleuron* (a European form) and it could then be called *Antrodemus*. In other words, *Antrodemus* was a second choice of genus. After all, the type specimen was half a caudal vertebra! It is now ganerally called *Antrodemus valens*, since the name *Poicilopleuron* had been previously used for another kind of animal and was therefore 'pre-occupied' and unusable in this connexion.

In 1877, Professor Marsh described a new genus and species on fragmentary remains of several parts of a skeleton which he called *Allosaurus fragilis*. Now the two type-specimens are not of the same parts of the body, so that they are not directly comparable, but later and more complete remains of *Antrodemus* have shown that one vertebra of *Allosaurus fragilis* is very closely similar to *Antrodemus*. Accordingly, C. W. Gilmore maintained that the two should be considered identical, and he referred the material to the name *Antrodemus valens* Leidy, 1870.

The text-books and works of reference vary in their usage. For example, A. S. Romer, 1956, uses *Antrodemus (Allosaurus)*; in 1966 he puts it *Allosaurus (Antrodemus)*; E. H. Colbert in 1956 used *Allosaurus (Antrodemus)*; in 1965 he says *Allosaurus* (more properly *Antrodemus*); and in 1968 writes *Antrodemus* (often known as *Allosaurus*).

Now there are few of the older genera of dinosaurs which are not complicated by nomenclatural problems of this nature, and the reader may wonder why so much stress on this instance has been laid. The reason is that among the Theropoda the genus which has been mainly responsible for shedding a flood of light upon the structure and habits both of *Ceratosaurus* and the English *Megalosaurus* is this *Antrodemus/Allosaurus*; and, having given a somewhat cursory glance at the synonymy, we shall refer to this genus from now on as *Antrodemus*.

The generic diagnosis as given by Gilmore (1920) states that in the upper jaws the premaxillaries have five teeth, the maxillaries fifteen to seventeen, and in the lower, the dentary fifteen or sixteen. There are nine cervical vertebrae (opisthocoelous, that is, with the hinder side of the vertebra concave), fourteen dorsal vertebrae (amphicoelous, i.e. with both front and back sides concave) and five sacrals. The pelvic and the metatarsal bones are not fused or co-ossified. There are only three digits in the hand and the first has a strong and curved ungual phalange, while the third digit is reduced. In the foot there are four digits, but the first (the hallux or great toe) is reduced. Dermal ossifications are not known, but abdominal ribs are present. It is distinguished from *Megalosaurus*, among other features, by having five instead of four teeth on the premaxillae, and from *Ceratosaurus* by having no horn-core on the nasals, five instead of three teeth on the premaxillae, by having a more numerous dental series, and by having the pelvic and metatarsal bones unfused.

It can be stated that like *Ceratosaurus* (but not *Tyrannosaurus*) *Antrodemus* had the lachrymal bones raised into a prominent crest above the antorbital fenestra: and that like *Tyrannosaurus*, but not *Ceratosaurus*, there was a second antorbital fenestra, small in size and on the maxilla.

In general, *Antrodemus* was a large carnivorous dinosaur somewhat like *Megalosaurus*, and up to about 40 feet in total length. Skeletons in good condition are in the United States National Museum in Washington, and in the American Museum of Natural History, New York, that in the latter museum being excellently mounted in a predatory position over part of the skeleton of the large herbivorous *Apatosaurus* (*Brontosaurus*). These, and other portions of skeletons upon which our knowledge of the genus is based, come from the Upper Jurassic of Colorado and Wyoming, particularly from the Como Bluff quarries, Wyoming. From these various pieces of evidence it is easy to visualize the appearance and habits.

The mount in the American Museum was based on the evidence of a portion of *Apatosaurus*, then called *Brontosaurus*, found by Dr Jacob Wortman at Bone Cabin, Wyoming, in 1897. Some of the bones, particularly the processes of the tail vertebrae, of this were apparently scored and bitten off, and comparison with the skull of *Antrodemus* showed that the spacing of the teeth of the latter fitted the spacing of the scorings on the bones. In addition several broken-off teeth were found beside the vertebrae. As no other remains were found associated with *Apatosaurus* (*Brontosaurus*) the natural conclusion is that *Antrodemus* fed upon such herbivorous dinosaurs. Other marks of teeth have since been found on the bones of other forms. The *Antrodemus* skeleton now mounted over it was collected in 1879 at Como, by F. F. Hubbell.

Antrodemus, like those other carnosaurs we have dealt with, was bipedal, with a stiff backbone of interlocking vertebrae, balancing on the strong hind limbs, the balance being adequately maintained by the long and heavy tail. The extended hind legs were 9 feet long in some specimens, and, of course, the knee bent forward and not sideways as is the case in modern reptiles, and the feet were digitigrade. The body must have been narrow and deep, like that of *Tyrannosaurus* and even of *Ornithosuchus*, not broad like a crocodile's, and the tail could only have had a limited movement up and down for balancing, although it may have been able to swing fairly freely from side to side. The large head was on a short but flexible neck and the mouth could undoubtedly open very widely; the teeth were strong, recurved and sabre-like, so that with the stout and sharp claws *Antrodemus* was no mean enemy.

Lying in wait, rather than by hunting or by cunning tracking, *Antrodemus* watched the coming of his prey. When close at hand he would rush suddenly forwards, and teeth, hands and feet would combine to subdue and tear to pieces the object of his attack. From our previous experience of the brain-casts we know that the quick vision, the acute sense of smell and the hunting instinct of the mammal were not his. It cannot be too often insisted that, if we are to understand properly the activities of these dinosaurs, we must think of them as the reptiles they were, rather than as the predatory mammals of our acquaintance. Much of the final rush on the prey and the attack by tooth and claw would be almost instinctive and not reasoned. In feeding, the shortish arms would be rested on the carcass of the victim while the teeth tore the flesh apart, but hands have been given too little part in this exercise and it is possible that small victims might be swallowed whole, for the gape of the *Antrodemus* skull is considerable, and the mechanism of the jaws is snake-like to a certain extent in that the bones can be moved to allow a lump of food to pass into the gullet.

Megalosaurus, Ceratosaurus and *Antrodemus* are often grouped in the family Megalosauridae although, as we shall see, each has its own place in the Jurassic and what appear to be family characteristics could be similarities, separately acquired. All these genera are known only from the Jurassic of the USA and Europe or from Wealden deposits in Europe.

The carnosaurs reached their maximum in a closely allied family often called the Dinodontidae, which is distinguished chiefly on account of minor characters in the skull, and whose members are only known from the succeeding Cretaceous period.

The dinodonts are carnosaurs that attain their maximum of development, whether we think of it as size or brutishness, in *Tyrannosaurus*—the 'tyrant reptile'—a name applied by Professor H. F. Osborn to the remains of a gigantic carnosaur from the Upper Cretaceous Hell Creek Formation of Montana, excavated by Barnum Brown in 1902. The type species is *T. rex* Osborn. Compared with this enormous creature *Antrodemus* was but a child.

In appearance *Tyrannosaurus* was unusually large, attaining a length up to 47 feet from snout to tail end, and carrying its head 16 feet or so from the ground. The great skull, 4 feet or so long, is unusually deep and laterally compressed, and has jaws containing numerous sabre-like teeth 3–6 inches long and an inch wide. The premaxilla has here four small teeth. In general the skull bones exhibit a more specialized condition, and have lost the slight tendency to movement which was apparently present in those of the megalosaurs. The neck is unusually short, to bear the unusually heavy skull. The remainder of the skeleton is similarly well-adapted for the habits of the creature, a

151

condition which we might reasonably expect in a group which already had a long history of bipedal and carnivorous activity. The hind feet had solid support and three large claws directed forward while the first claw still was short and backward. Through several discoveries the skeleton of *Tyrannosaurus* is well known, with the exception of the fore limbs, which appear to have been very small and with highly specialized hands.

Excellently displayed remains can be seen in the American Museum of Natural History, New York, where the type specimen is, and in the Carnegie Museum, Pittsburgh. Casts of the skull are in many museums including the Department of Palaeontology of the British Museum (Natural History) in London. This museum also contains a partial skeleton of *Tyrannosaurus* that is the type specimen of *T.* (*Dynamosaurus*) *imperiosus* Osborn, 1905. It was obtained by the present writer from the American Museum of Natural History through the financial generosity of Dr C. T. Trechmann and with the skeleton there came a small collection of intriguing bones and armour. The armour was soon dissociated from the true Tyrannosaur material and a skeleton, part modelled, was reconstructed by Mr B. Newman, until recently with the department. As the remains have frequently been found in association with those of the horned and armoured dinosaurs it is reasonable to assume that *Tyrannosaurus* battled with these creatures, massive and well protected though they were. There is some justification for the belief that in this genus the maximum development of bulk, tooth and claw in this particular type of animal mechanism was attained, and that any increase in these offensive agents and in general size would have lessened the effective activity. It is not easy to picture the scene in which the struggles and victories of *Tyrannosaurus* were laid. Some of the dinosaurs we have seen were light and apparently agile, but for purely mechanical reasons *Tyrannosaurus* could not have been other than a clumsy and awkward giant battling against other equally cumbrous forms. Not a cunning or highly brained creature, it would be guided largely by instinct and automatic reactions to the stimuli of sight and smell, even though practice through countless carnivorous ancestors had brought this co-ordination to a high pitch of efficiency. Still, the mechanical

152

limits of the body were all against sudden or leaping movements, swift pursuit, or the battle of wits that characterizes mammalian contests; and, no doubt, the contests of that Cretaceous world, could we see them now, would seem to have the stiffness of amateur activity rather than the smoothness of the professional even though the feud was real and terrible.

The real battles of these dinosaurs are not conceivable by us for we have no comparable animals and no comparable physiologies as guides. Indeed when we consider that *Tyrannosaurus* is illustrated in every vertebrate palaeontology text-book it would seem that we must know all about it. In fact we have fine skeletons in New York and Pittsburgh, the partial skeleton in London and a skull or two.

Of six specialists three give the total length from nose to tip of tail as 47 feet and three as 50 feet. The height of the head from the ground is variously given as 14 feet, 18 feet, 19 and 20 feet. The skull is 4 feet long and the teeth may project 6 inches from the skull.

E. H. Colbert went to very considerable efforts to try to discover the weight in life and obtained a figure of 7·6 tons—a very reasonable amount considering that an African elephant may weigh 6–8 tons according to its height and a 33-foot crocodile (*Crocodilus porosus*) may weigh 3 tons.

There are several great carnivores like *Tyrannosaurus*. The Russian *Tarbosaurus* is very similar in appearance and the diagnosis of *T. efremovi* Maleev (1955) gives it as 10–12 metres long (33–39 feet) and 4·5–5 metres high (14½–16½ feet). The premaxilla has four teeth, the maxilla twelve and the dentary (lower jaw) fifteen.

Like *Tyrannosaurus*, there is a small second antorbital foramen, a large antorbital with a smooth lachrymal surface about its upper and hinder corner, the eye has the vertical axis the greater and, like *Ornithosuchus*, *Gorgosaurus* and *Tyrannosaurus* there is a marked rounded flange-like projection of the squamosal into the lateral temporal fenestra. In the front of the skull there is a more strongly marked groove at the junction of premaxilla and maxilla than in *Gorgosaurus* (as figured by Lambe) and *Tyrannosaurus* as figured by Osborn.

Judging by these illustrations the USSR form is near to

Tyrannosaurus but is certainly not identical with it. Nor is a wider range of material lacking. On display in the Palaeontological Museum of the USSR Academy of Sciences in Moscow, the writer noted five more or less complete skeletons of *Tarbosaurus* with clear indications of a two-fingered hand. The three-toed feet show also a very small first digit.

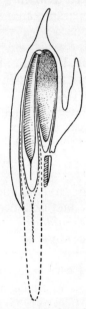

Fig. 36. Transverse section of maxilla of *Gorgosaurus*.

Tyrannosaurus is represented in *T. bataar* Maleev, of which there were two skulls and a partial skeleton. One of the beautiful skulls of *Tarbosaurus efremovi* is now well known for casts of it have been widely distributed. One is in the British Museum (Natural History) in London and another was sent to the author at the Royal Ontario Museum in Toronto.

Moscow has also a smallish skull labelled *Gorgosaurus lancinator* Maleev and a small *G. novojilovi* Maleev, from the Upper Cretaceous of Mongolia. Of this species, described in 1955, there is both skull and skeleton. The hand is clearly two-fingered and the feet three-toed. The skull is incomplete and the lower jaw is fragmentary. The length of the skull is about 2½ feet.

Of these specimens *Tarbosaurus efremovi* came from the Upper Cretaceous of Tsagan Ula; while *Gorgosaurus lancinator* came from Altan Ula and *Gorgosaurus novojilovi* from Tsagan Ula, Mongolia.

It should be mentioned that in 1965. A. K. Rozhdestvensky equates *Tyrannosaurus bataar* (=*Tarbosaurus efremovi* and *Gorgosaurus lancinator*.)

Gorgosaurus, with some seven specimens in the USA, is a well-known predator that is closely similar in its structure and habits to *Tyrannosaurus* and to *Tarbosaurus*, but is smaller in size and a little older geologically. The major account of this genus is still that of Lawrence M. Lambe, 'The Cretaceous Theropodous Dinosaur Gorgosaurus' (1917). The 1956 descriptions (in Russian) of the USSR specimens are brief and add but little to Lambe's account apart from the list of material and the figures of the skulls. Lambe dealt with the osteology and with the probable habits and appearance in life. *Gorgosaurus* was typically predaceous, for the restored skeleton shows admirably the characters of this group. The comparatively large head with prominent, sharp teeth, the forward stoop of the body, the strong, functionally three-toed and clawed feet, and the absurdly small two-fingered claw-hammer like hands, combine to form a picture that is peculiarly suggestive of truly reptilian and carnivorous habits.

Although 29 feet long and carrying its head 11 feet, and the back of the hips 9 feet, from the ground, the general construction is light. It was definitely a land-animal for the almost circular cross-section of the tail shows no water-living propensities. The form of the skeleton and the closely arranged series of abdominal ribs suggest that the erect position was not usually maintained, but that the animal walked with a definite stoop. It appears also to have rested on the bent hind limbs supported by the pubic bones. Feeding was probably accomplished in this squatting position. By bringing the body to the ground and lying flat upon the belly with the tail outstretched the dinosaur spent its periods of repose.

The hind legs were not spaced far apart and movement was

therefore not very speedy, while leaping would appear to have been impossible. The forwardly bent pose was maintained largely through the counter-balance of the tail, which would not therefore be of any great flexibility, so that when the animal turned sharply the tail would have to be swung round with a correspondingly quick movement.

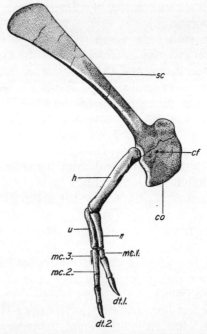

FIG. 37. Shoulder girdle and limb of *Gorgosaurus*. $\frac{1}{18}$ nat. size.
KEY: *co.*, coracoid; *cf.*, coracoid foramen; *dt.*, digit; *h.*, humerus; *mc.*, metacarpal; *r.*, radius; *sc.*, scapula; *u.*, ulna.

Lambe suggests that *Gorgosaurus* was a carrion-feeder which lived on the flat, wooded parts of the country. Its contemporaries were the very numerous herbivorous hadrosaurs and armoured dinosaurs as well as the other, generally smaller, members of its own kind, to say nothing of the now numerous small mammals and birds. There was bound to be, therefore, a great number of living creatures to pursue and of carcasses upon

156

which the scavengers could exist. Though it was not perhaps a lofty role in the scheme of nature that they were called upon to play, it must have been a very necessary one, and perhaps carrion feeding had a larger place in the giant carnivores' lives than has been assumed.

In the rapacious dinosaurs of the Upper Cretaceous it would appear that these creatures, rightly called terrible, had attained their maximum development. Further increase of bulk was impossible on purely mechanical grounds, if the necessary bipedal habit was to be maintained, and in any case bulk was becoming just a little too much for brain. Amongst the herbivores of that period, large and armoured as they were, the trouble again was lack of mental power. Such creatures would be practically immune today, even without the armour, if a mammalian intelligence guided their movements. Bulk and brain may form an inspiring combination but, of the two, the latter is by far the more important.

The importance of the theropods has long been known, for they have the longest line of any dinosaur group from Middle or certainly Upper Trias until the last days of the dinosaurs.

The unfortunate fact that so many are inadequately known is slowly being changed though at the moment it is the earliest and the latest that give most information and there are gaps, filled with names it is true in the middle. But these will be given more substance by the fact that there are trends from first to last that must also be found in a median representative.

That there are guidelines is obvious from the foregoing text. The number of premaxillary and maxillary teeth becomes standardized. The looseness of certain cranial bones disappears. The Cretaceous carnosaurs or dinodonts have two antorbital foramina. The fore limb grows smaller and the number of digits decreases.

The pubis, too, shows a greater expansion at its distal end where, in *Tyrannosaurus*, a great 'rocker' is developed.

The development of stiffening of the pelvis and the backbone, characteristic of *Ceratosaurus*, is an individual development that probably has no significance so far as relationships are concerned. Like *Ornithomimus* it learned a different way to pick or haul at its food and we must remember that in most cases,

157

perhaps in all cases except *Gorgosaurus*, there is too little material for us to speak 'as one having authority'.

None the less there are those who do and it is helpful that they make suggestions of relationships in the Saurischia.

To them these dinosaurs have origin from the pseudosuchian stem in the Middle and Upper Trias leading to the coelurosaurs, and the megalosaurs in the Jurassic. From the former came the Coeluridae and the Ornithomimidae (and perhaps *Ceratosaurus* which grew large and took on the manner of its betters—the distantly related megalosaurs and the tyrannosaurs).

To others the picture is more complete. The coelurosaurs had their own beginning and went their own lightly footed and long-fingered way. The carnosaurs were quite separate, with the little *Ornithosuchus* pointing the way to a far-distant Cretaceous with its *Gorgosaurus*, *Albertosaurus*, *Tarbosaurus* and *Tyrannosaurus* but without a clearly defined Jurassic member, for *Megalosaurus* and *Antrodemus* led their respective ways only to some little-known genera in foreign fields.

This story is by no means complete. There are many megalosaurs to which no reference has been made but whose founders' thoughts and ideas we have referred to elsewhere. There are megalosaurs in name (like the two-horned '*Megalosaurus*' *wetherilli* Wells that is no megalosaur but may find itself cast away on a nomenclatural island with *Ceratosaurus*.

If any of these classificatory dreams are true, it will be interesting to know, as it is interesting to speculate, why one branch remained comparatively small but developed long fingers and lost its teeth. And why the other branch became very big, and almost lost its forearms and fingers; and why the teeth of *Megalosaurus* are sharp but the teeth of *Tyrannosaurus*, which were so much more frightening, were blunt. And why abdominal ribs have less joints as the dinosaurs get bigger. We may be sure that these things did not happen just to aid the systematist!

CHAPTER IX

The Amphibious Dinosaurs: Sauropoda

There were giants in the earth in those days.
Genesis 6:4

The Sauropoda ('reptile-feet') are probably the most familiar of the dinosaurs to the general public, and their gigantic size, with the grotesque appearance as depicted in many restoration models and pictures, are never-failing sources of interest or amusement or puzzlement. As might be expected, they provide valuable material for the cartoonist and the advertisement artist, and, despite the fact that strange attitudes, habits and groupings are often portrayed, the result is that their characters are to a minor degree appreciated and accepted by the public. This is not unimportant for, when a bizarre form is discovered and represented, the non-specialist is apt to be sceptical, to consider the conclusions as the imaginings of a mind diseased from too long a sojourn in the abyss of the past.

Many years ago the author was standing in the Dinosaur Gallery of the British Museum (Natural History), looking at *Diplodocus* when a Yorkshireman came by.

'You don't mean to say you take it seriously, do you?', he said, and went on, 'where did it come from?'

'The USA,' I replied.

'Ah thought so', said he. 'They'd tell you anything there.'

But there was no tall tale about the low and long *Diplodocus*. There were such animals and our immediate purpose is to describe what is known about some of them and to explain their position in the dinosaurian scheme.

The Sauropoda range in geological time mainly from the Lower Jurassic to the close of the Lower Cretaceous, though several remarkable forms passed on into the Upper Cretaceous

159

and were comparatively widespread in the Southern Hemisphere. They were Saurischia, related perhaps to the Triassic carnosaurs and derived from ancestors as yet unidentified that may have been quadrupedal. There were no bipedal sauropods nor were any of them carnivorous though they may have ingested shell-fish or mollusca of various kinds in the course of gathering vegetarian food.

The earliest of these giant forms belongs to the family Morosauridae of Marsh and is *Rhoetosaurus brownei* described by Heber A. Longman in 1927. It came from the Walloon Coal Measures of Queensland, Australia, and the type specimen is in the Queensland Museum, Brisbane. Another early genus is *Amygdalodon patagonicus* Cabrera, 1947, from the Lower Jurassic of South America. Neither of these is known by any kind of complete skeleton, so that effectively the best known early dinosaur of this kind is *Cetiosaurus* which occurs from the Middle Jurassic upwards in much of central England. When the first fragments of *Cetiosaurus* were described by Owen (1841, 1842) he interpreted them as belonging to some crocodilian form, a natural enough assumption since the Sauropoda exhibit more crocodile-like features than any other dinosaurs. Then, secondly, in the important features of the brain-case and the scapulae the conditions in *Cetiosaurus* approach very closely to those of the earlier Plateosauridae. When we deal with that family of the Prosauropoda we shall see that *Plateosaurus* had a special significance and that it may have taken to the water in search of food. Further, its whole structure was only in part adapted for truly bipedal locomotion such as that of the later carnivores. The assumption of the bipedal mode of progression was a response to the aridity of the Trias, and *Plateosaurus* would most probably abandon it occasionally when in the marshy grounds or on the lake shores it is thought to have visited. No surprise need be evoked, therefore, by the assumption that some relative of *Plateosaurus*, in some less arid situation returned to the ancestral quadrupedal habit and, with virtually a clear evolutionary field before it, became highly adapted to an amphibious mode of life which provided it with ample succulent vegetable food and permitted great increase in the bodily size. In this way, and from such a source, the Sauropoda

160

ᴛᴇ I. *Iguanodon*. The earliest restoration of a dinosaur, erected at the Crystal Palace, Sydenham, ₃54 and designed by Waterhouse Hawkins. Courtesy of the Greater London Council.

PLATE II. *Dinosaurs of southern England.* This composite picture shows reptiles of land, sea and air in Lower Liassic times. The dinosaurs are *Scelidosaurus harrisoni* (top left) one of the earliest armoured forms; *Megalosaurus* (top centre), a flesh eater; *Stegosaurus* (on sand), another armoured dinosaur. Surrounded by other reptiles, pterosaurs, the earliest bird and an early mammal, the dinosaurs had ample competition and were not alone in a dinosaur world. 175 million years ago. Courtesy of the *Illustrated London News.*

PLATE III. *Dinosaurs of England.*
The Wealden deposits of Kent,
Surrey, Sussex and the Isle of
Wight have yielded a considerable number of dinosaur bones of
great historical interest. Here are
Iguanodon (right) a herbivore,
and *Megalosaurus,* and between
them, in the water, is *Cetiosaurus,*
an amphibious plant-eater some
25–30 tons in weight. On the left
is *Hypsilophodon,* a 5 foot high
small relation of *Iguanodon* that is
thought to have walked on the
branches of trees. In the foreground is the spined and plated
Polacanthus, and, near the trees, a
megalosaur in running position.
A turtle, a crocodile and a flight
of pterosaurs add to a picture of
a reptilian world of 135 million
years ago. Courtesy of the
Illustrated London News.

PLATE IV. *Dinosaurs of China*. A composite picture of dinosaur life in ancient China during the Mesozoic. In the background are Upper Jurassic stegosaurs (*Chialingosaurus*) closely allied to the African *Kentrosaurus*; on the left are typical Upper Cretaceous flat-headed hadrosaurs (*Tanius*) overlooking the large sauropod *Omeisaurus* (Lower Cretaceous). In the left foreground is an Upper Cretaceous ornithomimid, with a nodosaur (*Heishanosaurus*) in front of it. At lower right is a herbivorous biped like *Campto-saurus* (*Sanpasaurus*) and on the upper right *Szechuanosaurus*, an Upper Jurassic megalosaur-like flesh eater. Courtesy of the *Illustrated London News*.

may have been derived, although a great period of time elapsed between the appearance of their earliest-known representative and the last-recognized plateosaurid.

Until recently it would have been a relatively simple statement of this sort that would have explained the origin of the giant dinosaurs. The bipedal theropods had Triassic forms that were awkward, bipedal and shore-living and thus led to quadrupedal sauropods. There is no doubt that theropods and sauropods are closely linked in the overall Order Saurischia but recent discoveries and recent attempts at classification have altered this simplicity. Colbert, Charig, Attridge and Crompton, Romer and Kuhn have put forward schemes of classification and relationship for the Saurischia that add to, and in part clarify, the issues.

A whole series of remains of small, toothed carnivores and herbivores are known from the Triassic especially of England, Germany and South Africa. Many of these have long been known but the passing of the years has done little to explain them. The English Thecodontosauridae, the German Plateosauridae and the South African Melanorosauridae all contain forms of great potentiality, though there is no clear evolutionary connexion between them.

Perhaps in looking at early dinosaurs and their possible ancestry too much attention has been paid to the intermembral index (i.e. the relationships between the limb sizes) for many reptiles that seldom ran and were never bipedal have markedly shorter forelimbs as compared with the hind. Thus it is possible that the immediate ancestors of the quadrupedal sauropods were not bipedal just because they had shorter fore limbs than hind.

The relationship in general may be shown by stating that the Saurischia are divided into the Theropoda and the Sauropodomorpha (von Huene, 1932) and the latter term includes the Prosauropoda of von Huene, 1920, and the Sauropoda of Marsh, 1878.

To go back now to the Prosauropoda we may consider one of the best known, *Plateosaurus*, of which there are several entire skeletons and other related fragments from the Upper Triassic deposits of Germany, France and South Africa. Several well-preserved examples are in the Palaeontological Museum of the

161

University of Tübingen, and the genus was considerably studied by Freiherr von Huene of that institution.

The Plateosauridae, or family which contains *Plateosaurus* and its allies, are Prosauropoda of medium to large size, that is, up to 19 or 20 feet in total length, and with generally hollow bones. The appearance of the skeleton as mounted is undeniably clumsy. The smallish head, reputed to bear the vestige of a pineal foramen, was carried more or less in the same line as the longish and thick neck, while the body was barrel-shaped and the tail was long. The creature was bipedal and the clumsy hind legs, with the thigh bone curved and a little longer than the lower leg-bones, had five-toed feet which were very likely plantigrade during rest or slow movement, but digitigrade when the pace was quickened. It is interesting to note that the metatarsals were only loosely articulated. The fore limbs were also clumsy, five-fingered, although the outer two digits were reduced, and relatively large, which at first sight suggests that they may have been used for resting upon or occasionally in walking, but their position, when closely examined, goes against the latter, for so much are the scapulae rotated inwards that, when the arms were bent, the elbows would be away from the sides of the body and the hands together in the mid-line. The hands were strong with fingers as long as the fore arm and adapted for grasping small animals. The fore limbs were half the size of the hind.

The structure of the jaws suggests that they were capable of quick snapping movements. The teeth are also interesting because they are spatulate and laterally compressed, but serrated on both the front and the back edges. They extended over both premaxillae and maxillae in the upper jaws and along, at least, half of the mandible, and were of much the same size throughout. With such teeth, admirably suited for the capture of slippery prey, and associated with clawed fingers and toes and the not inconsiderable bulk of an animal 20 feet long, there can be no possible doubt that *Plateosaurus* was, for that time, an enemy of unusual power and terrifying aspect.

Von Huene, in 1928, dealt fully with the finding of the remains at Trossingen and with the habits and habitats of this family. During this part of the Upper Triassic, at what now is Trossingen, there appears to have been a wide belt of more or less desert land separating the high land on the east from an inland sea on the west. Further to the north and north-east was the main part of the continental land-mass, while further to the south were the great seas, part of Tethys and part of what is now the Atlantic. Just previously, in Stübensandstone times, a large river flowing from the north-east and running south-west had formed delta areas in the Trossingen district, and the banks of this river and the slopes of the higher ground were covered with coniferous trees. The climate was probably somewhat continental, with two seasons, a drier and a moister. During the drier times the Plateosaurs not unnaturally would be attracted from their hilly grounds to the shore of the inland sea about eighty miles away. To get there, however, they had to cross the sandy, dry and warm belt. Von Huene calculates that as the length of the legs of *Plateosaurus* was about 5 feet the stride would be 3 feet or a little more, and since probably two steps were or could be taken per second, the rate of progress would be about 4 miles per hour. Thus he visualizes herds of these animals crossing the dry plain and making the journey in two forced marches, perhaps by night, to the water's edge. It may be objected that this sustained effort is not very characteristic of reptiles, and the concerted movement of the herds is crediting them with mammalian attributes. Nonetheless the postulated speed is that calculated by Charles Darwin for the smaller journeys taken by Galapagos giant tortoises. It is by no means certain that such prolonged or speedy progress could be maintained by animals of such bulk, and even an elephant at the present day might find such marches a strain. Nonetheless, in whatever parties or at whatever speed, these dinosaurs strayed over the plains. The weak, the young, or the sick among them would become exhausted and fall down to die, and in time, be covered up by the dunes of wind-blown sand. Thus preserved they lay entombed until the hand of man uncovered them in the quarries of Trossingen. The material in these quarries is loess-like, and the skeletons thus far obtained are those of young, or weakly developed individuals, which supports this argument.

Arrived at the water side they may have found plenty of food in the shape of small reptiles, swimming reptiles, amphibians and fish, and there is a possibility that they might take to the water themselves to obtain food. As we have seen, the nature of the teeth and hands was suitable for the capture of fish. In this kind of way the origin of sauropods might have been brought about.

So far as the sauropods themselves are concerned their structure and classification are in many ways difficult to determine satisfactorily, chiefly on account of the large size of the body which, on the one hand, makes them very similar in estimated appearance, and which, on the other, introduces serious though mainly mechanical difficulties into the collection, preparation and subsequent examination of their remains. In addition, nothing very helpful is known about sexual, age, or individual differences in size. The result is that many genera of Sauropoda have been founded upon, and are inadequately known from, unsatisfactory fragments of the skeleton which are really indeterminable, and which would be readily admitted to be so in more easily collected Orders. The consequent difficulties in nomenclature form only one of the unfortunate results of this series of circumstances.

The Sauropoda were large, plant-eating dinosaurs with a long neck and tail but a relatively short body. The skull is proportionately very small and the dentition, which may consist of spatulate (spoon-shaped) or long and but slightly pointed (pencil-like) teeth, is feeble. The jaws themselves are weak and the quadrate slopes downwards and forwards for the articulation with the lower jaw, which has no coronoid process. Such jaws, coupled with the feeble dentition, do not provide a very efficient apparatus for mastication, so that the food must have been succulent vegetation although a certain amount of animal-food, such as mollusca, may have been included during the process of raking the food into the jaws. There is always one preorbital opening, but occasionally there are two (as in *Diplodocus*). Like the first preorbital opening, the orbits and the narial openings are usually large and the skull has often an exceedingly fragile appearance.

In the vertebral column the cervicals and some or all of the dorsals are opisthocoelous (i.e. with the hinder articular surface concave) and each side of them is considerably hollowed out.

The rest of the vertebrae may be amphiplatyan (with flat articular ends), amphicoelous (biconcave articular ends) or even, though very rarely, procoelous (i.e. with the anterior articular surface concave). The later dorsals have an additional and strengthening pair of articulations known as hyposphenes and hypantra. The dorsal vertebrae and some of the others often have large cavities which, as we shall see, were probably pneumatic during life and perhaps connected with the lungs as in birds.

The vertebral series is of considerable interest as it is obvious that, to support the massive weight of these animals, a structure of strength and stability, but as light as possible, was necessary. Lightness and efficiency were combined in the vertebral column, which is actually a very fine piece of anatomical structural engineering. In addition to the close articulations of the vertebrae themselves the whole series was given strength and some rigidity by ligaments and tendons connecting the neural spines of the vertebrae. In some Sauropoda the anterior neural spines were bifurcated and presumably additional ligaments lay between the two processes. To counteract as far as possible the weight of the more massive vertebrae the centra were excavated. The neural canal is greatly enlarged in the sacrum, so much so that this cavity is many times larger than the brain, and it is this part of the nervous system that controlled and co-ordinated the heavy hind limb and tail movements. Branca (1914) suggested that the innervation of the digestive organs was also part of the sacral brain's function.

It seems probable that the stomach in the sauropods was a powerful, muscular, and gizzard-like organ in which gastroliths, or stomach-stones, were ingested and helped to pulverize the contents.

In the shoulder-region there is an ossified, paired sternum. The limb-bones are solid and those of the fore leg are usually shorter than those of the hind limbs, although sometimes the two pairs are approximately equal in length, and in some forms of the family Brachiosauridae the fore actually exceed the hind limbs. The fourth trochanter, though present on the femora of sauropods, is not prominent. The pubes and ischia are comparatively long and broad and each bone is united distally with its opposite fellow by a cartilaginous joint. All four feet are semi-plantigrade and five-toed, but the two outer toes are reduced in size; the innermost toes had strong laterally compressed claws and in most cases the toes were enclosed in a pad like the feet of elephants.

The skin in all of them appears to have been smooth, although skin-impressions have been described which bear evidence of tuberculated but unossified areas.

In time the Sauropoda ranged from the Lower Jurassic to the Upper Cretaceous, and their remains have been found in England, France, Portugal, Spain, Switzerland, Tanzania, Australia, India, China, Madagascar; Wyoming, Colorado, New Mexico and Utah in the USA; and Brazil and Patagonia in South America. The centre of dispersal of the Sauropoda may have been in Africa, despite what we know about the German area in which the Triassic *Plateosaurus* ranged; the last refuge of the Infra-order appears to have been southern France, Spain and New Mexico.

There have been many attempts at classification over the years since Marsh outlined their characters in 1878 and divided them into the Family Atlantosauridae and the Family Morosauridae in 1882.

Marsh's fundamental statement (in *Amer. Journ. Science* (3), XVI, p. 412, 1878) was as follows:

SAUROPODA

A well marked group of gigantic Dinosaurs from the above horizon has been characterized by the writer as a distinct family, *Atlantosauridæ*, but they differ so widely from typical *Dinosauria*, that they belong rather in a suborder, which may be called *Sauropoda*, from the general character of the feet. They are the least specialized of the order, and in some characters show such approach to the Mesozoic Crocodiles, as to suggest a common ancestry at no very remote period.

The most marked characters of this group are as follows:

1. The fore and hind limbs are nearly equal in size.
2. The carpal and tarsal bones are distinct.
3. The feet are plantigrade, with five toes on each foot.
4. The precaudal vertebræ contain large cavities, apparently pneumatic.
5. The neural arches are united to the centra by suture.
6. The sacral vertebræ do not exceed four, and each supports its own transverse process.

7. The chevrons have free articular extremities.
8. The pubes unite in front by ventral symphysis.
9. The third trochanter is rudimentary or wanting.
10. The limb bones are without medullary cavities.

Since then the numbers of families has waxed and waned. Lull (1924) recognized four families; von Huene six in 1927 and two in 1932; D. M. S. Watson in 1931 had five and Smith Woodward (in Zittel's *Palaeontology*) had six though they were not quite the same six as those of von Huene.

In more recent times Romer (1956) has the family Brachiosauridae, with four sub-families, and the family Titanosauridae with four sub-families, a very agreeable distribution of the materials. Colbert (1961) also gives two families, the Brachiosauridae and the Titanosauridae and maintains this in his valuable paper 'Relationships of the Saurischian Dinosaurs' in 1964. In 1966 Romer (*'Vertebrate Paleontology'*—a household work for the palaeontologist) gives these same two families. In 1965 and 1967 Charig changes the names into the Family Morosauridae Marsh 1882 (= Brachiosauridae Riggs 1904) and Atlantosauridae Marsh 1877 (= Titanosauridae Marsh 1895). We are thus back to the classification given earlier in these pages by Marsh eighty-six years ago.

There is, however, a change that the present writer would make. *Morosaurus*, from which the family Morosauridae derives its name, is now generally regarded as a synonym of *Camarasaurus* Cope 1877 and the family Camarasauridae Cope 1877 predates the Morosauridae Marsh 1882.

The classification used here is therefore:

Infra-order Sauropoda;
Family Camarasauridae Cope 1877
Atlantosauridae Marsh 1877.

This represents a just division of the spoils between the two great rivals.

The general characters of sauropods as now recognized may be succinctly stated as usually large and sometimes very large Saurischia with large and heavy bones. The skull is small, compared to the rest of the animal very small, with weak jaws and teeth in the front of the mouth; the skull with one or two

167

preorbital foramina and with the nostrils high on the skull or in a raised bony protuberance. The neck is long; longer than the body; and the tail is very long. Fore limbs are usually smaller than the hind and the feet are short, broad and heavy (pachypod of Owen!) with the claws reduced often to one on the hallux or pollux. The large pelvis has a high but short ilium with a prominent process for the pubis. There are three sacrals but they are usually increased in number from the caudal series. Sauropods were all vegetarian and amphibious.

In the previous chapter so diverse were the structure, habits and environments of the different Theropoda that it was advisable, indeed necessary, to deal with the more important genera in some detail, but the sauropods, however different individually they are in the details of skeletal structure and size, appear to have led much the same kind of life in whatever period or place they lived, so that it should suffice to give short accounts of the principal genera of each family, and to follow these summaries with a discussion of the life-habits so far as they can justifiably be envisaged.

Cetiosaurus, a typical member of the family Camarasauridae, is the first-known sauropod, and comes from the Great Oolite (Middle Jurassic) of Oxford. In considering its skeletal structure it is of great interest to note that what is known of the brain-case has been claimed to resemble closely that of the Upper Triassic prosauropod, *Plateosaurus*. The teeth are broad and spatulate. The cervical and dorsal vertebrae are slightly opistho-coelous, while the bone in the centra is spongy and the neural spines are simple and not forked. The sacrum consists of five or six fused and solid vertebrae. The caudal vertebrae have flat or slightly concave articular surfaces, but the last centra have conical ends and together form a tail-lash. The proportionate length of the fore limb to the hind limb varies in the different species, but may be taken as about two-thirds to three-quarters, and the length of the thigh bone is about 5 feet. It was the shape of this considerable bone that led early workers to the idea that *Cetiosaurus* was a crocodile. The genus is only incompletely known, but interesting remains of the hind-quarters and tail, and also a fore limb, are on exhibition in the dinosaur gallery of the British Museum (Natural History). This particular specimen is named *C. leedsi*, and came from the Oxford Clay of the brick pits of Peterborough.

In England remains of *Cetiosaurus* have been found in many localities and in all the Jurassic horizons formed under continental conditions. Although the lowest in which they occur is Bathonian, there is ample evidence that there must have been a long developmental history, the details of which are, unfortunately, lost to us, as there can be no question that *Cetiosaurus* is quite a well-developed form. English readers will be interested to know that specimens have been obtained from a large number of localities, including Oxford, Stonesfield, Blisworth, Bibury, Enslow, and Cogenhoe, and the quarries in these regions have produced, and some still produce, interesting and valuable portions of the skeleton, particularly vertebrae and claws. The conditions under which the containing deposits must have been laid down give evidence of variation, but they suggest coastal waters or little lakes or lagoons where there were many other kinds of vertebrate and invertebrate life and apparently an abundance of plant-food.

As for *Cetiosaurus* itself, it was almost certainly a large, ponderous, slow-moving creature of considerable bulk and weight, with a long neck and tail (Plate III). The estimated length is something like 50 feet, which is in itself no little evidence of the length of time and of the sauropodous ancestry that must separate the genus from the original ancestor.

The other members of the sub-family Cetiosaurinae are incompletely known and are all from the Upper Jurassic of the United States, with the exception of one form, from the Jurassic of Switzerland, named *Cetiosauriscus greppini* by von Huene. This writer has made great contributions to our knowledge of the Saurischia and is a prolific author, not only upon the bones and genera themselves, but on the important question of classification. It is, therefore, only right to point out that he did not consider *Cetiosaurus leedsi* a species of the genus *Cetiosaurus*, but referred it to a new genus, *Cetiosauriscus*; further, in his conception of the Cetiosaurinae, *Cetiosaurus* became a member of a sub-family which he called the Cardiodontinae (after *Cardiodon* the name which Owen gave in 1841 to a tooth which probably is really from *Cetiosaurus*), while a second sub-

169

THE DINOSAURS

family consists of the Brachiosaurinae. In 1932, however, he placed *Cetiosaurus* in a sub-family Cetiosaurinae, and gives the Brachiosauridae the full familial rank (that we have equated, with the Camarasauridae). Nowadays we regard *Cardiodon* and *Cetiosauriscus* as synonyms of *Cetiosaurus*. The Australian *Rhoetosaurus* probably belongs to the same sub-family.

The sub-family Brachiosaurinae takes its name from *Brachiosaurus* ('arm-reptile'), a genus first described from America, by E. S. Riggs in 1902 (Riggs, 1902, 1904). Subsequent discoveries at Tendaguru, in what was German East Africa and is now Tanzania, have considerably added to our knowledge of this truly gigantic form. The Brachiosaurinae are closely allied to

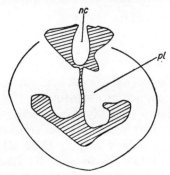

FIG. 38. *Brachiosaurus brancai*. Section of dorsal vertebra. (After Janensch.) ⅛ nat. size.

KEY: *nc.*, neural canal; *pl.*, pleurocentral cavities.

the Cetiosaurinae, but differ in two main characters—the vertebrae are much more excavated laterally, so much so that a cross-section looks rather anchor-shaped (Fig. 38), and the fore limbs are more slender than the hind limbs, but as long as, or even longer, these. In addition the extra (hyposphene–hypantrum) articulations on the vertebral processes are strongly developed. These characters are well borne out in *Brachiosaurus* itself, for it has the additional articulations very well developed and, a more obvious character, the humerus often exceeds the femur decidedly in length and both are not infrequently over 6 feet long. The length of some of the cervical vertebrae, about 28 inches, gives an idea of the great size of many of the bones.

170

From the remains now available for study in different museums throughout the world it is possible to build up a reasonably clear idea of the appearance during life. The skull was also small in this genus, the neck being very long and moderately thick at its base and the tail longish and thick-set, but not so long as that of *Diplodocus* which we shall mention later. W. D. Matthew (1915) summed up these features well in characterizing *Brachiosaurus* as 'a giraffe-like wader adapted to take refuge in deeper waters, out of reach of the fierce carnivores of the land'. Now, it is interesting to note that the neural spines of this genus are not forked and are at their highest just behind the neck and thereafter become low and broad. The reason would appear to be that with the humerus so long there was less need for the animal to raise itself up occasionally on its hind limbs, as sauropods might do in water when reaching after food, but that the long neck still needed lifting power. Incidentally, the nostrils were in a raised crest on the skull and thus very high in the air.

There is no doubt that *Brachiosaurus* was an immense creature, indeed it is the bulkiest of all dinosaurs, but there has been a natural tendency on the part of some to magnify unduly the proportions of the body. The earliest and most completely known forms of sauropods are those in which the humerus is shorter, often markedly so, than the femur. These animals are also of great size, so that when an unusually long humerus ascribed to *Brachiosaurus* was discovered it was concluded, naturally enough, that the proportion of the elements was in accord with that of the other sauropods and therefore that the new form was of proportionately larger size. Thus, estimates of the length of the animal varied from 100 to 150 feet. A fuller understanding of the structure of the limbs cleared up these difficulties and it is now accepted that *Brachiosaurus* was high and comparatively short instead of long and low. The height of the head from the ground when the neck was more or less erect must have been considerable, probably well over 30 feet, and is actually 40 feet in a mounted skeleton in Berlin, while the total length from skull to tail-end was from 60 to 80 feet. The weight was probably about 76 English tons for Colbert (1962) has calculated the US tonnage as 85·6.

171

Three species of this genus are recognized: *B. altithorax* Riggs, the type species, from the Upper Jurassic of Colorado, preserved in the Chicago Museum of Natural History; *B. brancai* Janensch, a slightly larger form, and *B. fraasi* Janensch, from the Upper Jurassic freshwater beds of Tendaguru, Tanzania, portions of which are in the museums of Berlin, Stuttgart and Frankfurt-on-Main, as well as in the Palaeontology Department of the British Museum.

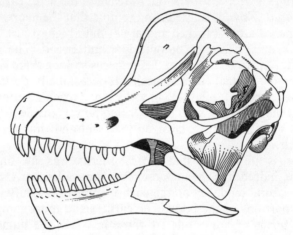

FIG. 39. *Brachiosaurus brancai*. Left side of skull. (After Janensch.) $\frac{1}{10}$ nat. size.

KEY: *n.*, narial opening.

Other genera of this family are found in the British Isles, the most important being *Bothriospondylus* and *Ornithopsis*, the type specimens of the genera and species also being in the Palaeontology Department of the British Museum. The former genus comes from the Middle and Upper Jurassic of Bradford and Swindon (Wiltshire) respectively, while the latter occurs in the Wealden deposits of the Isle of Wight and at Hastings in Sussex. Both genera are incompletely known, the remains discovered being merely some rather lightly constructed vertebrae and a few portions of pelvic bones.

To this family also belongs *Pelorosaurus* of Mantell (1850) which has now been made a sort of *omnium gatherum* of ancient

British genera, founded with enthusiasm and skill in the hey-day of early palaeontology. *Chondrosteosaurus, Eucamerotus, Dinodocus, Oplosaurus, Hoplosaurus, Ischyrosaurus,* and *Gigantosaurus* were all founded upon material that needed more bones and more elucidation for their firm establishment. Today a volume could be written on these alone and on the men who engendered them.

One of these genera, *Gigantosaurus,* based on the species *G. megalonyx,* was named by H. G. Seeley. The basic materials, which are now in the Sedgwick Museum of Cambridge University, are not of great importance at the present time but the name is important, as we shall see.

The next family, the Camarasaurinae, takes its name from *Camarasaurus,* the genus founded in 1877 by E. D. Cope on *C. supremus* from the Jurassic of Colorado. It was known by series of associated vertebrae which bore a close resemblance to those of Marsh's *Morosaurus.* However, since that date a skeleton of *Camarasaurus lentus* (Marsh) was taken out of the famous dinosaur quarry in Utah which is now set up as the Dinosaur National Monument.

This very complete skeleton is small, just about 18 feet long, and can be seen in the Carnegie Museum, Pittsburgh as a half-grown Camarasaur.

Camarasaurus ('vaulted chamber reptile') is so called because of its vertebral cavities. Most of the remains are not outstandingly large, so it is—perhaps erroneously—not regarded as a very large sauropod. It had a short high skull, with elevated nostrils. In general it appears to have been very similar in characters to *Morosaurus* ('dull-reptile') which is known to have reached 60 feet long, with fore limbs markedly shorter than the hind, and with a short and high skull which had very large orbital openings. The teeth, of which there are about forty-eight, are large, spatulate and somewhat crowned, and set in a long, close series. The neck (with twelve cervicals) was long and flexible, while the trunk was short (with twelve dorsals, the more anterior of which have forked neural spines). The tail was long, consisting of over fifty caudal vertebrae. *Camarasaurus* (*Morosaurus*) *grandis* (Marsh) from the Upper Jurassic (Morrison) of Wyoming, may have been as much as 55 feet

173

long. Fragments of this genus, or some very closely related form, have been recorded from the Wealden of Cuckfield, Sussex ('*Morosaurus' becklesi*). Our knowledge of the genus is derived from the material obtained from many American localities, chiefly in Wyoming, Colorado, Oklahoma, and Utah.

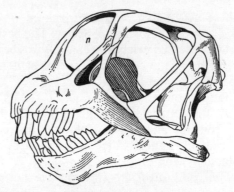

FIG. 40. *Camarasaurus*. Left side of skull. Approx. ⅛ nat. size.
KEY: *n.*, narial opening.

The last genus of this family with which we shall deal is quite an interesting Lower Cretaceous form from Shangtung, China, named *Helopus zdanskyi* by the Swedish palaeontologist, Wiman. The word *Helopus* means 'marsh-foot' and had reference to the habitat but the generic name had already been used in 1832 for a bird so the new genus *Euhelopus* has been given to the dinosaur by A. S. Romer, 1956. The description of the dinosaur forms the subject of a pleasantly written and excellently illustrated memoir of the Geological Survey of China (Wiman, 1929). In the skull and pelvic characters this new form approximates to *Camarasaurus* but the cervical and anterior dorsal vertebrae have only slightly forked neural spines. *Euhelopus* seems to have been about 35 feet long. It is placed in the sub-family, Euhelopodinae. Bones of this species are exhibited in the palaeontological museum of the University of Uppsala, Sweden. *Omeisaurus* is a related Chinese form.

One has to hesitate when asked what is the largest dinosaur.

174

Does largeness mean bulk or does it mean overall length? For *Brachiosaurus* is 40 feet high, 60 feet long and 80 tons in weight, yet despite that it is not and has never been a *popular* dinosaur. *Diplodocus* is long, nearly 90 feet, low in stature and about 10 English tons in weight. It is more popular: yet the favourite of them all is *Brontosaurus* (the 'thunder lizard', so-called from the supposed noise of its moving over the land). *Brontosaurus* appears in every book. It is hard therefore, almost painful, to demote this legendary giant to a lesser place, in the sense that it must become absorbed in a less appealing and less-known name.

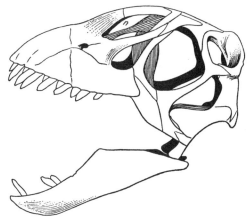

FIG. 41. *Euhelopus zdanski*. Left side of skull. (After Wiman.) Approx. $\frac{1}{8}$ nat. size.

KEY: *n.*, narial opening.

The second family of the Sauropods, the Atlantosauridae of Marsh (1877), contains as its first sub-family the Atlanto-saurinae and in this there are three important sauropod genera: *Atlantosaurus*, *Apatosaurus* and *Brontosaurus*.

Now this trio is not so easy to discuss as might appear. The skeletal remains cannot be equated satisfactorily and there have been considerable alterations in attribution. Romer in 1956, for example, makes *Atlantosaurus*, *Brontosaurus* and *Titanosaurus* Marsh (not Lydekker) all synonyms of *Apatosaurus* Marsh 1877. Now all of these genera, except *Brontosaurus*, were created in 1877. *Brontosaurus* dates from 1879 and this is important.

175

In his *Vertebrate Paleontology*, 1966, Romer gives *Atlanto-saurus* as a synonym of *Brontosaurus*, and *Apatosaurus* is placed in the other family of sauropods. If one looks up Marsh's 1877 paper in the *American Journal of Science*, one finds that in the first paragraph *Atlantosaurus montanus* is given as a replacement for *Titanosaurus montanus*, as Marsh's name *Titanosaurus* was preoccupied by *Titanosaurus* Lydekker 1877. The family name of Atlantosauridae was given in that paragraph too.

The following paragraph is headed by *Apatosaurus ajax*, a new genus and species, the type being a nearly complete specimen from the Morrison formation (Upper Jurassic) of Jefferson County, Colorado. This paper clearly differentiates between *Atlantosaurus* and *Apatosaurus* and, by the paragraph arrangement just mentioned, shows that *Atlantosaurus* has precedence over *Apatosaurus*.

The magnificent volume recently published by Ostrom and McIntosh under the title *Marsh's Dinosaurs* gives valuable information and illustrations of these nineteenth-century types. It seems to the present writer that *Atlantosaurus* is distinct enough to remain on its own and that *Apatosaurus*, of which some excellent materials have been discovered, is the same sauropod as *Brontosaurus* of which less satisfactory skull material is available. As has been pointed out the name *Apatosaurus* has precedence in time over *Brontosaurus*, thus all brontosaur species are therefore included here under the genus *Apatosaurus*.

In this century a very fine skeleton, named *A. louisiae* Holland, named in honour of Mrs Andrew Carnegie whose husband financed the explorations, was discovered near Split Mountain in Utah, in what is now the Dinosaur National Monument. This specimen, the type of its species, is exhibited in the Carnegie Museum, Pittsburgh, and gives an excellent idea of the massive build of these particular forms.

Apatosaurus (= *Brontosaurus*) may be described generally as a large sauropod with a very small skull (with a diminutive brain), a long neck, a short back, and a long tail. All the vertebrae are deeply excavated and cavernous. There are five centra in the sacrum; and the ischia are more slender than the

176

pubes. *Brontosaurus*, which attained a length of 72 feet, is known through a great deal of material obtained from the Upper Jurassic (Morrison Formation) of Wyoming and Utah. Perhaps the skeleton known best is that in the American Museum of Natural History, New York. This was discovered in 1898 at Medicine Bow, Wyoming, by Mr Walter Granger. It took the whole of the summer of 1899 to excavate the bones, and pack and transport them to the museum. There it took over two years to free the bones from the matrix and to piece them together and harden them sufficiently for handling. The difficult and laborious business of mounting the skeleton on its iron framework took even longer, so that it was not until 1905 that the skeleton was properly on exhibition. Matthew gave a very good account of its history and details in 1915. At that time knowledge of the general structure of such sauropods was slight, so that Dr Matthew and Mr Granger had to do a great deal of dissection of modern reptiles to obtain a good idea of the articulation of the limbs. On the tentatively mounted skeleton of what was then *Brontosaurus*, strips of paper were fastened in the position of the muscles and the mechanical requirements of the pose adopted were studied. By such elaborate and painstaking methods many of the public exhibits in our large museums have been made. The skeleton thus mounted is curious in many respects. The very small head seems inadequate for the needs of the great body, and the long neck appears to have had a considerable amount of flexibility. The body is short and compressed from side to side—'slab-sided' is Matthew's term—and supported on four solid and heavy limbs. The tail vertebrae are also heavy and the tail must have been a larger but unarmoured pattern of that of a crocodile or lizard and must have stuck out considerably behind the body. While the ribs, limb bones and tail bones are generally heavy, the cervical and dorsal vertebrae are so constructed that they combine lightness in weight with the maximum of articular surface and strength to sustain stress and strain. For this purpose they are constructed largely of thin plates and bars of bone, the bone between the bars being so much excavated that it really forms a network of air cavities.

The teeth of *Apatosaurus* indicate a herbivorous habit, and

177

the distribution of bone in the skeleton is remarkably arranged so that under a line joining the hip-girdle and the shoulder blade all the bone is solid and heavy, while above it the structures are light. The combination of such factors has suggested that *Apatosaurus* was a habitual dweller in coastal swamps or marshes, finding therein a luxuriant growth of water-plants to satisfy its large appetite, and having also the great weight of the body, which has been estimated at 30–35 tons, buoyed up by the water. On the other hand, the heavy limb bones would play the part of the lead on a diver's boots and enable the creature to walk comfortably despite the buoyancy of the water.

Much of this reconstruction of the living habits is, as we shall see, controversial, but the points at issue affect other forms than *Apatosaurus*, so that we shall defer the discussion of habit and habitat until we deal with these dinosaurs as a whole.

The other members of this family are *Atlantosaurus* (the name means 'Atlas-reptile', Atlas being one of the gods, and he who bears up the pillars of heaven), and *Uintasaurus* (the name is derived from the locality, the Uinta Mountains of Utah) which are found in the Morrison Formation, i.e. Upper Jurassic, of North America, and principally in the western United States, Wyoming, Colorado and Utah.

A sauropod from the Upper Jurassic of Tendaguru, Tanzania, is *Dicraeosaurus* ('forked reptile') of Janensch. The presacral vertebrae of this form are not excavated as those of *Camarasaurus* but the cervical and dorsal vertebrae have higher and more deeply forked neural spines, suggesting a more developed muscular arrangement and associated with the fact that the neck apparently is comparatively short (cf. *Brachiosaurus*, p. 171). Splendid material of *Dicreaosaurus hansemanni* (Janensch) was worked out and mounted in the Geological and Palaeontological Institute of the University, Berlin. It may be mentioned in passing that von Huene (1927 a and b, 1932) considered this genus to belong to a new family, the Dicraeosauridae, and that Romer has assigned it to the sub-family Dicraeosaurinae. It may also be pointed out that Lull in his excellent essay on 'Dinosaurian Climatic Response' (1924, pp. 235, 236), spells the name *Dikraeosaurus* and adds 'with

178

long neck'. These are minor points which have to be mentioned to avoid confusion.

A few years ago when the writer was at the State Museum of Natural History, Vernal, Utah, he recognized a series of old plaster moulds as those of *Diplodocus*. The moulds were there because the Museum had just cast a brown cement model of this old dinosaurian favourite to stand in the open, surrounded by an iron fence, in the museum grounds. At the same time an additional cast of the skull was made which is now in the dinosaur gallery of the British Museum in London.

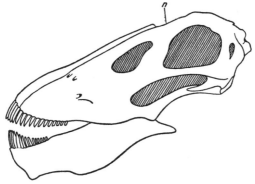

FIG. 42. *Dicraeosaurus hansemanni*. Left side of skull. (After Janensch.)
Approx. $\frac{1}{10}$ nat. size.
KEY: *n*., narial opening.

The dinosaur from which the original mould was taken was excavated from a quarry at the Dinosaur National Monument, only a few miles east of Vernal, at the junction of Utah and Colorado. The skeleton was an excellent one and when it had been studied it was named *D. carnegii* in honour of Andrew Carnegie, the Scottish–American steel millionaire.

Mr Carnegie was delighted with his namesake and, after the manner of millionaires, instructed Dr W. J. Holland, at the Carnegie Museum in Pittsburgh, to have casts made that could be distributed. Dr Holland was taken aback. To cast a skeleton, with its multitude of bones, points, angles, ribs and claws to a total length of nearly 90 feet was something never done before and presented awesome problems. However, Holland went down the street to the little shop where Serafino Augustini plied his trade, making holy medals and little plaster statues of saints. To him was entrusted this great task, which in due course he successfully undertook. The British Museum cast was the first to be made and was presented to the museum in 1910 in the presence of a distinguished audience including Mr Carnegie. The brown cement cast for Vernal was the tenth.

In between, similar splendid plaster skeletons, of full size and clear detail, were also given to the old Museum für Naturkunde in Berlin, the Senckenberg Museum in Frankfurt-on-Main, the Hof Museum in Vienna, the Capellini Geological Museum in Bologna, and the Musée National d'Histoire Naturelle in Paris. Subsequently copies were given to the Museum of Natural History in La Plata, Argentina and, with Mrs Carnegie officiating after the death of her husband, to the Natural History Museum in Mexico City. The moulds were destined to go to Japan from Utah.

So far as actual specimens are concerned these can be seen in the Carnegie Museum in Pittsburgh, the United States National Museum in Washington and the American Museum of Natural History in New York. The skeleton in the Natural History Museum at Denver, Colorado is *D. longus*. It is 75½ feet long. It, too, came from the Dinosaur National Monument.

In respect of complete skeletons there are more of *Diplodocus* than of any other sauropod. *Diplodocus* has become a frequent feature in restoration pictures, in cartoons and advertisements, on films and TV. The reason for this is not far to seek, for a skeleton, whether it be real or merely a plaster cast, that exceeds 85 feet in length is something of a rarity and sheds a new light on the mechanical possibilities of terrestrial life. This length is, of course, exceeded by certain whales, and in bulk *Brachiosaurus* outdoes it but *Diplodocus* represents the maximum development of the sauropods so far as length is concerned.

Diplodocus belongs to the sub-family Diplodocinae, and is characterized as having a rather long, somewhat horse-like skull in which the external narial openings are not paired but joined to form one large median opening at the apex of the skull (Fig. 43), and not near the tip of the snout. The orbital openings are large and had sclerotic plates, and in front of them, on each

180

side, is a large preorbital vacuity and, in front of that, a second preorbital vacuity. The two smaller openings are frequently mistaken for the nostrils. The teeth are pencil-like and developed only on the front of the jaws. The neck is very long and flexible with fifteen elongated cervicals, while the back is short and

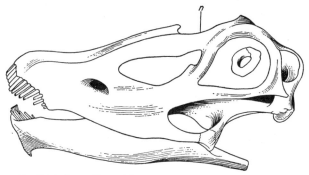

FIG. 43. *Diplodocus*. Left side of skull and narial opening. (After Holland.) Approx. ⅛ nat. size.

composed of ten dorsals, the lowest number of dorsals among the dinosaurs, and five sacral vertebrae; and there are at least eighty caudals, which is the largest number known in the dinosaurs. The tail was therefore long and appears to have been flexible over most of its length and ended in a series of rod-like

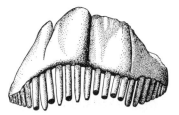

FIG. 44. *Diplodocus*. Front view of teeth. (After Holland.) Approx. ¼ nat. size.

vertebrae forming a whip-lash, the purpose of which is unknown. Some have suggested that it served as a defensive weapon, others that it bore a fin and was used in swimming. All the vertebrae are elongated, some being as much as 2 feet

181

or more in length, while many of the presacrals are much excavated and cavernous and thus very light in structure. The posterior cervicals and anterior dorsals have the neural spine divided into two symmetrical spines. The chevron bones underneath the caudals (to protect the blood vessels when the tail was dragged upon the ground) consist of two separate bars suspended in the middle, and it was these skids that prompted the name *Diplodocus* ('double-beam'). The scapulae are much broadened at the extremities, especially the proximal. The fore limbs are shorter than the hind. An asymmetrical, curved and long bone found with the original skeleton has been identified as either a clavicle or the os penis.

Diplodocus is almost perfectly known by four species: *D. longus* Marsh, 1878 (the type species), from the Morrison Formation near Canyon City, Colorado; *D. lacustris* Marsh, 1884, from the same horizon at Morrison, Colorado; *D. carnegii* Hatcher from Utah; and *D. hayi* Holland from Wyoming. Much of the type material of these species, with the exception of that of *D. carnegii*, was very fragmentary, so that although the complete osteology is now well known the synonymy is by no means clear.

The Washington D.C. specimen, *D. longus*, is just over 70 feet in length between perpendiculars, while *D. carnegii* measures over 85 feet, though this is measured along the backbone, and the maximum length is recorded as 87½ feet. The height from the ground of the neural spines over the hips in the former species is 12½ feet, in the latter is about 13 feet. As mounted, the National Museum skeleton has the head about 15 feet from the ground, but undoubtedly it could be raised considerably higher than this in life. The Denver skeleton is 75½ feet long and 12 feet 7 inches at the hips.

The skeleton of *Diplodocus* shows many adaptations for an amphibious life, not the least of which is the striking position of the external narial opening, and there can be little question that its environment was the coastal or estuarine waters, or the swamps, where there was plenty of succulent food to be pulled into the mouth by the rake-like teeth. The same water-line that was mentioned in connexion with *Apatosaurus* is evident in *Diplodocus*, while the clawed feet might have enabled the creature to obtain a hold on the slippery or sandy bottom of the lagoons and lakes. The structure of the skull shows that *Diplodocus* could have stood almost completely submerged in the water so long as the top of the head was clear. The roughness of the ends of the heavy limb bones shows that a thick layer of cartilage must have covered them for articular purposes, and this again speaks strongly for an aquatic mode of life. It is, therefore, possible to visualize the habits of *Diplodocus*, comfortably placed in the placid waters of a shallow lagoon, surrounded by ample food, and its burdensome body-weight materially eased, while protected by this watery shield from the fierce carnivores it could not hope to resist on land.

Diplodocus is not the only genus in the sub-family Diplodocinae, *Barosaurus* ('heavy-reptile'), is said to belong here. The genus is restricted to the Morrison Formation (Upper Jurassic) of the western states of North America, though it is reported also from East Africa.

The last sub-family of the Sauropoda is the Titanosaurinae, composed of Cretaceous forms much like *Diplodocus* in structure, but having six instead of five sacral vertebrae. It cannot be claimed that many of the genera are well known, but they are widespread and bear evidence of the great geographical range which the Sub-order had in the Cretaceous, especially in the Southern Hemisphere. The type species (*Titanosaurus indicus*, Lydekker, 1877) of the genus that gives the name to the family was described from Indian remains, while similar material has been obtained in England, France, Transylvania, Brazil, Patagonia and Madagascar. Other genera come from England, France (where remains of *Hypselosaurus priscus* have been found associated with great numbers of eggs), Egypt, East and South Africa, the United States, and Patagonia. In most characters they appear to resemble *Diplodocus*, but none, so far as we know, was so large, and they were, with the exception of the Tendaguru material, all Cretaceous, varying in time from the Lower to the Upper part of that period. A description of the South American genera and a reconstruction of *Titanosaurus* have been made by von Huene (1929) in a large and splendidly illustrated memoir. Two genera of some importance come from the Upper Jurassic of Tendaguru, Tanzania, the scene of the

183

several expeditions from the Berlin, Stuttgart, and British Museums.

The first of these is named *Gigantosaurus*, but the name was applied by Fraas in 1908 to material now in the Stuttgart Naturaliensammlung. As we have already said Seeley in 1869 named an English dinosaur by that generic name, and as the two genera are not by any means similar, it is clear that Fraas' name cannot be maintained. In 1911 Sternfeld suggested that the name *Tornieria* should be applied in place of Fraas' name but this has largely been ignored. Even at the present time the two genera named *Gigantosaurus*, when quoted, are differentiated by the author's name alone. There appears no necessity for this, and no reason why the German author's name should be regarded as so well known as to come under the 'nomina conservanda' rule which exempts certain very well-known and commonly used names from the strict application of the laws of priority. These African forms should be known as *Tornieria africana* (Fraas) and *T. robusta* (Fraas). (See notes in Janensch, 1914, and Nopcsa, 1930.) Many of the remains in Berlin are now exhibited and the bones indicate that *Tornieria* was a very large creature. A cast of the humerus in the British Museum is 7 feet long, which suggests that the height of the shoulder from the ground was nearly 20 feet. Others bones named *Gigantosaurus dixeyi* (which should be *Tornieria dixeyi*) have been described by S. H. Haughton from Nyasaland (Haughton, 1928).

How did such enormous animals move about on the land or in water? and were they truly amphibious? The two main questions really go hand in hand, for one cannot decide the suitability or otherwise of the articular surfaces for certain positions or kinds of locomotion unless one knows the medium in which they are to work. On the question of the pose of the skeleton there has been perhaps more controversy over *Diplodocus* than over any other extinct animal. On the one hand, Osborn (1899), Hatcher (1901), Abel (1901), Matthew (1901), and Gilmore (1932) maintained that the animal walked in upright, quadrupedal manner: on the other, Tornier (1909), Hay (1908 and 1911) and Hutchinson (1917) believed that the normal method of progression was like that of the

184

crocodile. Many of these gentlemen translated their conclusions into the form of restoration drawings and models, and the history of these efforts, and reproductions of some, were very engagingly set forth by O. Abel in his *Rekonstruktion vorzeitlicher Wirbeltiere* (1925).

It may be well here to state the problem, the method of approach to its solution, and what that solution may be. The sauropods were reptiles, and reptiles are generally cold-blooded, egg-laying (though occasionally ovo-viviparous), and their normal method of movement is by crawling, like lizards and crocodiles, with the elbows and knees well splayed out and the belly close to the ground. We have seen, however, that the bipedal dinosaurs had the body well off the ground and were occasionally swift runners. The assumption of a bipedal habit permits both an increase of speed in movement in certain kinds of animals and increases the probability of a warm-blooded condition, though this requires other characters too. We have little evidence that they laid eggs, or that they were viviparous, for only with one form, *Hypselosaurus*, have any eggs remains been discovered but they have been found in great quantity. As reptiles they would have laid their eggs on land unless, like the marine ichthyosaurs and many of the snakes, they had the eggs hatched within the body and the young produced alive. On these two points there is therefore no conclusive evidence one way or another.

As to the skeleton, we have seen that in the sauropods, and in *Apatosaurus* and *Diplodocus* especially, the heavy part of the skeleton is below a so-called waterline, which is coincident with a line drawn between the shoulder-blade and the hip-joint. In *Diplodocus* the openings of the external nostrils are placed together in a large foramen which occupies the same position on the skull as does the forelock of a horse. In most other sauropods the nostrils were in an elevated capsule or boss. Such positions can only indicate a water-living habit.

The heavy limbs again must have been sheathed in a considerable cartilaginous articular surface, which can also be associated with amphibious habits. The weight of such immense animals must have been considerable, in some cases so much as 80 tons, so that the weight of the body, it has been thought, would, unless buoyed up by water, crush the cartilage and irremediably destroy the bones for all articular purposes. It should be pointed out that there are no satisfactory criteria for defining the position of the heads of the upper arm bones and leg bones so that from the mere appearance of the bones the skeleton could be mounted with the elbows and knees out from the body and the limbs in a crawling pose. Tornier (1909) published such a reconstruction of *Diplodocus*, and a very grotesque looking creature it is, suggesting mechanical difficulties rather than their solutions.

If the weight of these animals was anything even approaching the 10–80 tons assigned to them, then obviously the stress and strain upon ligaments, muscles and cartilage was very great indeed, but doubt need not be thrown upon the mechanical efficiency of the sauropods on that ground. The sauropods gradually acquired size and, correlated with that, there must have been a compensating mechanical efficiency, and if at any point the latter failed then the particular dinosaur failed also. Thus *Diplodocus* did not bear any weight or burden which was in excess of that bearable on its straightened limbs. Vertically straight limbs or other structures sustain a greater load than bent structures, as every engineer knows.

Now, in man and many animals, considerable weight can be borne on the flexed limbs largely because of the accessory structures available. Thus the patella materially assists the maintenance of the flexed position of the leg. In dinosaurs this function may have been taken over by a muscular tendon or tendons or a wholly cartilaginous patella may have existed, but it is doubtful if either would be stronger or more efficient than the thick cartilaginous articular covering, and it seems unlikely that the crawling attitude could have been employed habitually. In crocodiles and other crawling reptiles the flexed position of the limbs is usually maintained by the aid of the belly, but in *Diplodocus*, *Apatosaurus* or *Brachiosaurus* there is no evidence whatsoever that this attitude could or would be adopted, though it must be remembered that the similarity of the sauropod femur to the crocodilian was one of the early reasons for assigning these animals to the crocodiles. The strength of the limbs of crocodiles is greater relatively than that of the dino-

186

saurs, for the simple reason that whereas bulk increases according to the cube of the linear increase, the supporting limbs can only increase their cross-section according to the square. When movement of any importance is made by a crocodile it is made on erect limbs, and, further, the sprawling attitude is no doubt largely associated with swimming powers, and with the adaptation of the limbs for the requisite positions.

There is no suggestion that the sauropods were swimming creatures with any more aquatic powers than, for example, the dog. It seems, therefore, that the larger sauropods might be able to maintain movement on the erect, elephantine limbs, but that the flexed position would be exceedingly awkward and clumsy, even dangerous, on land. In any question as to the power of cartilage in withstanding weight it may be pointed out that there are many normally aquatic mammals, sea-lions, walruses, etc., with modified flippers, whose joints are largely cartilaginous, and yet these animals progress on land, though clumsily, without the considerable weight relative to the size of the articular surfaces causing grinding of the limbs or of the cartilaginous articulations.

The question of brain organization must enter into the discussion, because highly efficient movement is usually associated with considerable nervous efficiency, not necessarily of an intelligent nature. Now the brain-case of these sauropods was small and the brain without doubt was also small and lowly organized, while the main control of hind limb and tail movements and reflex action was centred in the sacral ganglion or swelling of the spinal cord. Thus the movements could only have been slow and ponderous, and only restricted movement on land is therefore considered possible.

What of the habitat? As to this, three opinions were expressed and each had its followers. Owen, the great English anatomist and first Superintendent of the Natural History Museum in London, who described the first sauropod remains (*Cetiosaurus*), held the opinion that the sauropods were entirely shallow-water living, and were unable to come on the dry land. In the shallow waters the body-weight was eased by buoyancy and the mechanical difficulties were overcome. There would be abundance of herbivorous food and a good measure of safety from

187

carnivorous enemies, though the latter statement is probably over-optimistic. The many forms found since Owen's time bear ample testimony to this aquatic adaptation, as has frequently been pointed out. Professor E. D. Cope, the eminent American authority, strongly supported this view, and it has been widely followed by most modern specialists, particularly Wilfarth. Professor Williston objected to it on the ground that the females must have lived on land at least long enough to lay their eggs. Against this it has been stated that they were probably ovo-viviparous. As we have said already, these two opinions may cancel out, but what little evidence there is is on the side of the eggs! Osborn, however, believed that the sauropods must have resorted to the land occasionally.

The third opinion was that of Riggs and Professor Hatcher, that they were chiefly terrestrial. For this view there seems little good evidence to counter the overwhelming array of adaptations for a water habitat. The nostrils of *Diplodocus* and more special-ized forms are surely no osteological diversion. There is no denying the existence of a so-called waterline, and yet with all the adaptations and the long history of environment that must have gone to their acquisition the limbs bear a strong terrestrial significance, as compared with most aquatic reptiles and mammals.

Matthew stated that the heavy parts below the waterline would serve the same purpose, when the animal was in the water, as the lead on a diver's boots, but he did not believe that the body was wholly submerged. Hay (1911) on the other hand pointed out that lead is not needed on boots if one is only wading (and not diving). However, as many fishermen know, this is not strictly true, unless the wading is done in quiet waters, and in such waters a heavy animal could be submerged and thus comfortable, safe, and admirably placed for feeding.

The argument about sauropod life and activity runs on these lines if the skeletons are considered, and if weights are calculated on the basis of small models cubed in accordance with linear dimensions and without allowances. One can also disregard the sensational, for which there is not only no need in delineating the ancient environment but also no real evidence. We may notice the interesting and ingenious thesis of M. Wilfarth

(1949), who regarded dinosaurs as water-beasts, dwellers of the shore or shallow waters or even as submersible, drawing air by snorkels.

The ideas as well as the pictorially beautiful restorations of Zdenek Burian, done under the direction of the late Joseph Augusta (1962), create a lasting impression that appears to be decisive. The Czechoslovakian experts have placed us all in their debt and the life-restorations of *Brontosaurus*, *Diplodocus* and *Brachiosaurus* provide debating points as well as aesthetic satisfaction. (Incidentally the number of claws on the Burian pictures is incorrect.)

However, there are other aspects of sauropod structure that must be borne in mind. Attention has been drawn to the excavation of bone so that lightness is a prominent feature of the sauropod skeleton, but was this the only function? There is much probability, as we have already said, that these vertebral spaces and connected cavities in other bones were pneumatic, forming part of a very widespread system of pneumaticity which has close parallels with that of the birds, but which perhaps stopped short of a pleural connexion. Janensch (1929a) showed such a system clearly in *Dicraeosaurus*. In a later paper the same author (1939) drew attention to the spinal medulla (*Ruckenmarkkanal*) of the cervical vertebrae of the Dugong, *Halicore*, and the fact that it contains a network of vessels. It, and certainly that of sauropods, could have contained air sacs.

The enormous extent of air sac ramification in birds, even to the phalanges of the foot in some cases, suggests that in the larger sauropods, such as *Barosaurus* and *Diplodocus*, it is probable that air sacs arising from the lungs extended into the tail. Similarly the neurapophyses might have contained air sacs.

Janensch suggested that the cavities contained between the bifurcate neural processes (already mentioned) in *Dicraeosaurus*, *Diplodocus*, *Camarasaurus* and *Apatosaurus* could have held connective tissue that could eventually house air sacs. He held that pneumatization also affected the ribs.

It is improbable that in the sauropods the air sacs had a respiratory function as in birds. 'If the vertebrae of sauropods were pneumatic then the arrangement of sacs was important.

Those in the neck must have considerably reduced the weight of the neck and increased its mobility.' But the pneumatization did not stop in the cervical vertebrae but proceeded into the rump and, so Janensch repeats, into the tail in *Barosaurus* and *Diplodocus*. In a shorter-necked form, such as *Dicraeosaurus*, this pneumatization is less developed. Indeed it can be said to be characteristic of the larger forms, and therefore reaches an extreme in the long-necked and high-chested *Brachiosaurus* which, of course, parallels the avian condition in which the larger the bird, the greater the degree of pneumaticity. There is also another example, for *Baluchitherium* the giant rhinoceros of the Oligocene and Miocene, developed cavernous vertebrae as a weight-reduction process.

This last comparison raises the question as to how far this was purely a weight-reducing process and how far it can be taken as an additional indication of habit. The answer is that it was wholly associated with lightening the body load, and that the way of life took advantage of the condition rather than was dictated by it.

There are, fortunately, more direct methods of estimating the habits. The posterior and elevated postures of the nostrils, reminiscent in some ways of the crocodilian and ichthyosaurian condition, suggests that the skull was frequently in water. This does not mean that, as some artists have implied, that these great animals stood in water up to their eyes, but rather, that the neck and head were laid along the surface where they would be awash and float. The angle at which the head is joined to the neck allowed this.

The upright position in water was questioned more than eighty years ago on the grounds that the neck would be constricted, like a rubber tube, by hydrostatic pressure, and this objection was repeated by K. A. Kermack. None the less the sauropod neck was not a rubber tube, but a highly muscular passage-way that would be more resistant, if resistance was, in fact required and modern experience of skin-divers has suggested that this effect has been over-rated.

At Glen Rose, Texas, along the Paluxy River, south-west of Dallas and Fort Worth, there are series of footprints that are clearly those of sauropods. Some 200 miles to the south-west

190

of Glen Rose at Bandera, remarkable tracks of over twenty sauropods can be seen, young and older, which must have been splashing their way through deepish waters, with some of the youngsters afloat and the bigger ones also half-floating but bumping their way forward by pushing the fore limbs.

Taking all these things into consideration, we can truly imagine the sauropod life. The days spent in floating, aided by the buoyancy within of air spaces, intestinal and lung cavities and by the buoyancy of the water, with the neck stretched out, the great body awash, its dark colour mixing with the colour of the water, and with the hind legs stretched out. One sees now the meaning of the base of the tail kept high and horizontal, for the air sacs helped the buoyancy, and the end of the tail was trailing below as a sort of 'sea'-anchor, though these were freshwater creatures.

A lunge with the front feet ensured a slow movement and food was a little nearer. The vegetation was probably nothing like the water weed that has been so popular a diet in the books. Awash, almost invisible, and capable of reversing speedily into deeper water, they could lie, like animal castles surrounded by a moat, enjoying the vegetation of the shore and shoreward waters.

The carnivores watched and waited, hoping to catch a little one in the shallows. What thoughts could fill their little brains we shall never know. How slow was their nervous system in action? How long did stimuli take to reach a centre and how belated was the response? Was sauropod size a plain pituitary giantism?

It is possible that the development of such size with a very small brain led to nervous decentralization of which the large sacral ganglion was only an obvious part. A fundamental nervous and physiological disharmony was probably always imminent in these animals.

Mook (1918) investigated the conditions of the Morrison Formation. In North America, at this particular time, the high land was to the west, and the drainage system on the eastern side of it. The rivers flowed over the eastern plain, winding slowly, forming lagoons and islands, and frequently dividing up and joining again. There was an abundance of cycads and water-plants, while the animal life consisted of *Sphenodon*-like rhynchocephalians, dinosaurs, pterosaurs, and other reptiles, and occasional birds and mammals. The sauropods lived in these rivers and lagoons and without doubt they were largely immersed, like a hippopotamus. Although the teeth and jaws seem somewhat inefficient for dealing with the considerable amount of food that the sauropods must have required, it is idle to attempt to estimate the amount of that food. Comparisons based on the quantity consumed by large mammalian herbivores of the present day are misleading, as there is no assurance that the rates of metabolism and the energy requirements of the sauropods were anything like those of living mammals, indeed they ought to have been less.

Largely protected from enemies, well provided with nourishment, and able comfortably to move about—and in a temperate climate and warm water—they led a placid life favouring growth of body and length of life, to which the lines of Dryden might well be applicable:

> Supine amidst our flowing store,
> We slept securely, and we dreamt of more.

But the shifting sands would block up some channels and divert the streams; lagoons and lakes would dry up and others appear, and so from time to time the dinosaurs would leave their old haunts, lumber, but not necessarily sprawl, over the land, perhaps lay eggs, and pass on to new swamp lands.

The conditions in the other parts of the world where sauropods have been found were very likely similar, and visualizing such scenes it is easy to see that any pronounced change in land-level, however gradually produced, would result in the disappearance of the lagoons and a profound alteration in the conditions to which these dinosaurs were accustomed. We know that a general uplift occurred towards the close of the Jurassic, and would almost certainly have produced a drying up of the lagoons and a speeding up and alteration of the rivers. Cumbrous and highly adapted for the kind of environment in which they had spent so long, the sauropods would be unable to meet the new demands, or alternatively, to travel far in search of places like their old homes. Such large size as they possessed,

PLATE V. *Dinosaurs of Mongolia.*
The Gobi Desert has been the
scene of considerable discovery
both by the American Museum of
Natural History expeditions and
by several recent Soviet and
Polish palaeontologists. All of
these animals are of Upper
Cretaceous Age, from 70 million
to 90 million years ago. Dominating the left of the picture is
Tyrannosaurus some 50 feet long
and with its head 18 feet from the
ground Almost below, in its
13-foot stride, is one of two
Protiguanodon, small herbivorous
dinosaurs related to the larger
forms in the foreground, *Psittacosaurus*, with parrot-beaked skull.
On the right foreground are two
Protoceratops, related perhaps to
Psittacosaurus and to the later
ceratopsians of Asia and particularly North America. While
the large hadrosaur *Saurolophus*
faces *Tyrannosaurus*, the great
horned Ceratopsian, 30 feet long
raises its menacing head.
    Beyond, in the comparative
safety of water, are two sauropods, survivors in Mongolia of
forms already vanished in North
America.
    These dinosaurs are based on
restorations by Prof. K. K. Flerov
and are based on material in
A. K. Rozhdestvensky's *After the
Dinosaurs in Gobi* (Moscow,
1957). Courtesy of the *Illustrated
London News.*

PLATE VI. *Dinosaurs and their eggs.* The discoveries of dinosaurs' eggs in the Gobi desert are famo
but they were not the first nor the last. Never was there, however, such close association betwe
eggs and the developing young as in the specimens collected by the American Museum of Natu
History.

The illustration shows newly hatched Protoceratopsians, whose adults attained a length of f
feet. The nest (on left) shows the almost circular and spiral arrangement of the eggs which were l
to develop in the sand under the sun's heat. The lively event pictured occurred about 100 milli
years ago. Courtesy of the *Illustrated London News.*

PLATE VII. *Dinosaurs of Canada.*
The provinces of Alberta and
Saskatchewan have long been
famous for the dinosaurs that their
Cretaceous deposits have produced
and the illustration shows a selection
of the best known examples.

On the right, in the foreground is
the heavily armoured *Ankylosaurus*
and, beyond the tree, the related
Dyoplosaurus both with clubbed
tails; on the left, drinking from the
stream, is the curious ceratopsian,
Pachycephalosaurus, with a great
thickening of bone on its nose.
Farther over is another horned
dinosaur, *Chasmosaurus*. Centrally
placed in the picture are hooded
hadrosaurs, large herbivores with
remarkable extensions of their
olfactory organs (organs of smell)
in the helmet or spike-like processes
on their heads. To the left is
Corythosaurus; to the right is *Parasaurolophus*. On their right is a pair
of the lightly built 'bird mimics,'
Ornithomimus, which were toothless
and probably fruit eaters, who are
fleeing from the carnivorous inten-
tions of the great *Gorgosaurus*, 30
feet long.

On the hill to the left are the
small (10 foot long) herbivores,
Thescelosaurus, and, above them
and far away from the potential
troubles below, is the heavily
armoured *Scolosaurus*, the only
specimen of which is now in the
British Museum (Natural History).
The scene shows the advance of
modern kinds of vegetation, shrubs
and deciduous trees, all to be dated
about 90 million years ago. Courtesy
of the *Illustrated London News.*

PLATE VIII. *The last days of the Dinosaurs.* Towards the end of the Cretaceous, about 70 million years ago, there were significant geological and geographical changes that had inevitable effects on the dinosaurs. Illustrated are the characteristic late Cretaceous forms that seem to have lingered on when most others had disappeared.

In the middle ground on the left is the spiny and tank-like *Scolosaurus.* To right of it is *Gorgosaurus* (also known as *Albertosaurus*) 30 feet or so in length and to its right is the tyrant form, *Tyrannosaurus,* largest of dinosaurian carnivores. To the right is the massive ceratopsian *Torosaurus* with a 7 foot skull, and looking down on the scene, is *Styracosaurus* with its many horned skull margin. In the background, on the left, are perhaps the final performers of this long drama, *Anatosaurus,* the duck bill in the water and, beyond, the three-horned *Triceratops.* Giant pterosaurs, themselves doomed to extinction, fly overhead and on the foreground the little mammals, the heralds of the new world, play unconcerned with the great role that was shortly to be theirs. Courtesy of the *Illustrated London News.*

while probably associated with long life, would also entail prolonged adolescence, and a low birthrate, all factors which weighed against them in the struggle for existence in altering circumstances. The inevitable result was extinction, and many did not survive the Jurassic, though some, as we have seen, and mainly those of the Southern Hemisphere, managed to linger on into the Cretaceous, even to its closing stages, and then passed away with all the other dinosaurs.

CHAPTER X

The Beaked Dinosaurs: Ornithopoda

Nature hath framed strange fellows in her time.
SHAKESPEARE *The Merchant of Venice*

The dinosaurs with which we have dealt in the last two chapters belong to the Order Saurischia, while those we mention in this and the next are members of the Ornithischia. We have seen that the Saurischia have a simple, triradiate pelvis, large vacuities in the skull in front of the orbits, and the teeth are always in the front of the mouth and, if reduction took place, the back of the dental series was affected. The Ornithischia, on the other hand, have a quadriradiate pelvis, as the pubis has two branches, the forwardly directed pre-pubis and a post-pubic process (which is probably the true pubis rotated out of its original position) running backward and downward in close association with the ischium; there are either no preorbital vacuities or else they are very small; and the reduction in the tooth-series is at the front. Indeed, except in four genera, there are no teeth on the premaxillary bones, which, in the Ceratopsia, one of the armoured groups, have a 'rostral' bone developed in front of them; in most of the Ornithischia a special bone, the toothless predentary, unites the two halves of the mandible, and horny sheaths probably invested these anterior and prehensile parts of the mouth. The teeth are of a herbivorous pattern, spatulate or leaf-like, with serrated anterior and posterior edges, and generally arranged in a functional series composed of one or more closely set rows. The fore legs are generally shorter than the hind, but not so short as in the Theropoda, and the bones may be solid or hollow, and the feet plantigrade or digitigrade. Osseous tendons were often developed in the musculature of the back, but, except in the curious bipedal

194

Stegoceras, abdominal ribs were never present. The armour is either light or absent (in the bipedal forms), or very considerably developed (in the quadrupedal forms).

The earliest Ornithischia are known by remains from the Upper Trias of South Africa and of questionable footprints of the western states of North America. The Order includes the very last of the dinosaurs. Bipedal and quadrupedal forms occur, as in the Saurischia, but both kinds were vegetarian, and, although great variety of size exists in the many genera and species, the bipedal forms never attained the length or weight of the bipedal Saurischia—the Theropoda—and the largest of the four-footed forms are small in comparison with the great sauropods.

Among the Ornithischia are some of the forms which are most fully understood and numerously represented, and certainly the bipedal kinds occur widely in Europe and England, so that for English people the Ornithischia, both armoured and unarmoured, may be the more interesting Order of the dinosaurs.

The Order Ornithischia contains, properly, only one Suborder, called by Cope the Orthopoda and, by his rival Professor Marsh, the Predentata. Smith Woodward (1932) did not divide it into separate groups according to the different methods of locomotion or whether armoured or unarmoured. Lull (1947) on the other hand, splits it into three groups: the Ornithopoda, or bipedal forms; the Stegosauria, or plated quadrupeds; and the Ceratopsia, or horned dinosaurs. For convenience in description we shall divide it into two chapters: the Ornithopoda, or bipedal, herbivorous, mainly unarmoured dinosaurs; and the Armoured Dinosaurs, which are all quadrupedal. The remainder of this chapter will therefore be devoted to a description of the Ornithopoda.

The name Ornithopoda means 'bird-feet' and was given in virtue of the fact that nearly all of these dinosaurs went upon the three-toed digitigrade feet which much resemble those of struthious birds. Moreover, the feet are not the only bird-like characters, for, in addition to the horny bill or beak and the post-pubis mentioned in the previous pages, the structure of the sacrum and the proportions of the skull, shoulder- and hipgirdles, and the hind limb elements are all often suggestive of

195

the birds. It has been thought, therefore, that the Ornithopoda are the most nearly related of the dinosaurs to the ancestral stock that produced the birds. While the last-named took to flight and later became toothless the former persisted in terrestrial habits and retained at least some of the teeth. It may well be that these similarities imply no relationship and there are closer similarities between skeletons of theropods and the early birds.

The teeth of ornithopods are leaf-like, with serrated cutting edges, quite suitable for a herbivorous diet, and some, as we shall see in *Anatosaurus*, were well adapted for use as grinders although the method by which this was accomplished differs considerably from that of herbivorous mammals. The fore limbs were shorter than the hind and the hand may have been in some cases suited for prehension; it is clear, also, from preserved tracks that the fore limbs were frequently rested on the ground, which was probably not the case in most of the bipedal carnivorous dinosaurs. But, like these dinosaurs, the Ornithopoda are divisible into two kinds: small agile forms, such as *Hypsilophodon*, and larger and more slowly moving animals such as *Iguanodon* and the hadrosaurs.

The earliest traces of them have mainly been footprints, from Triassic rocks, often associated with the traces of the early Theropoda, such skeletal remains as have been obtained being fragmentary. The only remains of Triassic ornithischians have come from South Africa where in 1911 Robert Broom described *Geranosaurus* from the Cave Sandstone. Unfortunately only part of the jaws and none of the teeth can be observed in this specimen which is doubtfully referred to the earliest ornithopodous family, the Hypsilophodontidae. Quite recently, however, a British Museum expedition under the leadership of Dr G. W. Crompton of Yale and Dr Charig of the British Museum obtained a skull and lower jaw and associated skeletal remains from the Cave Sandstone (? Upper Keuper) of Cape Province, South Africa. This was briefly described by these palaeontologists in 1962 and discloses the existence of a remarkable small ornithischian with a peculiar dentition, to which they gave the name *Heterodontosaurus tucki*. (Heterodontosaurus = 'differentiated teeth reptile').

196

There is no doubt that this is an early ornithischian with some similarities to *Geranosaurus* and to later ornithopods. Its true place among the Ornithopoda must await the development and full examination of the material.

FIG. 45. *Hypsilophodon*. Mandibular tooth—inner view. × 7.

Hitherto the earliest undoubted ornithopod had been the little rather specialized dinosaur *Hypsilophodon*. This genus has been known in some detail, apart from its skull, since J. W. Hulke published a description of its osteology in 1882. The material he dealt with came from the Wealden of the Isle of Wight, from which locality there have since been obtained further specimens of great interest that are on exhibition in the dinosaur gallery of the British Museum (Natural History). The exhibit includes a mounted adult skeleton and that of a young individual.

Hypsilophodon has teeth on the premaxillae, five on each side and enamelled on one side only, and the maxillary and mandibular teeth are only in a single row in contrast to the multiple rows of higher forms. Each tooth has its enamel surface traversed by a few ridges which end in a serrated margin. The name *Hypsilophodon* means 'high-crested tooth' (see Fig. 45). The back-bone has slightly opisthocoelous cervical vertebrae, while there are five co-ossified sacrals, and the spines of the dorsals and caudals are traversed by ossified tendons. These

197

tendons are associated with the balancing function of the tail and it is important to note that they are absent in even the most advanced, yet also bipedal, Theropoda. The hand has five fingers, but the fourth and fifth are reduced, while the foot was functionally four-toed and traces of the vestigial fifth metatarsal are present. The femur is shorter than the tibia. Traces of bony plates in the skin have been found, and *Hypsilophodon* appears to have been clad in a thin but well-developed dermal armour consisting of flat bony plates.

The type species, *H. foxi* Huxley, is known by almost complete skeletons in the British Museum (Natural History), which show it to have been about 4 or 5 feet long, its skull alone being 6 inches. The short fore limbs have naturally led to the conclusion that this dinosaur was consistently bipedal, and the lightness of structure and the presumably active habit have suggested various kinds of habits to different authorities.

The earliest restoration, that of Hulke, shows *Hypsilophodon* on all fours, while Smit (in Hutchinson, 1910) restored it in two poses, a quadrupedal and a bipedal. Nopcsa (1905) threw great stress upon the traces of dermal armour that have been found and which suggest that of all the Ornithopoda *Hypsilophodon* approaches 'more closely the armour-clad Stegosaurs and Ceratopsia'. Heilmann (1916 and 1926) and Abel (1922 and 1925) published restorations showing the animal to be arboreal, and the latter author says it must have been closely similar in habits to the tree-kangaroo, *Dendrolagus*, a suggestion which Smith Woodward possibly implied in classifying (in *Zittel*, 1932) the Hypsilophodontidae as 'probably arboreal'. In 1926 Heilmann forcefully denied the similarity in structure of the Ornithopoda and the birds and, in discussing the structure of the limbs, clearly states that he 'cannot agree with O. Abel that *Hypsilophodon* was arboreal', a statement somewhat in conflict with his own reconstruction of 1916. He goes on to draw attention to the presence of dermal armour and adds, 'arboreal types, as a rule, do not seem to be equipped with dermal armour'. His earlier reconstruction clearly shows the armour. If the armour had been heavy it would be a serious objection to the arboreal theory, but there is no need to stress unduly such dermal structure. *Hypsilophodon* was not primarily an ornithopod-like armoured dinosaur, but an ornithopodous dinosaur with light dermal armour. The ultimate test must be the structure of the hands and feet; and there seems some possibility that the foot could be used for grasping, as it certainly appears more bird-like than Heilmann will admit and the slender, pointed unguals seem suitable for an arboreal habit. Nopcsa pointed out that the purpose of the ossified tendons, which increase towards the end of the tail, is 'entirely a puzzle', but it might be that it was associated with the use of the long tail in balancing which would be so necessary if the creature climbed in the trees.

We may pause here to consider two questions seldom posed in connexion with this dinosaur: first, what does arboreal really mean, and secondly how does *Dendrolagus* really live?

The word arboreal means, according to the largest dictionaries, in its zoological sense: 'adapted for living or *moving about* in trees'. Now living in trees and moving about are two different things. Opossums, monkeys and apes are highly adapted for living and moving about in trees, but many goats climb into trees and move about in them, so there are phases or degrees of arboreal life.

D. ursinus is a marsupial, a tree-kangaroo, that has less disparity in the length of its fore limbs as compared with the kangaroos, and it lives in New Guinea and Queensland, Australia, in mountainous country with high trees. Here it climbs trees with speed, dexterity and indifference to height. It is thus highly adapted to arboreal life, but its long padded feet have no hallux (big toe) and there are four closely approximated toes, 2 and 3 being small and 4 and 5 being large, but all have notable claws, by means of which the animal climbs.

Hypsilophodon had a hand that might have been grasping but the hind foot, with three functional toes and a possibly opposable hallux, would seem to have been more suited for walking along branches, and probably in that goat-like sense this dinosaur may have been arboreal.

The balance of probability is that *Hypsilophodon* lived, at least walked, in the trees, perhaps to escape its enemies. Protection from carnivores can be obtained either by the adoption of armour or by taking to a habitat inaccessible to the carnivorous forms. This is exemplified by the armoured dinosaurs and the sauropods, but both of these were large, and the feeble armour of *Hypsilophodon* could have been of no protection against the large Megalosaurid carnivores which were its contemporaries. On the other hand, the presence of such armour would be a hindrance to very rapid movement for which in any case the feet are not adapted, so the trees would form a natural refuge by no means unsuited to the structure of this small creature. The combination of unusual features makes *Hypsilophodon* one of the most interesting of the Ornithopoda, of which it is the most primitive, but it does appear to be, as Nopcsa has pointed out, a progressive and not a retrogressive form (Plate III).

A similar dinosaur, belonging to the same family, is *Thescelosaurus* ('wonderful reptile'), about 10 feet long, from the Upper Cretaceous of Wyoming, and Montana, USA, and Alberta and Saskatchewan, Canada. For some years the skull characters of this genus were incompletely known, but in 1925 C. M. Sternberg obtained a nearly complete skeleton in Alberta in which the teeth are shown. They are interesting because, although the skull and skeletal characters are close to those of *Hypsilophodon*, the teeth are of a more advanced character (and have both sides enamelled) and resemble those of a family of armoured dinosaurs. This was an active and perhaps agile dinosaur with no arboreal adaptation. We shall have to refer to both *Hypsilophodon* and *Thescelosaurus* later when dealing with the relationships of the interesting Upper Cretaceous ornithopod family, the Pachycephalosauridae. Other hysilophodontid dinosaurs were *Stenopelix valdensis*, from the north German weald described by E. Koken, *Parksosaurus* from the Edmonton Formation of Alberta and *Dysalotosaurus* from the Upper Jurassic of Tendaguru, Tanzania.

Meanwhile, we may turn our attention to the next family in order, that of the Iguanodontidae, the most important genus of which, *Iguanodon*, is probably the most completely known dinosaur. The dinosaur is especially interesting to the present author who has spent much time in investigating its history both in England and in Belgium and who has been able fortunately to solve some of the problems of the early years. These problems arose quite naturally because of the desire of the chief discoverer, Gideon Mantell, to keep the glory to himself. Thus localities were concealed from, or at least not disclosed to, others who might be rivals and, while this mattered little in 1822, it takes a great deal of unravelling 140 years later.

From 1818 almost till his death, Mantell kept a diary of his doings, his busy practice in the early years, his scientific excursions and of his family trials. On January 1, 1822, he wrote: 'I begin this new year with considerable apprehension; before the close of it should my life be spared I shall in all probability appear before the world as an author, and experience all the vexations and anxieties, inseparable from a first literary event.' The book was *Fossils of the South Downs* published early in that year when he was already busy compiling *Illustrations of the Geology of Sussex*.

An account of Mantell's interest and discoveries has already been given in Chapter II. It was in the spring of 1822 that Mrs Mantell, while waiting for her husband to visit a patient, discovered some teeth in a pile of 'road metal', broken stones for filling the holes in the country road. When Mantell emerged from his patient's house and saw the teeth he said, 'You have found the remains of an animal new to science.'

The teeth, and others found later, were figured in Mantell's *Fossils of the South Downs* and again refigured in *The Geology of the South-East of England* in 1833. In his endeavours to find more material Mantell naturally looked to the quarry from which the road metal had come. This quarry was not very far away (according to the writer).

As related earlier, it has been possible for the author to find the site of this excavation, now overgrown but still showing signs of former working. We can imagine the enthusiasm of Mantell in visiting the workmen on this considerable site. Bones there were in plenty, but none that he could associate with the teeth. Mantell had a good deal of advice from his friends but it was not always helpful. Even the great Cuvier made misidentifications. At that date it was not realized that mammal remains could occur in the Cretaceous, and as no reptiles were known with apparently masticating teeth it was naturally assumed, firstly, that Dr Mantell's specimens were mammalian, and, secondly, that far from being Cretaceous in age they were much more recent objects which had become buried or borne by water into the Wealden strata. Mantell was accordingly advised by some of his friends to avoid publishing the details of the find and thus, we must assume, keep from making a fool of himself. But he was made of sterner stuff and, unable to make headway with the palaeontological puzzle himself, he submitted, through Sir Charles Lyell, the first-found teeth to the great French anatomist, Baron Cuvier. And Cuvier reported that they were the incisors of a rhinoceros! Other and English specialists suggested that the teeth were those of some large fish.

Nothing daunted, Mantell continued to search for further material and enlisted the sympathy and enthusiasm of the quarrymen of Sussex, his sole scientific supporter at that time being Dr Wollaston, who was not a geologist. Shortly afterwards the intensive search brought to light some bones from the quarry near which the original find was made, and they were sent off to Paris amid great expectations on the part of Mantell. Back came word from Cuvier that they were bones of a hippopotamus! At this time also there was found a horn-like structure which was interpreted as the horn of a rhinoceros. Amid this welter of mammalian identifications or misidentifications Mantell worked steadily on, and at last some almost perfect teeth were brought to light, Mantell took them to London to the Hunterian Museum of the Royal College of Surgeons where a Mr Stutchbury showed him how closely akin they were to those of the American tropical herbivorous lizard, *Iguana*. Some of the teeth were submitted to Paris and Cuvier now recognized their true nature, as teeth of an unknown herbivorous reptile, and made predictions about the animal's structure which were subsequently proved correct. Cuvier very generously and boldly admitted his previous mistakes and withdrew the identifications. Mantell thereupon wrote an account of the animal and, in 1825, submitted it to the Royal Society of London, when he proposed to name the new reptile *Iguanodon*, or 'Iguana-tooth.' The similarity of the teeth with *Iguana* and the size of the bones thought to be of *Iguanodon* led naturally to some misleading calculations. Mantell's first reconstruction, discovered by the present writer, had an estimated length of 200 feet (see Fig. 46) but the mechanics of this reconstruction are obviously incorrect. Later Mantell worked out the length on a more conservative basis in the *Geology of South-east England* but he still made it 70 feet.

Real association of parts was not achieved until 1834 when a slab of Kentish Rag was blown out of a quarry at Maidstone.

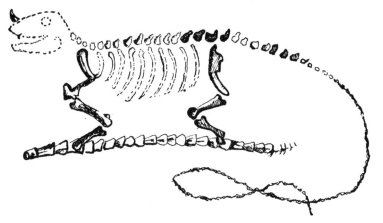

FIG. 46. *Iguanodon*. Mantell's first reconstruction of the skeleton, with an estimated length of 200 feet.

Little has been known of the details of the specimen or its discoverer. But once again the author was fortunate, for with the help of Mr L. R. A. Grove, the director of Maidstone Museums, he discovered a hitherto unknown document in the records of the proceedings of a small dining club that had an apparently short existence in Maidstone. The club called itself 'The Amici' for obvious reasons and this one volume of their Saturday evening exercises contains Mr W. H. Bensted's story of the Maidstone *Iguanodon*. No apology is made for reprinting this here although there is a copy in the British Museum (and now a photostat in the British Museum (Natural History). The British Museum Catalogue says that the contents are in verse. Two are certainly not and one of these two is the following story.

THE DINOSAURS

THE IGUANODON

'An account of the fossil remains of an Iguanodon, discovered in a quarry of Shanklin Sand near Maidstone, by Mr W. H. Bensted.

'In February, 1834, a portion of one of the lowermost strata in the above quarry, having been blasted, a quantity of some remarkable substance, resembling petrified wood, was observed in the stone. On inspecting a large fragment which had been reserved for me, I at once, perceived, that it was a fossil bone belonging to an animal of great magnitude.

'I immediately searched for the other portions and succeeded in finding many more fragments, some of which had been scattered and blown by the gunpowder to a considerable distance. I now felt that I had an object of great interest, and my gratification was much increased, as by degrees, I found myself enabled to fit the various fragments together.

'I erected a temporary shed over them and with mallet and chisel, cleared away the surrounding stone; following the outline of the bone until I had brought to view portions of the skeleton of an extraordinary animal, which had been buried in the bowels of the earth probably in the earliest ages of its existence. From the pleasure which I felt in this discovery, I can well imagine what must have been the feelings of Belzoni; when, bringing forth from their dark tomb the mummy, or richly wrought sarcophagus. He, by deciphering their hieroglyphical characters, revealed to us, previously unknown particulars, of the past deeds of Kings and mighty conquerors, who have long since bowed their heads to dust and have done homage to Death, the conqueror of all.

'The bones which I shall presently describe, were excavated from a sepulchre of rock, and, respecting their entombment, all would have been darkness and mystery, but for the hieroglyphics written in the fast-bound characters of Nature's records, records that have had successive creations for epochs; epochs that tell of the wrecks, changes, creations, and destruction of myriads of animated beings, which lived upon the earth before it was adapted to support the animals which now inhabit it.

'The era when reptiles of enormous size inhabited our planet, and the whole system of nature differed from the present, has been most appropriately designated by Cuvier "the age of reptiles"; and of the existence of these creatures there can be no more doubt, than there can be, when at the present day we see the print of a man's foot in the sand,—that man must have been there.

'The formation or deposit in which these remains were discovered is provincially called "Kentish Rag," but by Geologists Green-sand, from many particles of a green substance being found in it; or Shanklin-sand, from its occurring in large masses at Shanklin in the Isle of Wight. It is a formation of considerable importance in Kent, extending to Folkestone in an Easterly, and into Surrey in a Westerly, direction, and has long been celebrated for the variety and beauty of its fossil remains.

'Shells of the following genera have been met with in this quarry; Ammonites, Hamites, and Nautili, Terebratula, Gryphaea and Pecten,

204

all of which are of common occurrence together with the usual shells of the formation; and vegetable impressions, and fossil wood, are very abundant; the latter perforated by Lithodomi or boring shells. A large conical striated tooth assigned by Professor Buckland to the gigantic Plesiosaurus; Rhomboidal scales of a fish allied to the Lepisosteus or Pike; teeth of the Squalus Mustelus or Shark; and small palatal teeth of a fish resembling the Ray, with a Radi or dorsal defence of a fish of the Silurus species have been here discovered. Bones of Saurian type, but too imperfect to decide upon, have also been met with. A new and interesting Zoophite, Alcyonia Monilia, has been found, the restored figure of which leads to the conclusion, that the cylindrical stem had strips of attachment to the sands upon which it grew, and that, from the bulbs which occur in different parts of the stem, it had the power of projecting long beaded processes,—ending in attenuated threads—through the means of which it probably obtained sustenance. The beds of diluvium, covering and filling the faults and dislocations, contain the bones of the horse, deer, and elephant, with the remains of Mammalia that were probably buried in the last convulsion, all of which are of great interest to the Geologist, but of trivial importance when compared to the discovery of the bones of an Iguanodon in a formation decidedly marine.

'To the great research and superior acquirements of Dr Gideon Mantell, of Brighton, we are indebted for the first knowledge of this extraordinary creature. In his works upon Geology, we are informed that the Iguanodon was an herbivorous reptile, somewhat resembling the recent Iguana in general figure, and also in the structure of its teeth. Another curious resemblance is that between the osseous conical horn of the Iguana cornuta, of St Domingo, and a fossil horn of the Iguanodon, discovered in Tilgate Forest, by that gentleman. The enormous magnitude, however, of some fossil bones of an Iguanodon found in the Hastings-sand formation almost sets comparison at defiance. The recent Iguana has seldom exceeded four or five feet in length; whereas the bones of the Iguanodon lead us to suppose that there were individuals of that species one hundred feet in length. The peculiar structure and adaptation of their teeth, leave no doubt upon the mind of the comparative anatomist that the Iguanodon was herbivorous. With the detached bones of this creature, were embedded the fossil remains of palms and arborescent ferns, some of which had probably attained the height of forty or thirty feet, and doubtless, constituted the food upon which this monster of an ancient world subsisted.

'The whole economy of its structure was adapted to this purpose; and the following observations of Dr Mantell on the subject, are so conclusive that I beg to direct the reader's attention to them.

"The recent Iguana, as is well known, lives chiefly upon vegetables, and is furnished with long slender toes, by which it is enabled to climb trees with great facility, in search of food; but no tree could have borne the weight of the colossal Iguanodon, its habitation and movements must have been confined to the land and water; it is also manifest that its enormous bulk would require to be supported by feet of a corresponding solidity; accordingly we find that the hind feet, as in the Hippopotamus, Rhinocerous, and other large Mammalia were composed of strong, short, massy bones; and furnished with claws, not hooked, as in the Iguana, but compressed, as in the land Tortoises; the feet thus formed a massy base for the support of the enormous leg and thigh bones. But in the hands, or fore feet of the Iguanodon the bones are analogous to those of the fingers of the Iguana, long, slender, flexible, and armed with curved claw-bones, the exact counterpart of the nail bones, of the recent animal; thus forming a prehensile instrument, to seize and tear to pieces, the palms and arborescent ferns, and dragon's blood plants, which constituted the food of the original.

"Here we have another beautiful example of that admirable adaptation of structure, to the necessity and conditions of every form of existence, which is alike manifest whether our investigations be directed to the beings which exist around us, or to the structure of those which have lived and died and passed away, ere man, and the animals which are his contemporaries, were called into existence."

'Reflecting upon these extraordinary facts, may we not enquire with the illustrious Cuvier, "At what period was it, and under what circumstances, that turtles and gigantic lizards lived in our climate, and were shaded by forests of palms and arborescent ferns?"

'It is a very natural question to ask, "how came the bones of an animal which fed exclusively upon vegetable food in a marine deposit, surrounded with sea shells and the remains of fish which lived in the sea?" The Iguanodon could find no sustenance there!

'Geologists are now agreed that the Wealden, of which the rag-stone constitutes a part, was the delta of a mighty river, and it is supposed that the carcass of the Iguanodon floated upon the surface of that river, and was carried by its currents into the ocean; and the decomposition at length caused the separation of the flesh from the bones, which sunk to the bottom. The same currents brought down fragments of wood, the worn angles of which testify to the action of drifting waters; and pebbles, shells, wood, and bones are thus buried together. We have the same causes in full activity at the present time. The deltas of our rivers contain the remains of animals now existing, whose bones are buried in the sand and mud brought down from hills by streams, and carried onwards towards the sea, by the tides and currents. Thus the Nile, Niger, and Ganges, envelope the skeletons of Hippopotami, Turtles, and Crocodiles; our own rivers those of Man and the other Mammalia living upon their banks, together with shells, wood, etc. Thus we may see, every day, the same causes in operation which enveloped the bones of the Iguanodon in what is now solid rock, at a time too remote for conjecture.

'The science of Geology, which explains these operations, is of the highest interest; not only on account of the vast fields which it presents to the research of the enquirer, but also for its simplicity.

'If fossil wood is found embedded in the rock, we know that dry land must have existed and produced it; if bones are discovered, the comparative anatomist will be able, by analogy, to gain a knowledge of the whole skeleton and habits of an animal; although it may never have been seen alive by man.

'But other agencies have affected the earth's surface. Let the imagination endeavour to picture the tremendous scene, when the mighty Mont Blanc, with terrific roarings, burst through the crust of the earth, and shattering rocks of hardest granite, hurled mountains to its base; or when Chimborazo rose from the central fires and reared to the sky its burning summit, which is now capped with eternal snows,—the icy region of silence and solitude. These changes were produced by volcanic power. Water has also been a powerful agent in geological changes. It has rushed over precipices and overwhelmed hills and vallies; rounded large fragments of granite of many tons weight to the shape of pebbles, by grinding them against each other, and sweeping them hundreds of miles from their original position.

'Yet even this wreck of mountains had in it a design; for the earth which now smiles serenely in the verdure of Spring, or the rich glory of Autumn, was thus furnished with mould preparatory to the production of food fit for the beings that now inhabit it.

'Such are the scenes unfolded by the study of geology. It is a science still in its infancy, but it is a giant's infancy; and, unfettered by visionary theories, it rests upon facts powerful in their simplicity, and convincing to every unprejudiced mind; teaching us that the fatherly care of our Creator was, in times incalculably remote, preparing all the harmonies and beauties we now enjoy.

'The remains of the Iguanodon discovered in what is now called the Iguanodon Quarry, consist of the following bones:

Two thigh bones, each 33 inches long.
One leg bone (tibia) 30 ditto ditto.
Metatarsal and phalangeal bones of the hind feet which much resemble the corresponding bones in the Hippopotamus.
Two claw bones, (unguical phalanges), which were covered by the nail or claw and correspond with the Unguical bones of the land tortoise.
Two fingers or metacarpal bones, of the fore feet, each 14 inches in length.
A Radius (bone of the fore arm).
Several Dorsal, and caudal vertebrae.
Fragments of several ribs.
Two Clavicles or collar bones.
Two large flat hatchet bones which appear to belong to the pelvis; they are probably the ossa ilia.
A chevron bone, or one of the inferior processes of the vertebrae of the tail.
A portion of a tooth, and the impression of another. The discovery of these leaves no doubt of the identity of the animal with the Iguanodon Mantelli of Tilgate Forest.

207

'These valuable relics are now at Brighton in the Museum of Dr Mantell, who is preparing to publish a paper on the subject. From the well known talent and experience of that gentleman, this will doubtless be a highly interesting production.

W. H. B.'

Mantell offered Mr Bensted £10 for the slab, but the quarrymaster wanted £25. Eventually however a group of Sussex gentlemen contributed the amount, as one wag put it, to make a "Mantell-piece", and it found its way surely enough to Mantell's Museum in Brighton (where he had meantime moved to be nearer the royal entourage) and was placed near the fireplace.

Mantell hoped that his collection would form at least the basis of a county Museum but the collection was never acquired and he sold it in 1839 to the Trustees of the British Museum. Many of his specimens are now on exhibition in the Dinosaur Gallery of the British Museum (Natural History) including the Maidstone specimen, which, numbered R. 3791, was regarded by R. Lydekker as the type specimen of *Iguanodon mantelli*.

With this and other discoveries made later, and after the detailed descriptions by Mantell and Owen, *Iguanodon* was comparatively well understood. In April 1878, however, a fortunate discovery was made in Belgium which entirely transformed knowledge of the skeleton. It happens that the Coal Measures and the overlying deposits at Bernissart, near Mons, in Belgium, are occasionally interrupted by filled-in swallow holes (*puits naturels*) of great depth (about 1000 feet). During mining operations one of these, the Cran du Midi, was tunnelled into and by a piece of very good fortune a wonderful accumulation of fossil vertebrates was made. Here were found the remains of no less than thirty-three specimens of *Iguanodon*, and fossil fishes, turtles and crocodiles, together with remains of ferns and other plants. It would thus appear that the reptiles had met their end not, as has been assumed by some, through the falling of a herd over the edge of a cliff, or through a landslide, but by falling individually or being carried by water into the not quite bottomless pit where they became covered up and preserved. The remains were carefully excavated and transferred to the Royal Museum of Natural History in Brussels (now known as the Institut royal des Sciences naturelles de Belgique). The recovery of the materials, the reconstitution of the specimens and their description took many years, principally under the distinguished leadership of Professor Louis Dollo.

Today some thirty-three skeletons and partial skeletons are exhibited; eleven mounted as in life and the remainder in a specially constructed pit in the attitude in which they were found. Professor Dollo's astonishing industry upon them was mainly in the years 1882–84, but his solicitude for their individual welfare (even fossil dinosaurs get disease) continued to the last days of his life.

One great gesture which was made by the Belgian Government was the presentation of plaster casts of a complete upstanding *I. bernissartensis* to a number of museums and one is in the British Museum's Dinosaur Hall.

The whole story has been excellently told and well illustrated by Edgard Casier in *Les Iguanodons de Bernissart* published in 1960.

One of the discoveries in so well authenticated a series is that a sexual difference is probably obvious, in that the large, formidable creature known as *I. bernissartensis* is probably female and the smaller, more agile *I. mantelli* is male. Other species of *Iguanodon* have been described in England, notably *I. dawsoni, I. hollingtoniensis* and *I. prestwichi, I. fittoni, I. hilli, I. hoggii, I. phillipsi* and *I. seeleyi.* Most of these are based on inadequate material or are growth stages of some other species.

An excellent skeleton of a young individual was obtained near Atherfield in the Isle of Wight, by the late Mr R. W. Hooley, and placed on exhibition in 1934 in the Dinosaur Gallery of the British Museum (Natural History). Discoveries of isolated remains and casts of footprints continue to be made in the Wealden of Sussex, Dorset, and the Isle of Wight. Bones of *Iguanodon* have been found in Surrey, in the Ockley Brick Company's works, and finds have been made in North Africa that are now in the National Museum in Paris. *Iguanodon* is, therefore, one of the most clearly understood dinosaurs from deposits of Wealden (Lower Cretaceous) age.

Like *Hypsilophodon, Iguanodon* was a bipedal, herbivorous dinosaur, but with toothless premaxillae and without traces of any dermal ossifications. The skull is compressed from side to side and the large openings for the nostrils are placed at the front, near the tip of the skull. The frontal bones are fused, while the thin parietals meet to form a sharp median crest. Small supraorbital bones were developed above the orbits but there was no supraorbital projection in the orbit. Horny coverings sheathed the sharp premaxillae during life. In the dentary (lower jaw) and the maxilla (upper jaw) there are numerous spatulate and serrated teeth set closely together. The jaws turn slightly inwards so that the tooth rows do not represent the outer limits of the jaws as in many animals, and this would seem to indicate that *Iguanodon* performed a good deal of mastication for which a well-defined cheek and a certain amount of lateral movement of the jaws were necessary. The skull was carried at right angles to the shortish neck which consisted of 10 cervical vertebrae; the body was laterally compressed with 18 dorsal and lumbar vertebrae; there were 4 to 6 co-ossified sacrals; and about 50 centra in the long and laterally compressed tail. Ossified tendons are always present along the neural spines of the back and tail, but their distribution is rather different from that in *Hypsilophodon*. The fore limbs are about half the size of the hind, and the hand is five-fingered, but the thumb consists of a spike-like structure which was originally described as a rhinoceros horn, and which on some early reconstructions of *Iguanodon* was placed on the nose. Indeed it took many years to get it off the nose and on to the hand. In the hind leg the femur, which has a prominent fourth trochanter, is a little longer than the tibia (cf. *Hypsilophodon*), and the foot is digitigrade with four toes of which only three are functional, as is testified to by the not uncommonly found footprints, which show a more solid impression than those of the theropods. The first toe is represented by merely the vestigial metatarsal, and the fifth is entirely absent. R. W. Hooley has shown (on *Iguanodon atherfieldensis*) that the skin was covered by small polygonal epidermal plates arranged in rather asymmetrical groups, the tubercules being larger on the parts exposed to the sun. Several species are known varying in size from 15 to 30 feet as measured from the skull to the end of the tail along the backbone.

The type species, based on the material collected by Mantell, was named *I. mantelli* by von Meyer, and was about 20 feet long. Two of the Belgian specimens belong to this and the remainder to the larger species, *I. bernissartensis* Boulenger, and measure up to 30 feet. Both these species also occur in England, and it is interesting to note that Nopcsa long ago thought them to be the female and male of the same form. The specimen obtained from the Isle of Wight in 1917 by R. W. Hooley, and exhibited in the dinosaur hall of the British Museum (Natural History), is named *I. atherfieldensis* Hooley (Hooley, 1925; Swinton, 1933). All of these specimens conform to the generic specification and have been so frequently described that no purpose would be served by indicating the specific characters here. There are several other species and all the type specimens, with the exception of that of *I. phillipsi*, which is at Cambridge, are in the British Museum (Natural History).

In recent years undoubted *Iguanodon* remains have been found in North Africa. Footprints and casts of footprints of the three-toed hind feet are occasionally found in the Wealden at Hastings and Bexhill in Sussex, Swanage in Dorset, and the Isle of Wight, and they are known from North Africa and have recently been found in Spitsbergen.

There has not been the same controversy about the habits of *Iguanodon*, as we have seen that there was in connexion with *Hypsilophodon*, for the footprints show clearly that it walked upon the hind legs while the shorter front limbs were obviously not used at all in progression. The browsing kind of teeth help to complete the details for the picture so that we know that *Iguanodon* must have run about on its hind legs, pausing now and then to sit quietly upon the hind legs and tail for those periods of inactivity which are so common among the reptiles. As most modern animals avoid the kind of food most closely akin to those that existed during Wealden times, it is a little difficult to know what exactly formed the main food supply, though many ferns were found fossil at Bernissart.

We can think of *Iguanodon*, supported on the strong legs and perhaps also on the tail with the fore limbs resting upon a tree, while, with horny beak and busy jaws, the tree-fronds are ripped off and consumed. The flattened tail has suggested to many that

211

Iguanodon may have been something of a swimmer and thus partly amphibious in habit, and there is little doubt that it could take to the water when pursued, or if there were rivers or swamp-waters to cross. Otherwise, it was well suited to terrestial life. The main purpose of the front limbs and the hands was for occasional resting and for grasping and pulling off vegetation for which the spiky thumbs would be valuable, while the spike would also form a useful weapon.

Naturally enough, this dinosaur has always been popular with European authorities, and many restorations, some good, and some built on inadequate material and erroneous estimates, have been attempted. Mantell, handicapped of course by the slenderness of the evidence available to him, thought the thumb-spike was a nasal horn. This conception was maintained by Owen and by Waterhouse Hawkins, at the newly opened gardens of the Crystal Palace at Sydenham, in London. *Iguanodon* was one of this series and is represented as a somewhat awkward creature moving on all fours and with a prominent horn on the nose. These large models are still in the Crystal Palace grounds and smaller representations of them are in the Palaeontological Library of the British Museum (Natural History), but so different are they from the modern and accepted ideas that only by their labels are most of them identifiable. The large *Iguanodon* model was the scene of a famous dinner given in celebration of the erection of these models for public instruction! (Plate I.)

Of course, these earlier enthusiasts had not a great deal to go upon, and the period was one when people were greatly interested in the, wonders of creation. The more curious the form and immense the bulk, the greater the wonder was acclaimed, very much indeed as it is again today. F. A. Quenstedt, in a popular book published in 1856, estimated the length of *Iguanodon* as 100 feet, and he says its bulk 'must have exceeded all the animals of prehistoric times, if it did not attain that of the whale'. Fraas, another German savant, estimated the length at 60 feet. The discovery of the Belgian specimens reduced these estimates to humbler if more accurate figures, and the publication of the results of the examination of these fine skeletons made possible the creation of more natural reconstruction-

212

models and pictures. J. Smit (in Hutchinson), Professor Jaekel and P. Matschie all published drawings in 1910 which show the dinosaur on the hind legs though partly supported by the tail, and it should be realized that at this time there was considerable controversy about the possibility of a two-legged mode of movement in dinosaurs. The first of these three drawings is the best and has been widely copied; apart from its original sources, it has been reproduced by Abel (1925) and a fine copy of it hangs in the Palaeontology Department of the British Museum (Natural History).

Since that date Dollo has published a good outline drawing of the body-line (Dollo, 1914), and Heilmann has produced a very charming picture of two Iguanodonts running along side by side with rather too prominent thumbs (G. Heilmann, 1916 and 1926). More recent restorations were those in three dimensions by Abel (1924), by Mr Vernon Edwards and the author, and by Parker and the author in 1961. The whole subject of such reconstructions and their history is very adequately dealt with in Abel's *Geschichte und Methode der Rekonstruktion vorzeitlicher Wirbeltiere* (1925).

All the restorations agree in showing *Iguanodon* as definitely two-legged and the principal differences are the arrangement of the skin markings and the addition of various small scutes along the back and tail. Naturally, nothing is known about the colour of the skin, but Smit introduced some sort of colour-scheme in his restoration-drawing.

Iguanodon was, therefore, a large herbivorous dinosaur, sometimes 30 feet or so long measured over the backbone, and standing with the head 16 feet from the ground, whose normal method of walking or running was upon the two hind legs, while the front limbs, or arms as we can call them, were used only for resting and prehension. Although well accustomed to life wholly on land, in the course of its wanderings or in the endeavour to flee from its foes, it may have taken to the waters of the marshy regions where it lived, and may have been able to swim largely through the agency of the strong hind limbs and particularly of the tail which was flattened from side to side. So far, its remains are known from England, where it was found first, and from Belgium where the discoveries have been richest, from Morocco and as footprints from Tunisia and Spitsbergen; but dinosaurs belonging to the same sub-family, the Iguanodontidae, are known from Cretaceous rocks throughout Europe, and in South Africa and America. One of the more important genera is *Camptosaurus* Marsh from the Morrison Formation (Upper Jurassic) of Wyoming, and it is possible that an incompletely known English form (*Cumnoria*) is identical with it. Five species have been described, all from Como but they differ mainly in size. Apart from the shape of the neck vertebrae they are said to be close to Marsh's *Laosaurus*.

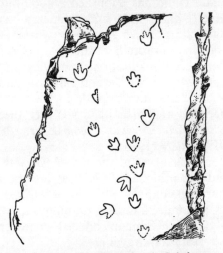

FIG. 47. *Iguanodon*. Footprints in Spitsbergen.

The structure and relationships of *Camptosaurus* have been well worked out by C. W. Gilmore (1909), who also restored the skeleton and published photographs of that and the more important remains. In many details it is more primitive than *Iguanodon*; the foot, for example, having four toes with hoof-like claws, though the first toe is smaller than the others, and there is a trace of the fifth metatarsal. The hand is five-fingered and the first three of these bear claws. Ossified tendons again are prominent. In size this American relation of *Iguanodon* grew from 18 to 30 feet or so, but the general appearance, as given by the mounted skeletons in the United States National

214

Museum in Washington and that at Yale, conveys the impression of a slightly more awkward, and generally less robust, animal. No doubt the habits were essentially similar, as the lizard-like teeth, the horny beak, and the structure of hands and feet imply. Such differences as there are can be well accounted for by the difference in the times in which they lived, for *Camptosaurus* was an earlier form than *Iguanodon*, and not so highly developed. Gilmore, however, considered that despite the difference in length between the fore and hind limbs there is 'some evidence to show that the bipedal mode of progression was not habitual'. He states that although the bipedal position was assumed, 'the quadrupedal posture was used more frequently than has been generally supposed'. Much of the evidence for this comes from the shape of the femur, which is curved in contrast to the straight femora of *Iguanodon* and the later, Cretaceous, Ornithopoda (*Camptosaurus* = 'bent-reptile'). The teeth are weak and it would seem that *Camptosaurus* did a lot of feeding near water. This would be done in a quadrupedal or semiquadrupedal position. *Camptosaurus* is represented in England by two species based on isolated thigh-bones from Peterborough and the Isle of Wight. Another English form which may belong to this genus is *Cumnoria prestwichi* (Hulke), known by an incomplete skeleton in the University Museum, Oxford.

If the Iguanodonts have supplied the dinosaur best known in Europe, the next family of the Ornithopoda has supplied one of the most fully understood in America, indeed one which has even been claimed to be the best-known dinosaur. This family is known as the Hadrosauridae and the original specimen was the first dinosaur to be discovered in the United States whose bones are still available to us. The story of this discovery has already been given (see p. 23). These hadrosaurs are all Upper Cretaceous in age and, although found chiefly in North America, have also been discovered in England, China, Transylvania, Siberia, Mongolia and Japan.

In general structure they closely resemble the Iguanodonts, but there are important differences in the structure and arrangement of the teeth, in the shape of the skull, and in the structure of the hands and feet. The skull is long and depressed with a curious broad duck-like beak or bill which causes these dinosaurs to be called the 'duck-billed' dinosaurs. Other members of the family, as we shall see, have even more curious modifications of the hinder part of the skull.

However, before we say anything about these dinosaurs there is, as usual, a nomenclatural problem. There is hardly anyone, whether a reader of popular books or text-books or visitor to dinosaur collections who will not come across the name *Trachodon* ('rough-tooth') which not so very long ago was regarded as the generalized duck bill and the starting point of their elaborations. *Trachodon* was a genus created by Dr J. Leidy with the type species *T. mirabilis* 1856. The specimen on which this was founded is a lower tooth (still in the Academy of Natural Sciences of Philadelphia, registered No. 9260) collected from the Judith River Cretaceous, near the Judith River, Montana. It is an unworn tooth, and though it has been measured and compared with many other duck-bill dinosaur teeth it cannot be matched. Today there are more than a dozen well-known genera of these dinosaurs and to relate them to the original tooth is impossible. The name *Trachodon* must therefore be abandoned.

The standard flat-headed hadrosaur best known is *Anatosaurus annectens*. It is known from a mounted skeleton in the United States National Museum in Washington, D.C., a skeleton in the Peabody Museum, Yale, the two famous skeletons exhibited in the American Museum of Natural History, and other skeletons in the University of Colorado, Boulder, Colorado and the Museum at the University of Michigan, Ann Arbor. This large and easily describable dinosaur is not, however, the simplest hadrosaur but is the end of a line of development and is among the latest dinosaurs. It is, incidentally, near in many ways to *Edmontosaurus* of which a part skeleton, obtained from the National Museum of Canada, Ottawa, by the writer, is in the British Museum.

The skull in *Anatosaurus* and *Edmontosaurus* has no vacuity in front of the eyes, and the paired openings for the nostrils are situated near the middle line on the front of the skull just behind the broad and flattened duck-bill. The orbit is larger than the lateral (infratemporal) opening and there is no projection into the orbit. The teeth, however, are perhaps the most remarkable of the skull features, for in their arrangement the dinosaurian battery of teeth reaches its acme. Each half of the jaws is provided with 45 to 60 vertical rows (actually 44 in *Anatosaurus* and 47 in *Edmontosaurus*) containing 6 or more compressed successional teeth, so that in a fossil there may be so many as 1600 to 2000 teeth in the jaws, quite apart from those worn out and discarded during life. Generally there are, however, less than this. All these teeth were not, of course, functional, but the battery consisted of the functional series which gradually became worn, and, from time to time, were replaced by the reserve teeth behind. Each tooth is enamelled on one face and is compressed from back to front. The lowers have a depression on the outer side and a ridge on the inner side, and the uppers show the reverse condition. The whole upper and lower functional series, which consist of several tooth-rows in different stages of wear, worked obliquely upon each other, for the upper series worked on the outer edge of the lower, so that the grinding surfaces were the lower and inner face of the upper tooth-rows and the upper and outer face of the lower. The gradual wearing down of the tooth-surface was compensated by the steady upward (or downward, in the upper jaw) growth of the teeth, so that the replacement was not like that of the crocodile or a mammal, but was an unceasing, slow, imperceptible, escalator-like movement of the tooth mass.

It may be thought that this constant renewal was an admirable and advanced arrangement far ahead of our own troublesome dentition or that of mammals generally, but actually it was not. We can only assume from the nature of the teeth that the diet was hard and abrasive, and although the dental series of hadrosaurs is comparable, at least mechanically, with that of the horse, the tooth-structure in the latter is much more complex and durable, though designed for a certain length of life, unlike the dinosaurs. The mammals, by reason of the nature and materials of their teeth, need a lesser series than the reptiles. The teeth of the hadrosaurs, as we have said, were an adaptation to hard food, such as the horsetail rushes which were common during the Upper Cretaceous and which contained much silica. It was on such rushes that the hadrosaurs probably fed, although

217

a very great range of grasses, ferns, palms, vines, water plants and deciduous trees and shrubs are known from the Cretaceous, as we shall discuss later. Very probably the beak was used for cropping off the plant-food, while the teeth chopped up the rushes, leaves, or stems into suitable fragments for swallowing. The mouth had also probably only a moderate gape because there must have been some sort of cheek to keep the food inside the mouth.

There was a ring of sclerotic plates in the eye, although these were absent in *Iguanodon*; on the other hand, a supraorbital crest was not developed.

The fore limb is about half the length of the hind though the proportion varies among genera, and, so far as bulk is concerned, is only about one-sixth that of the latter. It is clear that hadrosaurs walked upon the straight hind legs, using the arms merely occasionally while feeding. The hand is four-fingered, the thumb being absent, and the foot has three well-developed and hoofed toes. The tail may have had seventy or more vertebrae in it and was obviously long and strong, and laterally compressed, and was very muscular and mobile. The tail muscles were attached to the vertebrae by means of the ossified tendons like those we have already mentioned. Moodie (1928) investigated the histological nature of these structures and found that they are structurally unlike normal reptilian bones, but resemble more closely the long bones of mammals. The tendons as a rule are rod-like or like lead pencils. In the hadrosaurs as in *Iguanodon* they are concentrated around the base of the tail. Some of the tail muscles were attached to the prominent outgrowth, the fourth trochanter, on the inner surface of the thigh bone so that powerful side-to-side movements of the tail were possible. Now the shape and mobility of the tail strongly suggest that it was used for swimming, as well as for balancing the animal when standing or walking on land. Remains of the skin have been found and there is evidence that the hands were covered with a mitten of skin. So hadrosaurs would be able to swim quite adeptly, after the manner of some other reptiles, with the legs close to the side and almost motionless, the propulsive movements being made by the side-to-side movement of both body and tail. The fore limbs would be able to assist

218

this movement, so that on the one hand, this dinosaur was well adapted for swimming, and on the other, for terrestrial life, though it was less adept on land than the large carnivores.

Many species of hadrosaurs, some in an excellent state of preservation, are known, and vary in length up to 29 feet. Perhaps the most famous specimen is that known as the 'Dinosaur Mummy', exhibited in the American Museum of Natural History, New York.

In 1908 the famous collector of vertebrate fossils, Mr C. H. Sternberg, discovered in Wyoming a specimen of *Anatosaurus annectens* in which all the parts that have been preserved are covered by the shrunken epidermis. Actually no piece of the real epidermis is present because it has long ago disappeared, but it left its trace or imprint which has been beautifully preserved and which, for many purposes, is quite as satisfactory to the investigator. Probably this animal died naturally in a position where it was not disturbed by other animals or by water, but where the sun dried up the muscles so that the skin became hard and leathery and was drawn upon the bones. If this drying took place in the sandy and temporarily dry bed of a stream, and we imagine, at the end of the drying and toughening of the whole epidermis, a sudden flow of water in the stream, we can see how the specimen would be carried away and perhaps covered by fine sand and clay which would make a perfect mould of the surface of the skin before the skin disintegrated.

The impression thus obtained is so good that every detail will stand the most minute examination. There is no evidence of scutes or bony armour, but there are countless small tubercles which, according to further discoveries, seem to vary in shape and arrangement in different species, and which may indicate a colour pattern. The back and other portions more exposed to the sun have a concentration of larger tubercles, and the less exposed areas, such as the belly and the inner sides of the arms and legs, are covered with the smaller tubercles. Very likely, therefore, the back was of a dark colour and the under-surface light, just as in living lizards and crocodiles. Apart from this important evidence it is interesting to see that the epidermis forms a broad paddle-like extension of skin at the end of the arm, with a web between the fingers. This gives very weighty

219

support to the theory that these dinosaurs were good swimmers. Another mummified specimen of *A. annectens* discovered by Mr Sternberg is in the Senckenberg Museum, Frankfurt-am-Main.

A full and illustrated account of the dinosaur mummy was given by Professor H. F. Osborn (1911), and also by Dr W. D. Matthew (1915). A cast of part of the mummy and actual skin impressions of *Anatosaurus* are shown in the Dinosaur Gallery of the Department of Palaeontology in the British Museum (Natural History), where there is also a tail with fine skin impressions, of the Canadian hadrosaur, *Edmontosaurus*, already mentioned. Other mummified remains have been found, but that described above is by far the most important and illuminating, and its examination has greatly increased our knowledge of, and our ability to picture, the appearance of this group of dinosaurs.

In the Upper Cretaceous, there were several closely related forms of similar habits, but of strikingly different appearance. The difference was principally in the structure of the head, for these other forms frequently had extraordinary outgrowths on the top of the skull, some of which have been alleged to have been of secondary sexual significance. As a result of such outgrowths these animals are called the helmeted, crested or hooded hadrosaurs, although they all belong to the family Hadrosauridae. Most of the forms, including the elaborate forms, come from the Old Man (Belly River) and Edmonton Formations, and they have been specially discussed, figured and apportioned to some developmental line by R. S. Lull and N. E. Wright and by John Ostrom.

The origin of hadrosaurs is still in question and the earliest is not known satisfactorily. However, the climate and the ecological circumstances appear to have been favourable, especially in North America, to their mode of life and they rapidly evolved geologically in the space between the Old Man (Belly River) Formation and its equivalents and the Lance, a period of much geological importance. In general there appear to be two lines of development, the flat-headed dinosaurs start with hooked-nosed forms and progress to the flat-nosed and more slender-skulled kinds. The high-skulled Old Man form is

Kritosaurus ('excellent reptile'), a dinosaur known both from the Ojo Alamo Beds of New Mexico and from the Old Man Formation of Alberta, and which has two distinctive features in the skull: firstly, the prominent ridge running along the nasals and no doubt appearing as a crest on the living animal and, secondly, the height of the back of the skull. The skull is about 3 feet long, and its height about 20 inches. The result of this high cranial portion and the strong nasal crest is that the animals had decidedly arched, almost aristocratic, profiles. *Kritosaurus*

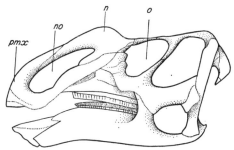

FIG. 48. *Kritosaurus*. Left side of skull. Approx. $\frac{1}{14}$ nat. size.
See key for Fig. 5.

is found in the Edmonton Formation where also there occurs *Edmontosaurus*. In the latter the skull is still large but there is no nasal elevation though the nasal aperture is still as large. We have already pointed out that *Edmontosaurus* is close in many features to *Anatosaurus* and we find this genus in *A. edmontoni* in the Upper Edmonton and *A. annectens* and *A. copei* occurring in the Lance Formation, the only survivors of the hadrosaurs.

Somewhat closely related to the high-skulled forms and with a crestless, rather depressed facial profile was *Prosaurolophus* in the Old Man series and this seems to give rise to, or be followed in the Edmonton by, a 'horned' type, *Saurolophus*. *Prosaurolophus* is crestless, *Saurolophus* is crested so that here there may be a connexion between the two groups.

Saurolophus ('reptile-ridge') is known by the skeleton of *S. osborni* Brown, from the Edmonton Formation, Alberta, a form apparently 30 feet long. The skull has a prominent horn above the eyes, pointing backwards and upwards, so that this

FIG. 49. *Saurolophus osborni*: sclerotic ring. (After Brown.) Approx.
⅜ nat. size.

animal is really a unicorn, but, remarkable as it is, there is no
evidence that it possessed the even more peculiar characters
of its mythical relation. Of the crested group there is a series of
quite remarkable skulls found in the Old Man Formation. Many
of these skulls are in the splendid hadrosaur collection of the
Royal Ontario Museum, Toronto. There is the small *Procheneosaurus* with a high, bumpy, "intellectual" forehead and there is
the well known crested *Corythosaurus*.

In the latter ridge formation appears to have reached its
maximum. *Corythosaurus* ('helmet-reptile') is quite well known
by nearly complete skeletons. It, or at least the species called
C. casuarius Brown, was nearly 30 feet long and was a good
swimmer. Remains of the skin are known and appear to be

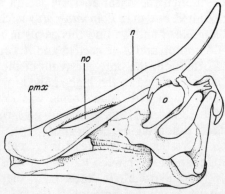

FIG. 50. *Saurolophus*. Left side of skull. (After Lull and Wright.) Approx.
1/20 nat. size.

See key for Fig. 5.

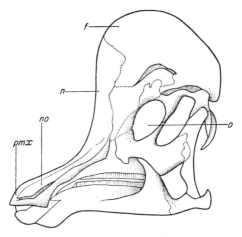

FIG. 51. *Corythosaurus casuarius.* Left side of skull. Approx. $\frac{1}{12}$ nat. size. See key for Fig. 5.

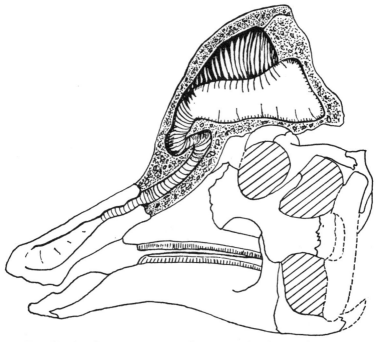

FIG. 52. *Corythosaurus excavatus.* Inner view showing nasal passage. (After Ostrom.)

223

much like those of *Anatosaurus*, but there were long rows of conical plates on the under-surface. The remains come from the Old Man Formation. The remarkable feature in the skull is that the nasal and premaxillary bones stretch upwards and backwards on the top of the skull and form a great crest or dome rather like a large bony, but hollow, coxcomb, the cavity of which is continuous with the nasal cavity (Fig. 52). As this is formed by the nasals, like the crest of *Kritosaurus*, it may be taken as a further development of the process seen in the previous genera, with which it is homologous. In *Corythosaurus* the facial part of the skull is small so that the appearance of the

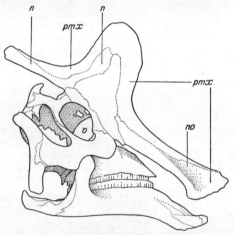

FIG. 53. *Lambeosaurus lambei*. Right side of skull. (After Gilmore.) Approx. $\frac{1}{12}$ nat. size.

See key for Fig. 5.

whole head is peculiar and is frequently likened to that of a cassowary. In another genus, *Lambeosaurus* ('Lambe reptile' = *Stephanosaurus* Lambe 'crowned-reptile'), from the same horizon and locality, the crest is even more pronounced and fits above the brain-case like a rather rakishly set cocked hat, being apparently the maximum development of the nasal arrangement. This structure is remarkable for the great part played in its construction by the premaxillaries which cover the whole length of the nasals in front of, over, and behind the dome, and actually project backwards beyond the posterior limits of the occipital elements.

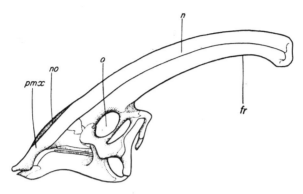

FIG. 54. *Parasaurolophus walkeri*. Left side of skull. (After Parks.)
See key for Fig. 5.

In *Parasaurolophus*, also from Alberta, the horn or spinous process is even more developed, for it projects backwards over the skull for a distance equivalent to the length of the skull. In profile the premaxillary and nasal curve of the skull (as can be seen in the British Museum cast of the skull) is strongly convex (Fig. 54). Another remarkable feature has been found in the dorsal vertebrae just over the fifth, sixth, and seventh vertebral spines, which are in contact and which were apparently

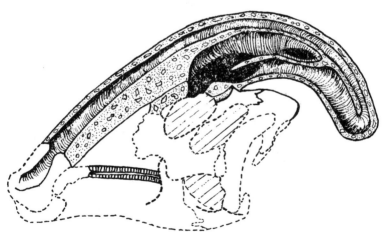

FIG. 55. *Parasaurolophus cyrtocristatus*. Inner view showing nasal passage.

225

capped by, and fused with, a curious ossification which seems to have been used for the attachment of a ligament from the tip of the crest. What the purpose of this structure and its muscular arrangement was is not known. Perhaps it had some connexion with aquatic life and the rapid raising and lowering of the head in feeding, if the feeding habits were anything like those of ducks. The fact that the central cavity of the nasal crest or boss is continuous with the nasal cavity was perhaps some sort of secondary adaptation for diving, but it is impossible to say. The occurrence of scutes on the belly of some of these forms suggests that they lived in shallow water, groping along

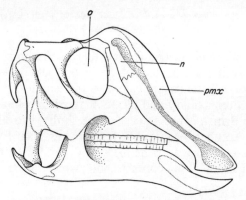

FIG. 56. *Procheneosaurus.* Right side of skull. Approx. ⅙ nat. size. See key for Fig. 5.

the bottom for water-plants, yet able to breath without coming to the surface at very short intervals. Of these forms *Procheneosaurus* is succeeded in the Edmonton by *Cheneosaurus* with a bulbous but not really domed head; *Lambeosaurus* is followed by the large-domed *Hypacrosaurus* and *Parasaurolophus* has a relative *P. tubicen* (Ojo Alomo Formation) as its later representative. Impressive as these large and peculiarly headed dinosaurs are, the use to which the skull spaces were put is even more intriguing.

Baron F. Nopcsa (1918, 1929a), believed that sexual differences are distinguishable in the skull, vertebral spines, forearm, and pelvis of these varied forms. According to him the male has these structures generally longer, and sometimes has excrescences on the skull, while the foot of the ischium is hammer-shaped. Nopcsa accordingly thought that several males and females have been placed in the wrong genera, and that, among these crested forms, *Parasaurolophus* is the male of *Kritosaurus*, and *Corythosaurus* the male of another genus closely allied to, and perhaps synonymous with, *Anatosaurus*. As L. S. Russell has pointed out (1930), the males and their supposed consorts do not always occur in the same horizon, which is quite a serious objection, but in any case the question is one of the greatest difficulty.

All these helmeted dinosaurs reached their maximum in the Old Man Formation and it is notable, if not surprising, that later, in the Lance Formation, only the conservative form, *Anatosaurus*, survived. As we shall see in the chapter on extinction, the grotesque forms often carry their own death warrant and are frequently the harbingers of racial disease and degeneration.

A very large number of these hadrosaurs are Canadian. Dale Russell records that in the Old Man Formation that there were 9 *Kritosaurs*; 9 *Prosaurolophus* forms and 72 *Lambeosaurus* (with extensive domes or tubes) and others which amount to nearly a half of the whole dinosaur population. In the lower and upper Edmonton, the proportion was even higher, at 50–60 per cent. In Lance times they had greatly dwindled to 10 per cent in the Frenchman formation. They are unrepresented in the Upper Edmonton of Red Deer River.

Of course, they occur elsewhere. One species has been found in England at Cambridge, *Anatosaurus cantabrigiensis* represented by a tooth and some foot bones which are now in the British Museum (Natural History). There is a good series, including at least one good mounted specimen, in Moscow and there are others from China, Japan and Mongolia.

From what has been said earlier it would appear that hadrosaurs had several adaptations that showed ability in water. The hand, the slightly awkward hind limbs as compared with the wholly terrestrial carnivores that were their contemporaries, the ossified tendons around the hip girdle (where incidentally there was a sacral nervous enlargement but only about two and a half

227

times that of the brain) and, above all, the fantastic air passages from external nostrils to the throat are all suggestive.

Surrounded as they were with luxuriant vegetation but with competitors of many kinds, it might be natural that they would find both safety and abundant succulent (if sandy) food in the waters, where there were no sauropods in competition. The list of contemporary vegetation is fantastic and has been analysed, with many other aspects of hadrosaurian life, by Lull and Wright (1942) and the nasal enlargements have been investigated by J. Ostrom (1962).

One remarkable fact in dinosaurian studies is the very few occasions on which fossils give any direct clue to food. One sees them against a background of vegetation, or compiles a list of contemporary plants but direct evidence is rare. However this direct guidance has been available to us for over forty years in the case of the mummy already mentioned as being in Frankfurt-am-Main. In the stomach of this *Anatosaurus* were seeds, twigs, fruits and needles of evergreens—a mixed bag of not unexpected things but none of them from water! Was this mummy unique in its habits or have we all been wrong?

Many writers have drawn the air passages and pointed out their use as water traps or air reservoirs. The present writer opted for the latter, and pointed out that the hooded or crested forms, with a greater air storage potential, always have an expanded foot to the ischium and therefore probably a more muscular base of the tail which could then with gentle movement keep the dinosaur moving under water.

Ostrom has shown that these passages were wholly sensory, not even sounding (resonant) chambers so that a hadrosaur could call to its mate amid all the press of dinosaur traffic and the wealth of trees. They heped their owners to smell enemies from friends, food from refuse and, who knows, even the scent of a mate!

The apparently scentless ones, the flat heads, probably more terrestrial in habit, seem to have done almost better in length of days if not in numbers. Parallels are not easy to find but the crocodiles do have complex nasal cavities, relatively long and lined to a considerable extent with olfactory epithelium and to a lesser extent with respiratory epithelium.

228

Once again the emphasis is on water, for the crocodile must use this scent-power while immersed. Fishes use their sense of smell in searching for food, locating mates or allies, avoiding enemies and, to some extent, for orientation. The writer has the idea that the hooded hadrosaurs used their receptors in the nasopharynx to inhibit respiration (as in the duck *Anas*) and that a postural reflex may have acted when the head was lower than the body. But this again lays stress on an ecology where water and marshland was dominant. One still has the feeling that hadrosaurs, especially hooded or crested hadrosaurs, were not usually far from water, though their relatively modest weights of 3–4 tons made recourse to water for locomotion only occasional.

Another curious form from the Old Man about which there is much controversy is *Troödon*, but it is not a hadrosaur, indeed, several authorities deny that it is an ornithopod. In 1856, Leidy established this genus and the species *T. formosus* on the evidence of a single tooth from the Judith River Formation of Montana, and it was not until 1931 that Gilmore (1931) was able to amplify the description of this species by the study of any fresh material. Meanwhile, however, other allied species had been described and are comparatively well known.

The characters of the genus are a heavy, thickened, dome-like skull which has teeth on the premaxillae, as has *Hypsilophodon*, a body that is quite ordinarily ornithopodous, *but with abdominal ribs*, and there is a general mixture of characters usually found individually in other groups of dinosaurs. Gilmore published a scientific paper in 1924, in which *Troödon* was figured as a bipedal dinosaur and described and very adequately figured *T. wyomingensis*, of Lance age, in 1931. In 1929 (1929b) and 1931 Nopcsa assigned this genus to a family of armoured dinosaurs, the Nodosauridae, on the characters of the shape of the skull, the co-ossification of certain skull bones, and the presence of apparently dermal ossifications on the skull. Further, Nopcsa contended that Gilmore's *Troödon* is an artificial mixture of the skull of an armoured quadrupedal dinosaur and the body of an unarmoured and bipedal form. L. S. Russell (1932) and C. M. Sternberg (1933) have replied to these statements.

229

Nopcsa's contention is fundamentally an objection to such a 'composite' form on mechanical grounds, and secondly a belief that such teeth as *Troödon* has are characteristic, both in appearance and composition, of certain kinds of armoured dinosaurs.

The grounds of the reply to this contention are also simple. Firstly, as to the composite nature of the skeleton reconstructed by Gilmore, both the skull and the body-skeleton were obtained from the same small quarry at the same time. Now it would be strange if in one such small restricted area the skull of an armoured dinosaur but not another piece of its skeleton, and the body and limbs of another kind of dinosaur but no trace of its skull, were to be found. No matter by what process the remains had been brought together and preserved, it would be a curious happening, and the site is not a bone-bed full of remains. Then again there is no great difficulty in associating the skull with the mounted skeleton; it is true, of course, that the skull is heavy and unusual.

If a skull is found associated with the rest of the bones, and if these articulate naturally, there is a strong probability that they belong to each other. If the skull of *Troödon* is that of a quadrupedal animal, the articular region at the base of the skull should be suited for quadrupedal life, but in this case the skull is so modified that it must have been at right angles to the neck. Either, therefore, the skull of *Troödon* was borne on a bipedal form and looked forward, like that of *Anatosaurus* and *Iguanodon*, or else it belonged to a quadrupedal form in which the skull faced downwards and where forward vision was impeded by strong overhanging orbital ridges.

C. M. Sternberg (loc. cit.) has proved that the thickening of the skull is due to thickening of the bones and not to dermal (i.e. secondary and external) ossification as in the Nodosauridae. With regard to the teeth, Nopcsa pointed out that they more closely resemble those of the armoured dinosaurs, because normally the bipedal beaked dinosaurs have enamel effectively on one side of the teeth and have simple crowns, while the armoured ones have both sides enamelled, have many cusped margins and a striated crown. This until recently was in accordance with our knowledge, but in 1925 Sternberg collected

THE BEAKED DINOSAURS: ORNITHOPODA

the skull and part of the skeleton of *Thescelosaurus* (see p. 200). This is a form closely similar to *Hypsilophodon* and an undoubted ornithopod, yet the teeth have enamel on both sides, and have multicuspid margins and a striated crown, in fact they are more like those of the armoured dinosaurs than are those of *Troödon*, and yet are certainly those of a member of the Hypsilophodontidae. Even the more primitive plated dinosaurs have no teeth on the premaxillae, but *Troödon* and *Hypsilophodon* have.

Therefore, as Nopcsa was convinced that the skeleton of *Troödon* is that of an Ornithopod, and as the skull characters do not exclude it from the group, and the skull and skeleton occurred and articulate naturally together, the only logical conclusion is that *Troödon* is an ornithopodous dinosaur. It was placed in a family of its own, the Troödontidae of Gilmore (1924), and the family would appear to be closely related to the Hypsilophodontidae, although, of course, it is more recent in time. Once again for various reasons we have to effect a change of name and the genus is now referred to *Stegoceras* Lambe.

C. M. Sternberg suggests that this strange creature lived on the higher ground above the marshy and low-lying grounds and deltas in Upper Cretaceous times in Alberta. This conclusion is based on the fact that few more or less complete skeletons are known although water-worn fragments of the heavy skull are abundant, which indicates that only the thickened skull bones would withstand the transportation to the deltaic deposits in which they have been preserved. The number of recorded remains shows that the genus must have been fairly common, and, had their habitat been the marshy ground, it would be reasonable to expect to find skeletons equally well preserved as are those of other Ornithopods and armoured dinosaurs. Dale Russell has recorded twenty-five *Stegoceras* skull fragments in the Old Man Formation (i.e. 7·8 per cent of fauna); and four in the Edmonton. In 1943 Brown and Schlaikjer described the remarkable bonehead, *Pachycephalosaurus*, from the US Upper Cretaceous which seems to be a magnified edition of the smaller genus.

Unfortunately, despite all that has been written, little more is known of the ecology of these animals. The present writer

231

believes the bonyheadedness is associated with the unusually large pituitary that can be presumed from the cranial cavities, and that here we have a case of dinosaurian acromegaly, though why it should be so common requires an answer from biochemistry or physiology.

The American Museum Expeditions to Mongolia from 1922 to 1924, which obtained so many interesting fossils, also secured the larger part of two skeletons of hitherto unknown dinosaurs that are referable to the Ornithopoda. They were named and briefly described by Osborn (1923-24), but they both belong to a new family, the Psittacosauridae, so called because of the parrot-like appearance of the skull. They were, of course, bipedal, and had a short, deep, and broad skull, with a highly arched profile and the beak much compressed from side to side so that it was quite like that of a parrot, at least in its front part. The beak was toothless, and the teeth in the jaws were few in number with only one row in use. The teeth themselves were compressed and sharp at the edge, but blunt on top, and the whole surface of the crown was enamelled. There is no vacuity in front of the orbits except the paired openings of the external nares, which are placed high up, above the beak, and midway between the front of the skull and the orbits. The orbits are large and were furnished, as in *Anatosaurus*, with a ring of sclerotic plates. The skull, according to Osborn's reconstruction, was placed at an angle of about 45° to the neck, and the latter was short, containing only six vertebrae, which is the smallest number of cervicals known in the dinosaurs. The fore limbs are stout, but shorter than the hind limbs, and the hand has only four fingers, the fifth being absent (cf. hadrosauridae). Osborn has reported that clavicles were present in *Psittacosaurus*, but they have not been described. If this identification is correct, this dinosaur, *Plateosaurus*, *Protoceratops* and perhaps *Oviraptor* are the only ones in which these structures are known. In the hind limbs the femur is shorter than the tibia, as in *Hypsilophodon* and contrary to that of *Iguanodon* or *Anatosaurus*, and the foot has four complete toes and the remains of the fifth metatarsal, but as the first toe was small the foot must have been three-toed in use. The ungual phalanges were pointed. The type specimen of the first genus, *Psittacosaurus mongoliensis* Osborn,

232

was about 5 feet long, and it was obtained from the Oshih Formation (Lower Cretaceous) of Artsa Bogdo in the Gobi Desert.

The other dinosaur, of an essentially similar nature but of more slender build, has been named *Protiguanodon*, the type being *P. mongoliense* Osborn (1923–24) from the Ondai Sair Formation (Lower Cretaceous) of the Gobi Desert. This species was apparently just over 4 feet long. It is not related to *Iguanodon*.

The presence of armour in these genera is doubtful, but until they have been more fully investigated their exact nature and their habits cannot be defined. Osborn considered that *Protiguanodon* was more cursorial than *Psittacosaurus*, but that both were less adapted to bipedal movement and arboreal feeding than *Iguanodon*. It is, therefore, interesting to see that they are specialized forms of an apparently primitive stock, just as *Stegoceras* is, and that they bear much resemblance in many characters to *Hypsilophodon*, though they are somewhat younger, geologically. It may well be, therefore, that the Ornithopoda developed from a hypsilophodont form some time in the early Jurassic and that the more terrestrial forms like *Hypsilophodon*, *Psittacosaurus*, and *Stegoceras* remained more conservative and were modified principally in the skull characters, while the aquatic or allegedly aquatic forms became generally more diverse, although in them also there was a tendency for the skull to become curiously modified perhaps in connexion with their habitat.

Osborn, as a result of the remarkable discoveries of these Mongolian expeditions, has suggested that Central Asia may well prove to have been a great dispersal centre of the land vertebrates, but nothing so far published on these dinosaurs gives an adequate basis for any statement on the probable place of origin or route of dispersal of the Ornithopoda. Indeed, the recent work of the Polish–Mongolian Expeditions suggests that parts of Mongolia contain highly specialized, rather than generalized forms. There is little to guide us in this quest, for the ornithopods had a wide distribution and the presence of remains of primitive forms in various localities of the same age is a geological, rather than a biological or geographical, effect.

233

As we have seen, the Ornithopoda ranged from the Trias to the Upper Cretaceous, and their remains have been found in England, Belgium, France, Germany, Austria, Hungary, Russia, China, Mongolia, Japan, South Africa, in North and South America and in the Arctic, and some of them were among those present at the closing stages of the Age of Reptiles.

CHAPTER XI

The Armoured Dinosaurs: Enoplosauria

Plate by plate the armour is made.
French Proverb.

The armoured dinosaurs are members of the Ornithischia and consequently share most of the features possessed by the Ornithopoda, but whereas these last were bipedal and un-armoured, the armoured forms were quadrupedal and protected by a series of heavy bony plates, or bosses, or spines, or had specially armed skulls. None the less they are similar to the Ornithopoda in the characters of the horny beak, the teeth, the structure of the pelvis, and the fore and hind limbs. Their appearance was, of course, greatly different, but most of the anatomical differences are due to the modifications consequent on the quadrupedal position and the weight of the armour. They all appear to have been herbivorous, and many were of great size. Some were bizarre in appearance and others rather like giant armadillos or rhinoceroses, yet many of the spiny forms are no more grotesque than would be such existing lizards as *Phrynosoma* or *Zonurus* if magnified to the appropriate size.

The oldest armoured dinosaur known is *Scelidosaurus harrisoni*, from the Lower Lias (i.e. Lower Jurassic) of Char-mouth, in Dorset, and the last of the armoured forms were in the very closing stages of the Cretaceous. They varied con-siderably in size, but probably none exceeded 25 or 30 feet in length; the smaller and earlier forms are represented best in Europe, and the larger forms in North America, and especially in Canada. Representatives of this group of dinosaurs have been found in England, France, Germany, Austria, Hungary, Portugal, Spain, Mongolia, South and East Africa, India, and in North and South America. They are generally supposed to have

235

THE DINOSAURS

been land-living, but one genus, from Kansas, is said to have been aquatic, while the cartilage-covered articular surfaces of the limb bones, so like those of the sauropods, have suggested to some writers that these dinosaurs were at least partly water-living.

The grouping of the Ornithischia into two smaller groups, the bipedal and the armoured dinosaurs, which is done in this book, is merely for convenience, for the armoured dinosaurs are properly classified into various families which all fall quite naturally under the Ornithischia. It is now customary to divide the armour-bearing forms into three groups each of which has the status of a Sub-order, based on the nature of the armour. Those dinosaurs which have an unhorned skull and plates of bone on the back are placed in the Sub-order Stegosauria; those with a more enclosing arrangement of plates are in the Sub-order Ankylosauria and those in which the skull is horned and a bony frill extends over the neck are called the Ceratopsia. The three groups have been variously named and have obviously different origins. Cope called some of them Thyneophora (shield bearers) but I suggest, for convenience, that a more embracing term for all of them is Enoplosauria (armed reptiles).

The armoured dinosaurs are descended from a bipedal ancestor, probably from a form whose nearest bipedal relation that we know is *Hypsilophodon*. However that may be, the earliest known quadrupedal ornithischians, though they are more feebly armed than the Cretaceous kinds, are already well adapted to a four-legged method of progression and are conspicuously armed.

The first family, the Stegosauridae, takes its name from *Stegosaurus*, which is one of the most familiar forms and one whose characters were extensively and admirably described by C. W. Gilmore (1914). *Stegosaurus*, the 'plate reptile', has a long, narrow skull with toothless premaxillae and a horny beak (or at least with horn-covered anterior mouthparts), but the size of the skull is small compared with that of the body. The nares are large and placed at the side and front of the skull. The teeth are small, spatulate, and somewhat flower-like, about twenty-three being in each half of the jaw (Fig. 57). They were

236

arranged in one functional row, the successional teeth replacing them from below. The brain cavity is relatively very small and indicates a small brain of low organization. The sacrum has four fused vertebrae, but sometimes it is larger through the addition of one or more lumbar centra, but it is remarkable in that the neural cavity is greatly enlarged, sometimes to as much as twenty times that of the brain cavity. The brachial, or shoulder, region has a much less expended neural cavity. The brain of this genus was, relatively, one of the smallest of the known land-vertebrates. Apparently the sense of smell was equally developed as that of sight, though how good this was

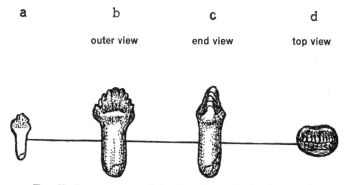

FIG. 57. *Stegosaurus ungulatus*. Tooth. *a*, nat. size, *b, c, d* ×2.

as judged by standards that we know, we cannot say. As to the other neural developments, the shoulder enlargement was the centre of innervation of the fore limbs, while that of the sacrum, to use Lull's words, 'was mainly the reflex and co-ordinating centre for the control of the mighty muscles of the hind limbs, but more especially of the powerful, active, and aggressive tail, which constituted the principal means of defence' (Lull, 1910, 1917; Branca, 1914). Another interesting feature of the sacral nerve centre or ganglion is that in young specimens the cavity is proportionately larger than that of adult individuals, which corresponds to the well-known law of brain-growth.

It is unfortunate that an amusing poem written about the sacral nerve centre should have called it a 'brain' or second brain, for this has persisted in popular accounts. This poem, entitled 'The Dinosaur' (Bert L. Taylor, in *The Chicago Tribune*, 1912), wrongly claimed that 'The creature had two sets of brains—one in his head (the usual place), the other at his spinal base.'

The vertebrae are slightly amphicoelous or have flat ends, and the first caudal vertebrae are the largest of the whole series: All are solid, as are the limb bones. The fore limbs are short and strongly developed, the ulna has a well-developed olecranon, or 'elbow-bone', and the fore feet are short, and semi-plantigrade, with five hoof-like toes. The hind legs are about twice the length of the fore, and the bones are long and straight. The feet are actually four-toed, but only three were functional as the fourth digit consists merely of a vestigial metatarsal.

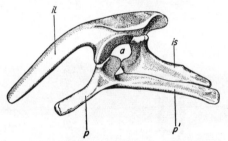

FIG. 58. Stegosaurian pelvis. Left side.

KEY: *a.*, acetabulum; *il.*, ilium; *p.*, pubis, *p'.*, post-pubis: *is.*, ischium.

The dermal armour consists of two rows of upstanding and flattened plates which extended along the whole of the backbone from behind the head to a little before the end of the tail. The space between the last plates and the end of the tail is taken up by four dermal, spike-like spines. In addition there were ossicles scattered over the skin and little dermal plates apparently upon the head and neck. As some of the main dermal plates and spines were as much as 30 inches high, and the whole animal was anything from 12 to nearly 30 feet long and over 5 feet high at the hips, it must have been grotesque in appearance, and has not unnaturally appealed to restoration artists. Now, in making any restored skeleton or reconstruction, whether model or picture, a great many questions arise that do not normally occur in a

238

mere description of the dry bones, and the case of *Stegosaurus* is no exception. The number, arrangement, and fixation of the great plates and spines has for long been a subject of controversy that is not settled yet.

In 1891, Professor Marsh made the first picture of the restored skeleton and this has been extensively copied by subsequent writers. In this picture the plates are placed along the back in a single row and four pairs of spines are set at the end of the tail. Later, in 1893, J. Smit, in Hutchinson's *Extinct Monsters* (1893, 1910), published a reconstruction-picture based on Marsh's restoration, clearly showing the animal crawling along with the knees well out from the body, and the back ornamented by twelve plates in single series and with four pairs of little, fine spikes on the tail. It is observable that the fore foot is clearly five-toed, but the hind foot has four functional toes, which is incorrect.

In 1910, in a drawing, Lucas was the first to show that the plates were paired, and his drawing shows nine pairs of large plates and four pairs of spines, but later he modified his views and under his direction a model was made by C. R. Knight showing the plates alternately arranged and the number of spines reduced to two pairs. Since that time Lull has prepared drawings and a model with the plates paired and the total number of spines as eight, and Gilmore has made a series of models, which are to be found in many museums throughout the world, with alternate plates and two pairs of spines. Lull also published (1924) a drawing adopting this plan. There have been many other restorations and a full history of this subject would fill a small volume in itself.

Gilmore, after a detailed study of the skeletal structure, established that the dermal plates were from twenty to twenty-two in number, and arranged in two rows with the plates alternating. The position of the largest plate was not over the pelvis, but just above the base of the tail, and the usual number of the tail spines was four, arranged in two pairs.

The main function of this armour must have been defensive throughout, although only the backbone and spinal cord were protected. Its power in an offensive sense must have been negligible, because the heavy tail with its battery of spikes was

239

apparently capable of only limited lateral movement on account of the close articulations between the vertebrae. The grooves and impressions on the surface of both plates and spines show that during life there must have been a horny covering to these structures, which would, of course, materially increase their size and render these features even more striking. The largest plate examined by Gilmore was 760 mm. (30 inches) high, 785 mm. (31 inches) at the longest part, and 87 mm. (3½ inches) wide; and the same directions on a spine measured 537 mm. (21 inches), 115 mm. (4½ inches), and 65 mm. (2½ inches), respectively. Neither plates nor spines were attached to any underlying bony element, or inserted into the muscles, as had previously been suggested. They appear to have been fixed only by their somewhat broadened bases into the unusually thick skin of the back.

Although *Stegosaurus* is one of our best known dinosaurs, to judge from the illustrations and restoration figures, in actuality few skeletons are known and only one is in a pose from which the position of the dermal plates can be estimated. This is the specimen in the National Museum in Washington, D.C., examined and described by C. W. Gilmore. It was lying on its side and the alternate arrangement of plates was seen on the ground. In view of the fact that very few vertebrates have an alternate arrangement of dermal structures (apart from dermal markings) and that the related forms described here (*Polacanthus*, *Acanthopholis* and *Kentrosaurus*) have paired plates and spines, we may wonder at the peculiarity of *Stegosaurus*.

If however the plates were paired, as this author now believes them to have been, and the animal died and lay on its side, the loosened plates would, or could, fall upon each other only to slide off into an intermediate position, thus suggesting alternation. It may be argued that an alternate series was more protective than a paired series, but since it is not at all clear what the armour of *Stegosaurus* was protecting it from, the whole function of these plates is in question.

As the teeth were relatively feeble and suited only for a diet of succulent plants, we may picture these extraordinary animals moving slowly along by the banks of the Jurassic lakes, rivers, and lagoons in whose placid waters the giant sauropods were to be seen. As they were sometimes over 25 and nearly 30 feet long their weight must have been in the region of 2 tons, so agility was not one of their attributes. Probably they walked with the small head very close to the ground and had the elbows and knees slightly out from the body (Plate 2). Thus they would pursue their herbivorous way, the lowly placed skull being admirably suited for shearing off the vegetable food, a process which Lull considers was aided by a prehensile tongue. This food supply, and the rugose articular surfaces of the limbs, would seem to argue a habitat akin to that of the sauropods though it is hardly possible to imagine the stegosaurs as aquatic, as Wilfarth did (1949). Consequently it seems natural to assign them a borderland domain, such as that suggested above, near the sauropods. But it is seldom that their remains are found in the same quarry as those of the giant dinosaurs, so there must have been a definite delimitation of habitats (although at Como, in Quarry 12, *Camarasaurus*, and *Diplodocus* were found with *Stegosaurus*). Although the two groups coexisted for a very long time, the stegosaurs did not survive the passing of Morrison (Upper Jurassic) times.

The principal species of *Stegosaurus* are *S. ungulatus* which was long, tall, and thin, and *S. stenops* which was of smaller build. Both species occur in the Morrison of Wyoming and Colorado, in the United States, and an English form, *S. durobrivensis*, is known from pelvic bones collected from the Oxford Clay of Peterborough and now in the British Museum (Natural History).

Another genus closely related to, if not actually identical with, *Stegosaurus* is *Omosaurus* ('arm-reptile') Owen, which was established in 1875 on material now in the British Museum (Natural History). The type species is *O. armatus*, which has a relatively shorter ilium and a longer humerus than any species of *Stegosaurus*, and shorter neural spines. Upstanding bony plates do not seem to have been present. This species comes from the Kimmeridge Clay of Swindon, Wiltshire, and other species have been described on material from Oxford, Normandy, Spain and Portugal. (*Omosaurus* Owen is pre-occupied as a name by *Omosaurus* Liedy and is sometimes called *Dacentrurus*. Both are now included in the genus

241

Pridontosaurus.) The oldest armoured dinosaur known is *Scelidosaurus harrisoni* from the Lower Lias of Charmouth and Lyme Regis in Dorset, and it is, in fact, also one of the earliest known Ornithischia. The type specimen consisted of part of the hind limb (now referred to a megalosaur), but a later discovery of an almost complete, though somewhat crushed, skeleton is the basis of our knowledge of this very interesting genus. It is placed in a separate family of its own, the Scelidosauridae.

In the general characters of the skeleton it differs in several respects from *Stegosaurus*; for example, the vertebrae are sometimes hollow as are the limb bones, and the neural canal is not expanded. Further, there is a definite coronoid process on the dentary, which *Stegosaurus* lacks. The tibia and fibula of *Scelidosaurus* are shorter than the femur and are not fused with the tarsals, but they are not so short as in *Stegosaurus*, in which they are fused with the proximal tarsals. The hind foot was perhaps functionally three-toed, for the first digit—the 'big toe'—is reduced, and the little toe is absent; the fore foot is four-toed.

The system of armament is very different from that of *Stegosaurus*, for instead of two rows of plates along the backbone, *Scelidosaurus* has a number of rows of small tubercles and keeled dermal ossicles or scutes running along the back. The tail had a row of vertical plates along its whole length just above the neural spines, but there were no spikes at the end. A restoration, by Mr Neave Parker and the author, of the living appearance of this animal, is given on Plate II. The length of the animal must have been about 12 feet. There were upstanding bony plates on the neck and tail but careful examination of the skeleton does not give support to the idea that there were two upstanding spikes in the shoulder region. These are prominent features on the reconstruction by Smit (in Hutchinson, 1893) where the animal is shown as bipedal, and it was similarly figured in 1905 in the *Guide to Fossil Reptiles, Amphibians, and Fishes* in the British Museum (Natural History).

The front part of the skull is missing so that there is no indication as to whether there were teeth on the premaxillae, but there is no question that *Scelidosaurus* is a primitive form and may consequently have had them. The teeth are set in separate sockets, but rather close together, and the jaws are so arranged that the teeth of the upper jaw came on the outside of those of the lower. Each tooth is composed of a cylindrical shaft or fang and a compressed, flower-like crown, somewhat triangular in shape and with three prominent ridges.

Now, the structure of the teeth is an important clue to the character of the food and consequently the nature of the habits. *Scelidosaurus* was found in a marine deposit that is famous for the remains of marine reptiles it contains. Owen, who first described this genus, thought the teeth were quite suitable for chopping up vegetable food, but that they were equally adapted for animal food, and he visualized the creature swimming out to sea in search of living prey. The truth of this supposition, he said, would be proved by the character of the premaxillary teeth if they should be found, and their absence would 'incline the balance of probability to the phytophagous nature of the Liassic *Scelidosaurus*' (Owen, 1861). There are two factors which seem to go against the suggestion that *Scelidosaurus* was carnivorous: firstly, the structure of the jaws shows that 'cheek pouches' may have been present; and, secondly, the strong probability that the remains of this dinosaur were washed out to sea. On the first point it may be said that 'cheek pouches' are most useful if plant food is to be chopped up and masticated. On the second point, it is noteworthy that the skeletons of several armoured dinosaurs have been found in marine deposits. In considering the habits of *Stegosaurus* we have said that probably these animals lived on the banks of the lakes, lagoons, or rivers, where the supply of succulent plant food would be abundant. In such positions a slip into the water, or the sudden rush of a flood-stream, might result in the heavy creature being drowned and the body carried out to sea. The circumstances of the burial of *Scelidosaurus* are, therefore, not necessarily a strong argument in favour of a living prey, but they help to substantiate a herbivorous diet, and a low-lying marshy habitat for this particular dinosaur.

Scelidosaurus is, therefore, structurally different from *Stegosaurus*, and altogether more primitive. It seems to play the part among the armoured dinosaurs that *Hypsilophodon* played

243

among the unarmoured beaked forms, although it is geologically older. There are significant similarities between some bones of the two genera and *Scelidosaurus* may be a descendent of a hypsilophodont ancestor. Some years ago a small partial skeleton was recovered from the Lias at Charmouth which the present writer identified as a young *Scelidosaurus*. The imprint of the small rump and tail plates could be seen and their centres of ossification.

There are two other genera of the Stegosauridae to which we must refer. The first is *Kentrurosaurus* from the Upper Jurassic of Tendaguru, Tanzania. A good, mounted skeleton of *K. aethiopicus* Hennig is on exhibition in the Geological and Palaeontological Institute and Museum in Berlin and portions of the armour, also fom East Africa, are in the British Museum (Natural History). This genus closely resembles *Stegosaurus*, but the neural spines of the later vertebrae of the tail lean forwards, while the armour consists of paired spines on the beginning of the back and the tail and small plates on the middle of the back. *Kentrurosaurus* (now more correctly referred to as *Kentrosaurus*) was about 17 feet long. Secondly, a lower jaw from the Oxford Clay of Peterborough, named *Sarcolestes leedsi* by Lydekker, also in the Palaeontological Department of the British Museum, shows the very characteristic sigmoid curve of the tooth row of these armoured dinosaurs, and may well belong to this family. *Chialingosaurus* (Plate IV) is near *Kentrosaurus*.

The second Sub-order of armoured dinosaurs is called the Ankylosauridae, whose first family is the Acanthopholidae. *Acanthopholis* Huxley is an English form whose remains have been found in the Lower Chalk at Folkestone and the Cambridge Greensand (Cretaceous) of Cambridge, and is remarkable in that the long axis of the head appears to have been nearly at right angles to the neck, in the deeply serrated teeth shaped like lancets, and in the nature of the armour. There were a few paired upstanding plates along the centre of the neck, and paired series of oval, keeled scutes were along the dorsal surface of the body, and there were flat plates of bone on the tail. Nopcsa considered that there were probably small spines on the shoulders. The type species, *A. horridus* Huxley, attained a length of 13 feet. The family occupies a position intermediate

244

between the Stegosauridae, on the one hand, and the Nodo-sauridae, which is also included in this Sub-order, on the other. The genera included in the family Nodosauridae are all Cretaceous in age and are among the most interesting armed forms we known. Many of the best-known genera are North American, and particularly from Canada, where very rich discoveries have been made. Fortunately two of the most famous specimens are in the Palaeontological Department of the British Museum at South Kensington.

The members of the family may be characterized briefly as four-footed armadillo-like dinosaurs armed with paired series of bony plates and spines, the plates being usually almost circular or oval and often keeled. The broad, triangular skull was covered by a number of coalesced dermal bony plates, and was not carried at right angles to the neck. The teeth were small and the whole dental series was reduced. The limb bones were massive, the fore limbs being shorter than the hind. The sacral region was armoured by a remarkable bony shield of con-siderable size which was sometimes co-ossified with the ilia.

The oldest member of the family, from a geological point of view, is one of the British Museum specimens, *Polacanthus foxi*, from the Wealden of the Isle of Wight. Originally described by J. W. Hulke in 1881 the specimen was examined by Baron Nopcsa (1905), and set up in the then Geological Department under his supervision. It is a very interesting form and it is most unfortunate that the skull, fore limbs and hind feet are all miss-ing. Some of these elements were, in fact discovered, but vandalism in the Isle of Wight during the 1939–45 war removed these also. The armour is, however, almost completely known, though the position of some of the elements is conjectural. The most noticeable feature of this dermal armour is the large, roughly quadrangular plate of bone that rests upon the sacral region and hip-girdle somewhat after the manner of a saddle-cloth placed rather far backwards. This structure has been called the sacro-lumbar buckler and is composed of a large number of irregularly shaped plates of varying size fused together. The condition of the underlying ossified tendons clearly indicates that this shield was not co-ossified with the ribs, and such co-ossification, if it did occur (which is not proven), would have

245

been with the upper borders of the ilia and along the surface of the neural spines. Along each side of the neck and back in front of this buckler was a row of long, sharp pointed spines, the exact position of which has caused some difficulty. Nopcsa worked out their probable position in a manner that certainly agrees with the longitudinal data of the remains, and they were so mounted on the skeleton, but it is almost certain, from the investigation of other dinosaurian material received by the British Museum subsequently, that the spines, though correct in arrangement from front to back, are on the wrong sides. The result of the rearrangement would be that the spines would point much more laterally.

The tail of the animal bears no such spines, but has two rows of divergent, bony plates, which are broad and sharp-edged, running along its length, and in the space between the plates are set button-like ossicles. There are some additional plates whose position is not known, though it is likely they were on the sides of the body below the row of spines.

In many ways the armour of *Polacanthus* resembles that of *Scelidosaurus*, and many of Nopcsa's conclusions were based on this similarity. Smith Woodward (*Zittel*, 1932) gave the length of the animal as 'about three metres long', and Nopcsa (1905, p. 250) says the 'height at the rump did not exceed three feet', but the skeleton as mounted under their direction is about 13 feet long without the skull and is 4 feet high at the rump. In life it was, therefore, about 15 feet long and with the rump at least 4 feet from the ground, and was consequently a large, long, and broad creature, rather low in stature and like an armadillo (Plate III). The bones bear evidence of considerable muscular power, and it was no doubt a heavy and slowly moving plant-eater. Nopcsa has called it, very justifiably, 'a Glyptodon among the Dinosaurs'.

The family Ankylosauridae takes its name from the genus *Ankylosaurus*, known from the Upper Cretaceous of Montana, USA and Alberta, Canada. *Ankylosaurus* ('rounded reptile') was a massive creature; long, low, and broad, like *Polacanthus*, but with a heavy, triangular skull and rather feeble *Stegosaurus*-like teeth. The fore limbs are again relatively short. The dermal armour consisted of flat plates fused to the surface of the skull, and a continuous series of oval, flattened but keeled scutes over the whole upper and lateral surfaces of the neck, body, and tail. These scutes are more or less symmetrical and, as arranged over the body, fall into definite longitudinal and lateral rows. It is noteworthy that in *Ankylosaurus magniventris*, the type species (B. Brown, 1908), the armour increases in size, weight, and solidity towards the pelvic region. There are no elevated plates or spines as in *Stegosaurus, Kentrosaurus, Scelidosaurus,* and *Polacanthus*, so that the complete armament was a series of flat and solid plates. The head was heavily armoured and the eyes and forwardly placed nostrils were all overhung and protected by bosses of bone, and the tail, equally heavily armed as the body, has a heavy mace-like club of consolidated plates at its tip.

The length of this animal was about 17 feet and the over-armour breadth just over 6 feet, so that its weight must have been very considerable. As a modification associated with the support of the armour, the widely spread ribs are co-ossified with the vertebrae and the neural spines are short. *Ankylosaurus* has been well described as 'the most ponderous animated citadel the world has ever seen'. The short, massive legs ending, possibly, in elephantine feet, would make the animal of low stature, and when attacked it would merely have to lower its body slightly to become an impregnable block of almost solid armour, against which even its giant contemporary, *Tyranno-saurus*, might launch itself in vain, unless, of course, it could turn it over on its back. Like the other members of this group it was herbivorous, probably very slow-moving, and inhabiting the low-lying grounds.

A somewhat similar form from Canada is named *Dyoplo-saurus* (Parks, 1924; Gilmore, 1930). It is known from an incomplete but highly interesting skeleton from the Upper Cretaceous of the Red Deer River of Alberta, and from a skull from the Two Medicine Formation (also Upper Cretaceous) of Montana. The type and only known species is *D. acutosquameus* Parks, and is in the Royal Ontario Museum, Toronto. In general character it resembles *Ankylosaurus*, though the shape and other details of the skull readily distinguish it from that genus.

The armour is only partly known, but that of the back appears

247

to have consisted of oval, keeled scutes which gradually increase in size and height as they are traced towards the tail, but as only the most posterior scutes were found there can be little certainty as to the features of the general body-armour. The surface of the belly appears to have been studded with irregular, polygonal tubercles, closely set together, but traversed by the wandering and irregular markings of canals.

The most remarkable feature of the armament is the long tail-club formed by ten or eleven caudal vertebrae. In these not only are the centra fused, but also the neural spines and arches and the chevrons, while running on each side are masses of ossified tendons. Bony plates embrace the end of the tail to form a knob at the end of the vertebrae, and although the plates are firmly attached to the end vertebrae, Parks thought they were of dermal origin. The knob is just 10 inches long and just under 7 inches broad, while the whole 'club' is 4 feet long. It is probable that the series of scutes also entered the surface of the

FIG. 59. *Dyoplosaurus*. Tail-club. (After Parks.) Approx. $\frac{1}{32}$ nat. size.

club so that it must have been a heavy as well as an unusually rigid structure, and a valuable organ in defence or attack (Fig. 59). In general habits we must conclude that *Dyoplosaurus* was closely similar to its contemporary 'dreadnoughts'. The teeth are much like those of *Stegosaurus* but are asymmetrical. The ilium is large, broad and horizontal and is reminiscent of that of the rather peculiar *Talararus plicatospineus* Maleev. This 14-feet-long nodosaur is in Moscow.

In 1914 W. E. Cutler obtained the major portion of a skeleton of a large dinosaur from the Upper Cretaceous of the Red Deer River, Alberta. It came from sandstones in the Old Man Formation at Dead Lodge Canyon near Happy Jack Ferry, on the Red Deer River. Cutler was working for the British Museum (Natural History), where, in 1915, the excavated fossil, still largely surrounded by matrix, duly arrived. It was not possible to deal with it then because of the war and the consequent absence Mr L. E. Parsons whose duty it was to develop and prepare such material. The specimen was, however, unpacked and made ready for its subsequent treatment. In 1919 the active work of preparation commenced, and the matrix was slowly and carefully removed from the bones, until, upon one side of the slab, the greater part of the limbs and vertebral column was exposed. The preparator's attention was next given to the other side of the slab so that the remaining matrix might be removed and the bones freed. While engaged on this task he encountered a brownish layer of sandstone with peculiar ornamentation which, on further investigation and after extremely careful work, proved to be the impression of the skin. The actual epidermis had, of course, disappeared long before, and the impression was merely that made by the skin on the fine sand on which the dead animal lay. The conditions of burial and preservation must have been similar to those in which the *Anatosaurus* mummy was made (see p. 219).

The very greatest care and skill were exercised by the preparator in disclosing the epidermal structures that remained, and these were found to be of several distinct kinds. There were paired series of spines and plates, numerous polygonal plates of different sizes, and, in what must have been the more flexible regions of the skin, hundreds of little ossicles.

In 1925 the specimen was examined by Baron Nopcsa, whose report was published in 1928 (Nopcsa, 1928), and who made it the type of a new genus and species named, in virtue of its spinescence. *Scolosaurus cutleri*, the word *Scolosaurus* meaning 'thorn reptile'. In skeletal characters *Scolosaurus* falls naturally into this family. The skull was unfortunately missing, but it must have been similar to that of the rest of this group. The vertebral series is extensively shown, but the actual number of cervical centra cannot be determined. The front limb is markedly shorter than the hind, and the humerus is unusually well developed and is by far the most prominent bone in the skeleton. The left front limb is preserved in its natural position; namely, with the short and stout humerus horizontal and at right angles to the stout radius and ulna. Unfortunately the whole manus is wanting except for two metacarpals. There can be little doubt that the more slender hind limbs were similarly set in life, so that

Scolosaurus, like other reptiles of this family, walked with the feet wide apart and, consequently, with a very small stride. The hind foot is very incomplete, but one complete toe and the impressions of two others remain. The toes had broad and flat claws, and the foot was plantigrade. As Nopcsa remarks, 'altogether there is no decided fossorial adaptation, although the feet might have occasionally been used for scraping'.

The armour may be briefly described as follows. The neck region is protected by two bony transverse strips, the nuchal plates, which are separated by a short strip of flexible granular skin. They are followed by a large, broad, and comparatively long patch of flexible granular skin, the lateral borders of which are indented where the fore limbs, with their protective cover of skin and spines, meet the body. Then come four transverse strips of inflexible skin averaging 10 inches in length from front to back, and separated by narrow belts of flexible skin. These four strips and the nuchal plates serve to protect the front half of the body, while the hinder half is covered by a large, rigid plate apparently formed by the fusion of three segments of inflexible skin with polygonal scute-traces. This is suggested by the fact that, though each of the preceding segments bears only one transverse row of spines, this plate has three rows. It thus forms a lumbar shield comparable to that of *Polacanthus*. The shield or buckler is followed by the alternating, polygonally marked segments and granular skin of the tail. The complete tail is not preserved, but it was probably protected by some five segments.

The spines, bosses, and plates are distributed symmetrically over the segmented cuirass. Their remains show that, starting at the first segment, two longitudinal rows of spines ran along each side of the back; while, starting at the third segment, a third series was intercalated between the members of the other two and ran to the hinder end of the lumbar plate. The anterior spines of the innermost series are blunt, conical, bony projections, 6 inches high, posteriorly becoming flatter, and eventually passing into round plates. The outermost series are somewhat similar, but show greater variation, while the intercalated rows consist only of flat plates of more or less circular outline. Spines also occur on the two cervical plates, while a whole battery of sharp-pointed spikes is arranged to cover and

250

protect the upper arm. On the tail the spines again increase in size until the last segment but one, which carried two great spikes, whose use it is rather difficult to imagine. This part of the tail was no more vulnerable than the anterior portions, while the tail appears to be too thick and clumsy to have been used in offence like a Crusader's mace. No doubt during life the spikes and bosses had a sharper horny covering.

The whole animal must have appeared something like a very large, spiky, and heavily tailed tortoise. The total length is nearly 18 feet, the greatest breadth 8 feet, and the height 4 feet. Nopcsa estimated the weight at nearly 2 tons, which is slightly more than that given here for *Stegosaurus* (1·75 English tons). When attacked by even its most formidable contemporaries *Scolosaurus* must have been a difficult proposition, and the low, broad body would be almost impossible to upset, though if once turned on its back the animal would be absolutely helpless.

Scolosaurus, though so heavily and adequately armed, had, no doubt, only a small and lowly organized brain like the other members of this family. The sandstone in which the remains were found is of aeolian origin, and the fact that a dried but well-preserved leaf of a plane tree was found in the body cavity indicates that the creature did not become embedded in water-laid sediments. Unfortunately, the skull was missing so there is no direct evidence as to the adaptation of the teeth. What then were the habits of this dinosaur, and how did it obtain its food?

In his original description of the remains, Baron Nopcsa held that *Scolosaurus* was desert-living, basing his assumption not only on the conditions of its burial, but on the general similarity to such modern lizards as *Moloch* and *Phrynosoma*, which live in semi-desert or desert regions, where their bodies lie flattened and largely hidden on the sandy surface. Their spines protect them from attack; and they eat insects. Since *Scolosaurus* died in such a sandy region and was obviously so clumsy that it could not have travelled far or fast in search of food, Baron Nopcsa made the ingenious suggestion that it was insectivorous, and he calculated that it probably ate 7000 grasshoppers and beetles a week. If this were true, *Scolosaurus* was the largest insectivore that we know. In allied forms the feeble quadrates certainly indicate that no great pressure was brought to bear upon them, and that the food was probably soft. On the other hand, the teeth are frequently reduced, which suggests that the food was not cut up, and consequently most types of desert vegetation can be excluded as articles of diet. Nopcsa had, therefore, quite good grounds for his interesting suggestion.

In 1929 the author pointed out that there are, however, equally good grounds for a less sensational view: 'If we study the rocks of the region where *Scolosaurus* was found, we see that this district was a great well-watered delta, quite capable of supporting a good vegetation—indeed, the leaf found in association with the skeleton is proof that trees existed at no great distance from the sandy spot where the animal died. Much of the ground must have been swampy, and entirely unsuitable to the heavy, slow-moving *Scolosaurus*; but there is no reason why vegetation should not have been close to the numerous sand-dunes which must have occurred, and this sandy ground would provide good foothold and adequate vegetable diet for the dinosaur. His contemporaries, *Palaeoscincus* and *Panoplosaurus*, are generally supposed to have lived under these conditions, and the insectivorous diet suggested by Baron Nopcsa for *Scolosaurus* does not appear to be by any means inevitable. It is almost certain, then, that an abundant supply of suitable trees and plants existed in the area in which *Scolosaurus* lived: the heavy armour was sufficient protection against the very large carnivorous dinosaurs of the time; while the low body position made it almost impossible for the creature to be pushed over when attacked. Very likely the soft sand of the dunes gave way suddenly under one side of this particular dinosaur, which then rolled on its back, a position in which it was quite helpless, and in which it met its death. Then apparently the body cavity opened letting in the sand and the plane leaf, and finally the whole carcass became embedded in wind-blown sand. In the course of time the sands hardened into sandstone, which were later excavated by the Red Deer River, and once more the dinosaur was brought into the light of day.'

In 1933 C. M. Sternberg, who had visited Cutler during the recovery of the specimen, and who is very familiar with the locality, published a note on the 'Habitat of *Scolosaurus*'. In it he pointed out that all the nodosaurs he had collected or observed in these beds were buried upside-down, and he believes that this is because they died in water, or were carried off by flood under decomposition, when the gases in the abdominal cavity on the one side, and the heavy plates on the other, would cause the carcass to float upside down. It would continue in this position until it lodged against a sand-bar or sank to the bottom. He suggests that the presence of wind-blown sand and a plane leaf is due to the fact that the carcass lodged on a sand-bar during flood, but that it was later exposed to the sun and the wind. He concludes, 'while it is true that the recent spiny lizards which Nopcsa mentioned, are desert or semi-desert dwellers, we also know that most of the broad-bodied short-limbed turtles inhabit swamps or streams', and says, 'eight years' field-work in the Belly River and Edmonton formations leads me to assign a lowland habitat to the Nodosaurs.' He makes no statement as to the food habits of *Scolosaurus*, but it is evident from the context that he does not support Nopcsa's contention.

On the whole, it seems more probable that this dinosaur was a soft-plant eater inhabiting the lowlands in this great delta region, which is precisely the sort of habitat we have specified for the other nodosaurs. *Scolosaurus* has been dealt with at considerable length because it is a form of unusual interest, and the type, and only known, specimen in the British Museum (Natural History) is almost certainly the finest armoured dinosaur so far discovered.

To this family also belong *Hierosaurus*, from the Niobrara Chalk of Kansas, which is considered to have been as aquatic as a turtle, and *Lametasaurus*, the only Indian armoured dinosaur of which we have evidence. Once again Dale Russell gives useful information about the occurrences of these dinosaurs in Canada. In the Old Man Formation there were thirty-five nodosaurs, 10·9 per cent of the fauna: In the Edmonton altogether ten or 7 per cent of the fauna. There were two or 11 per cent in the Lance (Upper Edmonton) and none in the Frenchman.

The families Nodosauridae and Acanthopholidae, which have much in common, are sometimes placed together under the name Thyreophora, of Cope; indeed this name was early suggested for all the armoured dinosaurs. It means 'shield bearers'. The genus *Nodosaurus* which gives its name to the Nodosauridae is not well known, and frequently the family is referred to as the Ankylosauridae, after the much more fully understood *Ankylosaurus*.

If we consider the Acanthopholidae and the Nodosauridae as one group we find that all the armoured dinosaurs fall into three fairly natural divisions. Firstly, there are the Stegosaurs, with only a paired row of alternating plates and two pairs of spines upon the tail, and a moderately tall and thin body. Secondly, the Acanthopholid–Nodosaur group, or Thyreophora, of Cope, with plates and spines all over the body and tail, and the body low and broad; and thirdly, the Ceratopsia, with horns upon the skull, and a bony frill over the neck, but no plates or spines upon the rhinoceros-like body.

This last group is the only one that remains for description. The members are usually grouped as two families, the Protoceratopsidae and the Ceratopsidae (Romer, 1966) and are placed in a third Sub-order of the Ornithischia called the Ceratopsia. The Sub-order and families take their name from the genus *Ceratops* Marsh 1888, which is derived from the Greek words meaning 'horned eye' or 'horned face'.

These horned dinosaurs may be characterized generally as having a large skull which is sometimes more than a third of the length of the whole animal. The skull may have no horns or may have as many as three horns on the face, And there is a backwardly projecting frill or crest, with or without fenestrae (or openings) over the neck. The borders of this frill may be plain or may be ornamented by dermal bones or produced into spinous processes. The neck-frill is formed by the parietal and squamosal bones, and sometimes there is a secondary roof with a pseudopineal foramen over the frontal bones. There is usually no vacuity in front of the orbits, except the nasal openings, and in this antorbital region the skull is much compressed from side to side to form a beak-like front. *Protoceratops* had premaxillary teeth (but no opposing teeth); in all other forms they are absent: there is on the upper jaw a median unpaired element (the rostral bone) which bore the turtle-like cutting beak and met the corresponding toothless predentary part of the lower jaw. The teeth, which are set in a groove, may be in one or more functional rows, and may have simple roots, as in the Protoceratopsidae, or bifid roots, as in the Ceratopsidae, and they are above the successional teeth, which pressed closely upon their predecessors between their roots. The teeth in general are unique among the reptiles, not only on account of their possessing a double fang with an internal and external root separated by the crown of the succeeding tooth, but in that the teeth are held in an open groove in which alveoli are but slightly indicated. So slight is this bony connexion that the decomposition of the gums has usually resulted in the loss of the teeth. The skull was borne with its long axis in the same line as that of the neck. The vertebrae have flat articular ends, and are of solid construction, like the limb bones. The fore limbs are shorter than the hind, and the fore feet have five hoof-like toes and the hind feet four, but in *Triceratops* only three of the latter were functional. The protoceratopsians had clawed toes, the ceratopsians had hoofed unguals. The skin had a thick mosaic-like covering of scales.

All the members of this group are Upper Cretaceous in age and are among the last products of dinosaurian activity. We have had frequent occasion to refer to the work of the American Museum expeditions to Mongolia and it is not an overstatement to say that their discoveries have put an entirely new complexion on some of our conceptions of the dinosaurs. The Ceratopsia are one such group whose history and evolution have certainly been greatly clarified as a result of these discoveries in Mongolia.

In 1887 Professor O. C. Marsh published a short description of what he considered a bison horn found fossil in Colorado. Some time later expeditions working in Wyoming and Montana, under the leadership of J. B. Hatcher, found skulls and skeletons of new dinosaurs to which the so-called bison horn of Marsh was clearly referable. It was also found that certain teeth and bones at Philadelphia in the possession of Professor Cope should be referred to this new form. Cope had previously named his material as *Agathaumas*; Marsh now named the horn *Ceratops*, and he gave the name *Triceratops* ('three-horned face') to the animals collected by Hatcher. Since that time many remains of Ceratopsia have passed below the examining eyes of palaeontologists and the group is very fully known so far as the skeletal structure is concerned and much progress has recently been made in phylogenetic and evolutionary studies (Colbert, 1948 and Ostrom, 1966).

It may be said that in general characters, in habits and habitats, the various genera are much alike, but there is considerable variety in size and in the nature and ornamentation of the facial and frill regions.

The most primitive genus is undoubtedly *Protoceratops* Granger and Gregory, from the Djadochta (Upper Cretaceous) of Shabarakh Usu in the Gobi Desert, Mongolia. This genus is known by several specimens which have comparatively large skulls that are wide behind but narrow rapidly in front. The premaxilla is furnished with two long and cylindrical teeth, while the other teeth succeed one another in closely arranged vertical series of not more than two teeth. There are thirteen to fifteen functional teeth in each half of the jaws. The orbits are relatively larger than those of the later ceratopsians, and there are deep preorbital foramina. The fore limb is shorter and more feeble than the hind limb, and in this as in many other of the skeletal features, *Protoceratops* bears evidence of its bipedal ancestry, and has many resemblances to that other rather primitive, but bipedal, Mongolian ornithopod, *Psittacosaurus*.

The skull of *Protoceratops* is the simplest form known among the Ceratopsia. There are no horns on the face, and the frill is merely a bony scaffolding at the back of the skull for the attachment of the powerful neck and jaw muscles. Already, however, this frill is perfectly formed, but has two large fenestrae of transversely oval shape (Fig. 60). The purpose of this frill was largely for muscular attachment and its protective function, for it spread backwards over the important nerve and blood systems of the neck, was merely secondary. In the primitive forms, such as *Protoceratops*, the neck vertebrae were not fused together (the first three being only partly joined), but in the later and more heavily skulled kinds the first few cervicals were fused to form a stronger support. The margins of the frill, or collar as it is often called, gave attachment to numerous muscles so that it not only helped the opening of the jaws, but also the

256

raising and lowering of the head. The mechanisms of the jaws have been very fully discussed by J. Ostrom (1964 and 1966).

P. andrewsi Granger and Gregory, the type and only species, is known by a large number of specimens of very different age, from the newly hatched stage to that of the adult. The largest skull so far mentioned (Gregory and Mook, 1925) has a frill 20 inches wide, and the skull is about the same length. Some skulls are relatively longer than others, and this may be a sexual difference, but it may be that two species are represented in the collection. The length of the complete adult dinosaurs is about 5 to 6 feet. Excellent specimens are exhibited in the Dinosaur Hall of the British Museum (Natural History).

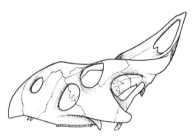

FIG. 60. *Protoceratops andrewsi.* Left side of skull. Approx. ¼ nat. size.

In connexion with its probable habits it is interesting to note that the neural spines of the tail are long, whereas those of the later ceratopsians are short, and this, with the characters of the feet, has suggested that it may have been partly aquatic. It certainly was also terrestrial and did lay eggs, for this is the dinosaur which laid the eggs that aroused such interest in the press and in scientific circles generally in the mid-twenties.

The eggs were found in close association with both adult and very young remains, and are undoubtedly those of *Proto-ceratops*, but remains of other dinosaurs have also been found with them and are probably the relics of those that came to steal them or suck their contents, though to give them the benefit of the doubt (to which they are entitled), they may just have been passing by.

The eggs themselves are about 6 inches long and are rather elongated ellipsoids. Apparently quite a large number were

laid in a clutch, and they were laid in a sort of spiral arrangement (Plate VI), the slightly thinner end of the egg being towards
the inside of the ring. Professor Osborn told the writer that it
appeared that the dinosaur when laying them walked round in
an ever-decreasing circle; which, as Pepys would have said, is
very strange! The structure of the eggs was fully investigated
by Dr van Straelen (1925, 1928), and it is sufficient here to say
that the nature of the shell is quite unlike that of all modern
reptiles, but the prismatic layer, at least, is closely similar to
that of the eggs of modern birds.

Protoceratops, as we have said, is the most primitive Ceratopsian known, and forms the basis of the artificial lineage
which we shall now proceed to detail. It is important to mention
at this point that the structure of the frill in *Protoceratops* affords
very strong evidence that the central part of this frill is a
parietal, not a dermosupraoccipital, element.

Now, while this Mongolian dinosaur differs in many respects
from the late New World forms, there is one American genus,
Leptoceratops, of Brown (1914), that shares many features with
it. This dinosaur, of which at least six have been found in the
Upper Edmonton Formation (Upper Cretaceous) of the Red
Deer River, Alberta, seems to be a little-modified survivor of the
ancestral group. Its skull is similar in general characters to that
of *Protoceratops*, but three of the cervical vertebrae are fused
together, and the feet are somewhat different. The neural spines
on the tail are also rather long so that it may also have been
partly aquatic. Both these genera are very properly placed in
the family called the Protoceratopsidae, with two less-well-
known forms, *Montanoceratops* (from Montana) and *Micro-
ceratops* from Asia. All the other horned and frilled dinosaurs
are placed in the family Ceratopsidae, and all are of Upper
Cretaceous age and from North America.

There is a good deal of variation in body-size, in the length
and direction of the nasal and orbital spines, and in the nature
of the frill openings of these Ceratopsidae, so that there have
been frequent attempts to form some classification that would
show the relationship of the different genera.

It would seem that the Ceratopsia can be grouped in three
main series. The first series (*Protoceratops* to *Torosaurus*) has

258

Protoceratops for its basis, and proceeds to *Chasmosaurus*, *Anchiceratops, Pentaceratops* to the last of this line, *Torosaurus*. From this line there may have come the second series (*Brachyceratops* to *Monoclonius* to *Triceratops*;), while the third series is based on some ancestor of *Leptoceratops*, bypassing *Styracosaurus* which is out on a Ceratopsian limb. In the first series *Chasmosaurus* Lambe, the Old Man Series representative has all three horns short and stout, both the nose and the orbital curving backwards. The fontanelles in the crest are large and somewhat triangular, and the marginal bones have secondary dermal bones upon them. *Chasmosaurus belli* Lambe comes from what used to be called the Belly River Formation of Alberta. In this species the longitudinal diameter of the fontanelles exceeds the lateral (Fig. 61). There are excellent

FIG. 61. *Chasmosaurus.* Right side of skull. Approx. $\frac{1}{30}$ nat. size.

mounted skeletons of this genus in the National Museum of Canada, Ottawa. The Edmonton formation (and Fruitland–Kirtland) has three considerably sized representatives with their own contrasting series. *Anchiceratops*, from the Edmonton Formation of Alberta, shows a tendency towards the closing of the frill openings (or fontanelles as they are often called). As we shall see, the later forms all show a secondary tendency towards the reduction of these openings. This genus has a long and low skull with the horns directed forwards and the contemporary genera, *Pentaceratops* and *Arrhinoceratops*, show increase in height of skull, increase in length and forward direction of horns, and decreasing length of face and size of fontanelles in the frill.

Pentaceratops Osborn with a horn on the nose, one above each orbit and two jugal horns, comes from the Kirtland shales of New Mexico, USA, and *Arrhinoceratops* Parks, with two large horn cores and a great frill, comes from the Edmonton of Alberta. The Royal Ontario Museum has excellent material of this genus.

259

'The logical outcome of this line of development', to use the words of Gregory and Mook, is *Torosaurus* from the succeeding Lance Formation. This genus has a short nasal horn, broad at its base but sharp at the apex, and directed forwards and upwards. The orbital horns are very large, laterally compressed and directed well forwards and outwards. The neck-frill was very large and had circular fontanelles, but no dermal bones on the borders. The skull of *T. gladius* Marsh was eight or more feet long, and perhaps this is the largest Ceratopsian with an overall length of 30 feet but the post-cranial skeleton is not adequately known. The second evolutionary line, that from *Protoceratops* to *Triceratops*, includes *Brachyceratops* and *Monoclonius* in its Old Man–Judith River–Two Medicine stratigraphical series.

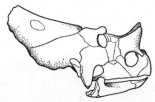

FIG. 62. *Brachyceratops*. Right side of skull. Approx. $\frac{1}{12}$ nat. size.

Brachyceratops is a primitive member of the Ceratopsidae and all its horns are small. *B. montanus* Gilmore had a skull a little over 18 inches long and the length of the whole animal was no more than 5 feet (Fig. 62). The type specimen came from the Two Medicine Formation, Montana.

It may be that *Monoclonius* is a direct descendant of that primitive genus, for it has a prominent and straight horn on the nose, but the horn over each eye is merely incipient. The openings on the occipital crest or frill are long, and are each overhung by a bony process from the hinder margin, while there are dermal bones arranged along the hinder and lateral borders of the frill. A species, *Monoclonius nasicornis* B. Brown, is known by a complete skeleton about 17 feet long. The skin was ornamented with polygonal plates. Remains of *Monoclonius* have been found in the Two Medicine Formation, Montana, and the Old Man Formation, Alberta.

The last member of this series is the famous and historical

Triceratops (see Plate 8). In it the skull is very large and more elongated but less deep while the orbital horns point forwards and outwards, and are sometimes nearly 3 feet long. The nasal horn persisted, but was small, and pointed upwards and forwards; but the long and wide neck-frill was completely bony and had no openings. On the margin of the frill is a row of small, rather limpet-shaped dermal bones. *T. prorsus* Marsh from Wyoming had a skull 6 feet long. This form is familiar from the many actual specimens and casts of the whole animal

Fig. 63. *Monoclonius nasicornus*. Left side of skull. Approx. $\frac{1}{30}$ nat. size.

Fig. 64. *Triceratops*. Right side of skull. Approx. $\frac{1}{40}$ nat. size.

in the museums of America and Europe. There is a mounted skeleton in the National Museum, Washington, and in the American Museum of Natural History, New York, while a complete skull, and a plaster cast of a whole specimen, are in the Dinosaur Gallery of the British Museum (Natural History).

The skull, as has been said, is large, and the bony frill is marked by the many vascular channels that once ran into its covering of skin. It must be remembered that the horns are not really horns, but horn-cores covered during life with a horny

261

covering which no doubt considerably increased their length and size. The neck-frill (and the fontanelles also where they occurred) were buried, no doubt, in a thick epidermis.

It is not difficult to visualize the living appearance of this great animal, for the body must have been curiously like that of a rhinoceros, though in bulk it more closely matched that of an elephant. Skeletons are known which show that it must have been as much as 25 feet long, and have weighed perhaps 8 or 9 tons. The head was carried low and was no doubt sufficiently mobile for the defensive use of the horns. When attacked *Triceratops* had only to manœuvre the body so that the head faced the enemy, and with head lowered and horns presented, awaited the attacker, which was in danger of being impaled. It must have been a formidable animal in attack when, as in appearance and perhaps in habits, it may well have been comparable to the black rhinoceros of Africa.

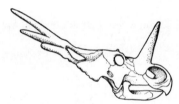

FIG. 65. *Styracosaurus*. Right side of skull. Approx. $\frac{1}{10}$ nat. size.

With its shearing horny beak and teeth well suited to a browsing habit, it would find ample suitable food in the everglades through which it roamed. The vegetation was nearly all of modern type, and in these rapidly modernizing scenes were the last of the horned dinosaurs, the great *Triceratops* and *Torosaurus*, and their bipedal relations, the duck-billed hadrosaurs.

What strange fellows they must have been in those fast-closing stages of the Cretaceous. All with curiously modified skulls, all grotesque, the last products of an old and mighty race upon whom, for ever, the curtain of the Cretaceous was so soon to ring down. Before this end, however, the Ceratopsia had produced *Styracosaurus*, which we have mentioned, in which the nasal horn is very large and straight and the orbital

262

horns are not developed. The frill has large fontanelles and on the margin, long spikes, three on each side, that project backwards and outwards. The type species is *S. albertensis* Lambe from the Old Man Formation of the Red Deer River, Alberta. In the Edmonton Formation is *Leptoceratops*, perhaps a direct descendant of *Protoceratops*. Here there are no horns, and a small frill. It is, as we have said, already, included in the Protoceratopsidae. It is North American, being known by skulls from Alberta and Montana and the postcranial skeleton is known too.

An aberrant and remarkable form, whose place in the stratigraphical table is about all that can be given, is *Pachyrhinosaurus* ('thick-nose reptile'). Four skulls of this are known and they are hornless but, perhaps in their place, a thickness of nasal and prefrontal bone up to 10 inches is developed. The frill of this small dinosaur is a rounded scuttle-like projection and the purpose of the arrangement of mass and hornlessness, back and front, is unknown, though perhaps it was a battering ram, and the horns of ceratopsians were used for felling, or pushing down little trees, and not entirely for the head-to-head battles that have been envisaged.

In the Old Man Formation of Alberta there were seventy-seven ceratopsians—24 per cent of the fauna—a proportion exceeded only by the hadrosaurs. In the Edmonton there were together only about 15 per cent of the fauna, and much overshadowed by hadrosaurs. In the Upper Edmonton they accounted for two-thirds of the dinosaur population and, finally in the Lance and Frenchman formations, they made their last stand—80 per cent of the population, dominating in numbers the few remaining hadrosaurs (*Anatosaurus*) and in size the coelurosauria and the hypsilophodonts.

The last dinosaurs were *Triceratops*, nobly built and well armed, but as James Shirley wrote more than 300 years ago:

> The glories of our blood and state
> are shadows, not substantial things;
> There is no armour against fate:
> Death lays his icy hand on kings.

CHAPTER XII

Dinosaurs and Disease

There are many who regard disease as an inevitable result of civilization and of habit upon the life of Man. But for Man's activities, they believe, the world would be care-free and without the ills that now beset us; in fact, to them, 'every prospect pleases and only Man is vile'. What we call civilization has, of course, brought limitations as well as blessings in its train, and the increase of Man's intelligence and means of perception has naturally greatly advanced our knowledge of the ills that 'the flesh is heir to'. Thus the number of recognized diseases has constantly increased, but that need not necessarily mean that disease itself is increasing. There may be cycles of incidence and phases of infection. However, there is ample proof that Man and disease did not originate together.

Readers of the previous pages will realize that our knowledge of many forms of life is sufficiently complete that a difference in structure of a particular organ or bone at once attracts attention, and examination may show the nature of the change and may even reveal its cause, whether due to pathological conditions during life or sustained after death. The histological examination of fossil remains has already accomplished much, and the structure of the bones of many groups of fossil reptiles is known as intimately as that of recent forms with which it often shows close correspondence.

Such examination by the unaided eye and by the microscope clearly and undoubtedly shows that many fossil remains, including some from dinosaurs, bear the traces of what can only be regarded as disease. The evidence is sometimes direct, sometimes circumstantial, but during the last century many students, palaeontologists, anatomists, and pathologists, have contributed observations, so that already a considerable literature has accumulated. The histological knowledge thus obtained has been used for other purposes than the study of pathology, for some workers, such as Baron Nopcsa and Dr Adolf Seitz, have brought their studies to such fine detail, and tabulated their results so well, that it is claimed that a fragment of bone can be identified generically by comparing a microsection of it with an identified series, particularly if the same bone (rib, limb bone, etc.) is examined.

The survey of this science or art of Palaeopathology, as it is called, made by Roy L. Moodie (q.v. 1923) is still the most comprehensive for our purpose and the imposing evidence he submits is, for the greater part, convincing. It is shown that disease is a phenomenon of great antiquity, and that forms of parasitism, commensalism and bacterial action are probably almost as old as life itself, although not all of these are in the strict sense forms of disease and the first bacteria may not have been infective. The evidences of disease in the dinosaurs are given by the conditions of the bones and by the appearance of the skeleton as a whole. Naturally, nothing can be deduced directly concerning epidemics or conditions which affect the blood, lymph, muscles, or internal organs and only where the disease affected the surface or structure of the bony internal skeleton, or the plates of bony body-armour, can the palaeopathologist find the signs that interest him.

Of the cases recorded many are directly attributable to disease in the strict sense, and others are the result of accident where the fractures and wounds were infected or where the animal made sufficient recovery to go on living.

It will be convenient here to discuss, in the following order, those cases which show simple uninfected fractures, those which have become subsequently infected, bones with traces of actual disease, and skeletons with a general condition indicative of death under spastic distress. Although the number of cases on record is considerable it is only just to point out that it forms a very small percentage of the actual number of dinosaur remains known.

The rarity of fractured bones is largely due to the structure

265

of the bones themselves. Dinosaur bones, particularly limb bones, are of unusual weight and strength, as they are generally of much more solid construction than those of the mammals. In the fossil state this weight is great, and a typical, large limb bone, 5 or 6 feet long, can weigh 500 pounds or more. Few fossil skeletons are discovered in which the bones are unbroken, but in most, if not all, of the other cases the fractures are post-mortem. Amongst the dinosaurs, uninfected fractures which have taken place during life, as is shown by their subsequent healing, are mainly known from the ribs. This is only as might be expected to result from the fall of heavy and cumbrous bodies or from the attacks of other animals. The latter cause is well exemplified by *Triceratops*, in specimens of which fractures of the horns, neck-frill, and jaws have been reported; in fact, just in those places that would be affected by the offensive or defensive functions which we have supposed them to have. On the other hand, the best-known case of fractured ribs occurs in one of the large, and more or less defenceless, sauropods, *Apatosaurus*, and in this case the fractures healed imperfectly and with the formation of a considerable amount of callus, or new bone growth. A left ischium of *Iguanodon*, which was on exhibition in the Palaeontological Department of the British Museum, clearly shows in the middle of the shaft a thickening due to fracture and callus. The line of fracture remains a plane of weakness, for when the specimen was developed the bone broke readily in the same place. The proximal part of this bone is somewhat misshapen, and it is possible that the whole bone suffered injury during a fight at the breeding season.

Hypertrophy following on fracture has been seen in the scapula and coracoid of *Antrodemus* and is figured by Moodie (1923b, pl. XXIII).

Examination of these fractured bones by x-ray gives no interesting or informative results.

Several cases are known where the fracture was followed by acute bacterial infection, and the most interesting of these has been fully described by Moodie. In this case, an isolated left humerus of a hadrosaur, *Hypacrosaurus*, now preserved in the American Museum of Natural History, New York, had been obliquely fractured and suppurative periostitis, or infective inflammation of the bone covering, supervened, with the result that the periosteum was raised up and a bridge of bone was formed extending over practically the whole anterior surface of the humerus, and covering a great subperiosteal abscess. This evidently contained several litres of pus, and the sore must have discharged throughout the remainder of the life of the animal, although death did not apparently follow very quickly on the injury or infection.

Another infected condition of the bones observed in some of the dinosaurs is that known as osteomyelitis. So far, this diagnosis has been limited to some lesions observed in the caudal vertebrae of *Apatosaurus*, one of the large sauropods. This form of necrosis is well known today and results from the activity of certain bacteria, principally Staphylococci, which have spread from an infecting focus in the mouth or throat or from a wound. It is interesting to note that at the present time long bones are more liable to this disease than short ones, and that it is essentially a disease of young people (the epiphyses of whose bones are not yet united) and is much more common in boys than in girls. This cannot be taken to mean that the dinosaurs in question were either young or males, but the comparison of pathological conditions is interesting. The long and comparatively defenceless tails of the sauropod dinosaurs would be particularly liable to attack or accident, and the wounds received would be difficult to heal and very susceptible to infection. The wonder is not that osteomyelitis is known in these ancient forms of life, but that it should be so rarely seen.

Numerous remains have been found bearing traces of necrotic sinuses. The necrosis was no doubt generally the result of osteitis and osteomyelitis. Simple sinuses have been observed on the dermal plates of *Stegosaurus*, and an excellent case is shown on a skeleton of *Camptosaurus* in the United States National Museum, Washington, where a large necrotic sinus occurs on the right ilium, which is, in addition, somewhat malformed. Abel has suggested that the specimen was a female and that the injury was sustained in the breeding season. The suggestion is interesting but, like that earlier suggested for an *Iguanodon* bone, is purely speculative.

Evidence of hypertrophy or hyperplasia is by no means

267

uncommon. Bony outgrowths of an unusual nature are sometimes found, some of which must have caused great distress and
others must have been a continuing nuisance to the creature.
These outgrowths are known as hyperostoses.

Evidences of tumours are, as might be expected, very rare.
The most studied structure of this nature occurs on a specimen
referred to *Apatosaurus* and affects two caudal vertebrae, most
of the surface of which is involved. The actual determination of
the cause is very difficult, but the American pathologists who
have examined the bones believe that the lesion resulted from a
haemangioma, or tumour affecting blood vessels. It seems more
probable, however, that it is a spongy exostosis, or homologous
osteoma as it is called.

A dinosaur bone from the uppermost Cretaceous of Transylvania, and therefore some 70 million years old, shows a
periosteal lesion of some interest. The bone went to the British
Museum (Natural History) with the Nopcsa Collection in 1924
and was diagnosed in a London Hospital as a periosteal sarcoma. It was figured by the writer in 1934 and was for a time
part of a small exhibition of dinosaur diseases in the Palaeontological Department. The sections show (R. 5505 and R. 5506) a
marginal area with many cavities among radially orientated
laminae or osteophytes. The sections were re-examined in much
detail in 1966 by Dr J. G. Campbell who rejected the idea of a
sarcoma and suggested that the disease involved is an avian
one, osteopetrosis. This virus disease is of RNA type and
different in origin and location on the bone from the human
form (Albers-Schönberg disease)

The association of a disease of warm-blooded birds with a
cold-blooded dinosaur is of interest, for although the possession
of a common ancestor is probably true for these groups it was a
long way away even in the Upper Cretaceous.

Other tumours or alleged tumours are the instances of
multiple myeloma (malignant tumour of bone marrow) that
seem to have occurred in the skulls of Ceratopsia. Hatcher,
Marsh and Lull recorded the bony openings in their classic
United States Geological Survey Memoir, *The Ceratopsia*, of
1907, and Lull made further observations in his own memoir,
A Revision of the Ceratopsia, of 1933. In both memoirs attention

is drawn to the occurrence of closely situated openings which are of sufficient frequency to have caused remark. They are alleged to be pathological and the fenestrae of myeloma tumours. It is remarkable that they all appear to occur on squamosal bones.

The lesions of which we have the most complete historical knowledge are those resulting from the various kinds of arthritis, although, of course, we only know those forms which have attacked the articular cartilages and bones, that is to say the forms of osteo-arthritis. The history of this disease when it attacks the vertebrae, and is then known as spondylitis deformans, is particularly well authenticated and we have specimens illustrating it in Mesozoic reptiles, Tertiary mammals, Palaeolithic, Egyptian, and modern man. When the spine is affected there is often such a widespread growth of new bone that the articular surfaces, and even the general outlines, of the vertebrae are obscured and the bones fused together. The milder form, in which the vertebrae of the tail are not fused but merely roughened and worn, is well shown in the large exhibited portion of *Cetiosaurus leedsi*, a sauropod dinosaur from the Oxford Clay of Peterborough, which is in the Dinosaur Hall of the British Museum (Natural History).

In the same hall is the well-known plaster cast of *Diplodocus carnegii* on which are faithfully reproduced two caudal vertebrae united as a result of spondylitis deformans. Examination of the original specimen, preserved in The Carnegie Museum, Pittsburgh, USA, has shown that the articular surfaces are unaffected and are merely hidden by the unusual lateral 'lipping' of secondary bone (osteophytes) which connects the two vertebrae. Formerly it was suggested that the fusion had been brought about by the trailing of the heavy tail on the ground, but there now seems no doubt that arthritis is the real cause. Coalescent vertebrae are not uncommon among the great sauropodous dinosaurs as a result of old age, but even the expert palaeontologist or pathologist cannot easily distinguish the vertebral conditions alleged to be caused by senility, osteo-arthritis, or osteomyelitis. So far no undoubted case of rheumatoid arthritis, in which the articular surfaces are destroyed, has been reported in dinosaurs.

269

The description of the pathology of dinosaurs is, however, not exhausted by accounts of the external features of the bones. As has been pointed out in previous pages, so well preserved are the minute structures of the bones of many vertebrate fossils that the hope has continually been raised that careful and wide histological investigation of sections of bones would reveal the presence of bacteria or blood-corpuscles: and, indeed, both of these kinds of bodies have been described. Of the two, the presence of bacteria has been the more convincingly established, but the chances are that they are the remains of bacteria of decay rather than the infective bacteria of disease from which the animal suffered in life, though the possibility of contamination must be borne in mind.

The so-called traces of blood-corpuscles are much more to be doubted. It is true that the appearance of some of the minute bodies found is strongly similar to that of corpuscles and they are even of reddish colour. But it is doubtful if the little crystals are either haemosiderin or haematoidin which are the final products of the breaking up of blood-corpuscles, and they are more probably small crystals of a natural iron product or iron-stained osteoclasts (or bone-absorbing cells) which have been thus fossilized and preserved. These structures were described as blood-corpuscles by Adolf Seitz (1907), who found them in bones of *Iguanodon bernissartensis*, but an important clue to their real nature was given by Moodie, who, when examining sections of a footbone of *Apatosaurus*, found them in close proximity to Howship's lacunae. These lacunae are semicircular 'bays' in the walls of the little canals in bone which is undergoing absorption, and are named after John Howship, the early nineteenth-century English anatomist who discovered them. It is only natural that they should be in close association with the absorptive cells, or osteoclasts; thus Moodie's discovery makes it almost certain that at least some of the so-called blood-corpuscles are iron-stained osteoclasts. This does not, of course, lessen the interest of such histological investigation, but it must be confessed that, at the moment, there is no established instance of the preservation of blood-corpuscles or blood-stains in the dinosaurs, or, for that matter, in any of the other Mesozoic reptiles.

270

Perhaps the least convincing field of palaeopathology is that based on the attitude of animals in death, that is, the circumstantial evidence of accident or disease. It is well known by all students of medicine and pathology that certain substances or diseases produce toxins which act upon the central nervous system and lead to spastic distress and spasmodic contraction of muscles and paralysis of the body. The most widely familiar cases of this nature are those resulting from strychnine poisoning and tetanus or lockjaw. In both these disorders during the severe spasms the spine and limbs are strongly recurved so that a patient rests on the back of his head and on his heels, with the length of the body between strongly arched. Remains of many fossil reptiles and mammals have been discovered in which the appearance strongly suggests that death occurred during a similar type of spasm. The head may be thrown back, the vertebral column arched, and the limbs and phalanges extended and directed backwards. Such a condition is known as opisthotonos and, if the opisthotonic attitude is interpreted correctly, the animals probably died from tetanus or from some form of poisoning or disturbance of the central nervous system. Only two dinosaurs are known preserved in this condition, and if it is questionable how far one can generalize on such limited evidence, there are available records of many similarly preserved fossil vertebrates. One of the cases, that of the small carnivorous dinosaur *Compsognathus longipes*, a cast of which is in the Fossil Reptile Gallery of the British Museum (Natural History) in London, certainly exhibits an opisthotonic attitude, but the arrangement of body, skull, and limbs is not wholly inconsistent with post-mortem movement of these elements. On the law of probability one must choose the latter explanation and reject a diagnosis of toxic poisoning. Moodie, however, has described and figured (1923b, pl. LXVII) a more probable case, that of another little theropodous dinosaur *Ornithomimus* (*Struthiomimus*) *altus*, from the Old Man Formation (Upper Cretaceous) of Alberta, Canada, which certainly suggests opisthotonos very strongly. But it can only remain a suggestion as there is no positive test. There is no evidence that the bacilli (*Clostridium tetani*) which produce tetanus existed in those far-off times, though other bacilli are known in the Palaeozoic and the

Mesozoic, nor have we proof that *Strychnos nux-vomica*, the source of strychnine, spread its seeds on the land in the Cretaceous. The first fossil example of *Strychnos* comes from the Eocene of the United States.

These, then, are the evidences we possess of disease among the dinosaurs, and it is worthy of note that, although we know many fossils, the incidence of disease, at least upon the bones, is slight. Affections or infections of the soft parts, the occurrence of epidemics, or other causes of speedy death, might leave no trace upon the hard skeleton, but at least palaeopathology produces no evidence of widespread disease or large scale infections of any kind, and gives no clue to the extinction of the dinosaurs. The question of pituitary hyperfunction has not been included here for its manifestations are mentioned elsewhere in the text and its influence on extinction is referred to later. But extinction is a larger problem to which we must now direct our attention.

CHAPTER XIII

The Extinction of the Dinosaurs

Fate cropped him short, for be it understood
He would have lived much longer, if he could.
W. B. RHODES *Bombastes furioso*

The unexpected or unusual death of a human being is generally
followed by an impartial inquiry or inquest, and the demise of a
whole section of the population would certainly be the subject
of a searching and prolonged investigation. It is, therefore, only
to be expected that we should spend a little time considering the
cause or causes that led to the disappearance of the whole group
of creatures that we have been studying. There are no dinosaurs
alive today, and none has existed since the close of the Cretaceous, despite the rumours that occasionally are found in popular
fiction. The great race, entrenched on earth for so many million
years, widespread over the continents, and consisting of forms
which were certainly majestic for their time, silently passed
away, leaving the reptilian field to a few relatively unimportant
orders, but having no descendants of its own. Of course, during
the age of the dinosaurs some forms were slowly becoming
extinct. Many of the sauropods left the field early, as we have
seen, and other minor groups followed at various times, but the
great and glorious company of dinosaurs was not appreciably
weakened by their loss, for they were replaced by other dinosaurs. Then, almost suddenly, towards the end of the Cretaceous, and for no obvious cause, the candle flame of their life was
extinguished; the wind of some unknown circumstance had
blown over it and it was gone. So closed one of the most memor-
able chapters in the history of life on the earth.

Among animals and plants many other groups, orders, races,
call them what you will, have similarly disappeared, and the
problem of extinction is not primarily a problem of the dino-

saurs. Whole orders of invertebrate animals, many kinds of fishes, reptiles, and mammals have had their day and silently passed from the record of living things, without leaving descendants. Thus the general question of extinction has exercised many minds and has provoked a considerable discussion, the main products of which are recorded in the bibliography at the end of this book. The general suggestions and causes among the vertebrates are closely similar, so that the consideration of the problem as it affects the dinosaurs takes notice of the circumstances affecting, at least, the other land-living groups of vertebrates and also of the early Tertiary mammals.

The main problem before us, then, is why, towards the close of the Cretaceous period, there were numerous forms of dinosaurs alive and apparently comfortably settled in their respective habits and environments, yet, when the Tertiary era dawned, none was left and the mammals were assuming the dominant position among the land-living forms. Was the cause some world-wide cataclysm of a physical nature, or some widespread epidemic whose ravages have left no trace upon the bones? It is true, as has been hinted, that a few reports have been made that dinosaurs lingered on into the Eocene, but all of these have so far been found to be misidentifications of bones or of strata. So the problem remains unmodified, and we must now attempt some solution.

The cataclysmic hypothesis can receive no support. We have shown that dinosaurs were world-wide in distribution, and, of course, they did not live alone. Many other kinds of creatures lived on land, in the air, and in the sea whose history would have been profoundly affected by any great catastrophic change in environmental or other conditions. So far, the largest number of dinosaurs which were thought to have died through one cause at one particular time are the thirty or so specimens of *Iguanodon* which were carried into a ravine, and subsequently entombed, at Bernissart in Belgium (see p. 208). Examination of the strata in which many of the skeletons lie, in the Institut royal des Sciences naturelles in Brussels, shows that considerable deposition, and therefore time, passed between the burial of separate skeletons. The accidents were therefore several and separate rather than a single accident to a herd. There is no

274

evidence for a cataclysmic theory for the extinction of the whole group of dinosaurs.

What, then, are the causes which may generally be supposed to lead to the suppression of one particular set of animals, and yet not greatly change the characters of the remaining population? They must be of two kinds—firstly, internal, that is within the physiological or anatomical make-up of the animals themselves, or secondly, external, that is, in the biological, geographical, or geological environment which the animals inhabit; or, it may be, a combination of both. The internal causes may be due to the characters of the animal's heredity; to acquired or impressed characters affecting the life and habits of the creatures themselves. To simplify this statement we may assume that every animal has at the time of its birth certain inherent, that is, genetic, characters governing principally the trend of its evolution, its reproduction, and its conformity to type on main lines. These evolutionary characters may from time to time become slightly modified, for the history of a race of animals is like the life of a man; it has its youth, its period of adaptability, its settled and, we may suppose, comfortable middle-age and, lastly, its period of senility. The members of the race at any particular time have much the same fundamental traits: not only the same anatomical structure, but similar trends or tendencies in the germ-cells; the same plasticity of response to external circumstance. Where external factors are quiescent, and the members of a race are endowed with much the same evolutionary characters, the end-products will be almost similar; but if there is slight divergence of evolutionary trend the end-products will be somewhat divergent, but probably all equally adapted for life in the same habitats. Where, however, there are differences both in evolutionary characters and in environmental conditions the successive individuals will become divergent—even widely so—and any stock more plastic or adaptive than its neighbours, relations, and competitors, will tend to succeed at the expense of the less fortunate of these.

Now, in their long history, the dinosaurs became profoundly modified, so that, as we have seen, a great variety of forms became evolved, though we must remember that they started

275

not from a common source, but diphyletically. These various lines of evolution in the dinosaurs we have already seen. If we imagine a group or family of any sort of animals dwelling over long periods of time in favourable conditions, free from undue competition, with abundant food supply and well adapted to the prevailing climatic conditions, it is easy to see how con-servative it might become, and how easily adaptability might be lost. It is easy (though it is not an exact parallel) to apply this test to everyday life and the lives of men themselves. In animals such equable conditions frequently produce forms which become progressively larger, and one result of this is loss of adaptability to new conditions. Any geographical change would seriously affect the race, as will readily be seen. But change would occur in the habits and nature of the animals themselves, for increase of size is often correlated with longer life, longer adolescence, later sexual maturity, and, as a result, a loss of fecundity. It tends also, as might be expected, towards specialization and towards the development of accessory skeletal structure, as if the hormones became restive and did anything rather than nothing at all. Thus there is commonly to be observed in old and what seem to be effete races a tendency to develop spines-cence, as is well exemplified by some of the armoured dinosaurs and the bizarre forms of large, early Tertiary mammals. Baron Nopcsa once said to the writer, when discussing hormones and the growth of accessory structures on the skulls of Tertiary mammals, that 'when there are many passengers some are bound to get out at the wrong station'. In these reptiles and mammals the proportion that did so was apparently high.

In a long-lived race there is also the fact that gradually the more effete and the less adaptive forms die off, leaving the more safely ensconced successful forms. This will appear axiomatic, but its important result is that by the elimination of the less adaptive the adaptability of the remainder is decreased, and the ultimate effect is somewhat similar to that of interbreeding. Numerous examples of this could be cited. Among the dino-saurs we have ample evidence of the extraordinary increase in size, and of the development, even over-development, of spinescent and otherwise grotesque forms. It is noteworthy that the earliest main group of the dinosaurs to become extinct were the

276

sauropods, and the last forms, those of the Upper Cretaceous, were the heavily armoured, slow-moving, and cumbrous ceratopsians and the grotesque hadrosaurs. As examples of mammals which suffered from increase of bony structure or excessive growth of parts may be cited the titanotheres; and, more recently the giant Irish deer, in which the increase in the size of the antlers made them unsuited for their established habits and environment; and the elephants, the primitive members of which were apparently doomed because of the increase of the length of the limbs which brought the skull, and consequently the mouth, out of reach of the ground. The present elephants are those whose ancestors overcame the latter handcap by the lengthening of the teeth and jaws with the ultimate formation of tusks and a trunk.

No such fortune attended the latest dinosaurs, and they continued with increase of size, armour, or spinescence, or other over-elaboration of skeletal structure, which has been interpreted as a condition of racial old age, which made them easy victims of any change of climate or alteration of general topography, well adapted though they were for life in their existing habitat. Amongst senile forms toothlessness is common, not only individual toothlessness, but a tendency for whole families to become thus handicapped. This tendency has been observed and described by Sir A. Smith Woodward in a theropod dinosaur, *Genyodectes*, from the Upper Cretaceous of Patagonia, while we have described the toothless *Ornithomimus* and *Oviraptor*. Yet, senile or decadent as these forms are alleged to have been, there is little indication that they could not have carried on for a considerably longer period, and there seems no doubt that although this so-called racial senility was a predisposing factor towards extinction, it was not in itself sufficient cause.

Endocrine deficiency and disease, especially of the pituitary gland, have also been cited as possible factors, since, among other things, they may cause loss of fertility, but for this we have no evidence, nor do these seem likely to have been so general (1933a). Such hormonal imbalance may have been of great physiological disadvantage. There is one remaining internal factor which must be considered and the proper place for its

277

treatment is in connexion with some of the external circumstances. It is the question of brain. Now, the qualitative estimation of brain is based not only on the size, weight, and structure of the brain itself, but on its comparative size to that of the body it controls. The dinosaurian brain, as we have already seen, was small and lowly organized, no larger than that of the common kitten and much less efficient; Professor Dollo held that the extinction of *Iguanodon* was due to the inadequacy of its brain.

In the Pleistocene period we know that the great climatic changes produced wholesale extinction, and that, from the welter of the doomed, Man escaped largely owing to his superior mental ability. In the Upper Cretaceous dinosaurs then, we have not only inadaptive feet, teeth, and bodies, but lowly-organized brains, and, as Lull remarked, they were 'finally indicted on the last count'. But not, be it noted, on it alone, but on account of its failure to rescue the animal from the consequences of changed external conditions. Thus we are brought face to face with the conditions outside the dinosaur's physiology and anatomy which might afford a clue to extinction. One such condition, which deserves more consideration than it has received, is Albert Schatz's ingenious suggestion of high oxygen pressure in the Cretaceous atmosphere and its resultant stress effect on large reptiles (Schatz, 1957).

The possible external causes are of two kinds, and both are environmental: they are the biological environment and the geographical environment.

The first of these includes all the plants and animals, friends or foes, of equal, lower, or higher zoological rank, that were present in the normal environment of the dinosaurs and whose presence might be passive, helpful, or deleterious to them. The suggestion has been made that the dinosaurs perished through rivalry and warfare amongst themselves, which is a perfectly plausible theory if the habitat were overpopulated and restricted so that competition was unduly severe. Colonies of dinosaurs, like those of other animals, no doubt were diminished in this manner, though there is no direct evidence for it, and their world-wide distribution proves it to be on no account a general cause, which is what we must seek. Other possible sources of competition were the contemporary reptiles, the birds, insects, parasites, or the early mammals, as yet small and apparently unimportant faunistically. The other reptiles had always been a source of some competition which must have been largely suppressed during the passage of time, nor are the birds likely to have been a serious menace. As for the mammals, although their remains are now known from many parts of the world, they do not seem to have been decisive competitors though they became decisive successors. It was formerly thought that the dinosaurian stock decreased and finally died out as the result of the little mammals sucking the eggs; but although many modern mammals and reptiles suck or devour eggs, there is no evidence that any race has been seriously reduced through this agency. When, as is indicated, the mammals appear to have been relatively few, and in some areas the eggs were many, this hypothesis would seem to be inadequate to explain, at least, a wholesale result, quite apart from the fact that, as we have said, some of the dinosaurs may have been ovo-viviparous. Of the competition of the insects or effects of parasites there is no evidence and probably they were unimportant save as the cause of disease. We have already considered this question of disease and have reached the conclusion that, so far as disease which leaves a trace upon the bones is concerned, there is no support for it as a prominent or even predisposing factor in extinction. From the consideration of other orders of animals and plants we find that disease has seldom, if ever, been the entire cause of their disappearance, and, on the contrary, there are many orders, known in the fossil state, which were extinct before there is evidence that any form of disease, as we know it, existed. Among the dinosaurs, as among the early Tertiary mammals, there is no proof that epidemics did not occur, because death from such causes would be comparatively speedy and leave no trace upon the fossilized remains. It is, however, unlikely that such epidemics would be world-wide or would leave untouched other kinds and groups of animals. They may have formed a local cause and a contribution towards extinction but not a world-wide agency. It is true that nowadays epidemics, such as those of influenza, have widespread effects, but these are due to the presence of highly mobile agents such as man. Among

279

the Oligocene deposits of Colorado there have been found evidences of the existence of *Glossina*, the tsetse fly and the carrier of the dread nagana or sleeping sickness, but we do not know if it carried the trypanosome in those far-off times. If it did it may have produced widespread disease and extinction among the cattle and horses of the plains, but we have no similar discovery to help us with the epidemiology of the Cretaceous.

Similarly, there is no direct evidence that the plant-life was inimical to the dinosaurs though E. Baldwin (1964) has drawn attention to the suggestion that diminution of the number of ferns (and thus the good effects of *Filix mas*) may have led to the death of vegetarian dinosaurs through constipation. During the Cretaceous, of course, as was said in an early chapter, there were gradual but massive changes in the flora, principally by the introduction of the deciduous trees and flowering plants and the decrease of the cycads, for so long the food of many dinosaurs. These changes were so slow, however, that the dinosaur population should have adapted, and apparently did adapt, itself quite successfully to the altering circumstances. The possibility of plant poisoning must not be overlooked, for, at the present day, certain seeds, berries, and leaves do occasionally poison animals, but again we have no evidence of the existence of poisonous plants in the Cretaceous, nor is anything known of their relative toxicity or of the tolerance of the contemporary fauna. To take examples from present-day experience, while man is sensitive to small quantities of belladonna, aconite, and strychnine, rabbits are largely insensitive to the first two substances, and horses and oxen show great tolerance to the last named. On the other hand, the frog is so acutely sensitive to strychnine that the physiological test of its tetanic convulsions is more reliable than the delicate chemical tests (1933b). It would thus appear that this field of research does not help to solve the vexed problem of extinction. The lack of certain chemical constituents in the plant food, it has been suggested, might affect the pituitary gland and thus lead to the curious bony over-development characteristic of the latest forms or it may have led to hormonal changes affecting reproduction. Very recent research has shown, for example, that clover has

280

unexpectedly deleterious effects upon sheep and similar effects may well have affected dinosaurs in the new vegetation.

As a mild corrective to the view that animal competition may be disastrous to a group of animals, it may be stated that there is abundant evidence from the condition in modern protective reserves and national parks that its absence may be responsible for excessive increase in numbers owing to unusually favourable conditions, with a consequent inadequacy of food supplies. In the dinosaurs we have seen that rapid increase would be unlikely on account of the later sexual maturity and loss of fecundity which increasing size brought in its train. On the other hand, increase in numbers would mean an increased demand on the vegetation, and local though not universal extinction of the animals and their plant-food might result.

The elimination of these considerations leaves one further field for exploration, that is, the geographical environment. This includes the factors of climate and physical environment. Any survey of the geological history of the world shows that climatic and structural geographical features have never been constant, and the main alterations in both during the Mesozoic era have been outlined in Chapter III. The climatic variations largely depend on the topographical changes, and both are usually slow in operation and effect, but any change of climate, whether it becomes more moist, or drier; warmer or colder, must have an effect on both animal and plant populations. At the present time the important reptilian areas are all tropical and it may be presumed that the dinosaurian centres were all moderately warm, thus a cooling of the general temperature would be adverse in its effect though the work of Colbert, Cowles and Bogart (1946) showed that alligators, acting as stand-ins for dinosaurs, could tolerate lower temperatures than had been expected. S. Rodbard (1949) discovered that cold-blooded animals have thermosensitive brain-centres that affect blood pressures and other functions. Any drying or moistening of the atmosphere would also react upon the vegetation and thus ultimately affect the animal population. These changes would not profoundly disturb the more resilient stocks, but the effete groups would not respond satisfactorily. When we remember how settled the late Cretaceous dinosaurs were, how cumbrous

281

mentally and physically, and how little adapted for change of their long-established habits and habitats, we must realize that climatic variation would definitely tend towards the elimination of the least responsive and might well predispose the whole to extinction. Any increase of temperature can embarrass reptiles of large size since they find it hard to find cover or shade while continued cold also affects them as they cannot hibernate or burrow and cold would affect the eggs and young.

Change in climatic conditions usually follows upon alteration of physical environment. The geological processes known as weathering and erosion tend towards the reduction of the continents to a nearly level surface, or peneplain. Frost, ice, snow, rain, and winds attack the mountains, the rivers thus formed drain and erode the lands, carrying the waste material, or detritus, towards the seas, and if these processes could be continued indefinitely all land surfaces would be reduced to base-level. Periodically, world-wide 'revolutions', or epochs of continental uplift, have occurred which arrest this process, and put back again the geological clock. Naturally these movements are slow, some are of small intensity, yet others are of great magnitude and extent and obviously profoundly affect the plant and animal life. What are the effects of all these processes upon the population? One series of minor results are earthquake, volcanic activity, and flood, all of which are powerful agents of destruction in limited, though occasionally large, areas. The objection against them as exterminating factors for the dinosaurs is that such catastrophic agencies are no respecters of persons or classes of animals. The young and old perish alike, and it is difficult to understand why the dinosaurs should have suffered so severely while so many other orders survived unchecked.

On the whole, diastrophism has not of itself been a cause of extinction, though it may well have accelerated the process. Clearly this is no satisfactory reply to our main query. But there are many other ways in which environmental changes work. Any difference in land- or sea-levels or distribution may result in the extension of land or the cutting off of portions of it forming protected areas, or isolated portions such as islands. The expansion of boundaries gives room for expansion of the animal

282

population and, often, for its improvement, while its restriction, on the other hand, has varied and interesting results. Thus, to take a well-known example, the isolation of the Australian Continent has preserved the marsupial fauna and favoured its development, whereas elsewhere the competition of later and higher forms led to its extinction. Again, in smaller islands, the protection of the existing stock was followed by what approximated to overcrowding with a consequent diminution in size of the individuals, producing, for example, the dwarf elephants, whose remains have been obtained from the Mediterranean islands, and the existing small Shetland ponies. Any profound alteration in purely geological conditions, with its inevitable climatic and physical geographical concomitants, would demand a general response on the part of the fauna. Food supplies would be affected, climate and habitats generally changed, and fresh competitors might be introduced, particularly in the shape of hitherto subordinate and adaptable orders, whose evolution might be increased by these new stimuli. An effete or ageing race would be precisely in the condition of aged human beings subjected to increased difficulties or abrupt changes in life; that is, they would be unable to meet the demands. They would be, in other words, in the condition of a mediæval man in armour in the quickened life of today.

Now the Cretaceous saw two important geological movements. The Cenomanian transgression, in the earlier part, produced a wide advance or invasion of the seas in Europe, Asia and North America. By flooding low-lying lands and deepening pools and swamps it must have hastened the departure of some, even many, dinosaurs.

Towards the end of the period, the contrary condition, the Laramide revolution with its uprising of land, was more important. For long there had existed a vast northward extension of the Gulf of Mexico that formed a great inland sea on whose low-lying banks the carnivorous, the armoured and the hadrosaur dinosaurs lived.

Their disappearance must have been hastened by the draining of swamps and the acceleration of rivers and by the gradual disappearance of the everglades. Yet this process was slow (and, as Loris Russell has pointed out, no stratigraphical break can be seen in Canada) and it is thus doubtful if any sudden or widespread destruction of forms would take place. Nonetheless it must have brought profound changes in its train, and this must have supplied the basic geological cause of extinction.

Not a great deal is known about the influence of this revolution throughout the world, partly because its effect was less noticeable away from the North American area, and partly because of purely geological difficulties in identifying and correlating the evidence in many places. In North America it was accompanied by widespread uplift-movement and volcanic activity principally on the Pacific border, but the eastern area was also affected. In the Northern Hemisphere, both east and west, it has left traces, but in the Southern Hemisphere its effects are much less clearly seen.

It is generally agreed, however, that considerable uplift-movements of the land, and a consequent diminution in the extent of the seas, followed, and there was very probably a decrease in the temperature though this was not so marked as that accompanying other great revolutions. Such cooling as there was, was apparently too slight to make any great impression on the plants, although, somewhat unexpectedly, glacial deposits have been found in Australia.

Now, uplifting of the continental areas, besides bringing a certain diminution of temperature, would cause a drainage of the low-lying marshy lands which we consider to have been the principal haunts of the dinosaurs. Thus the Laramide revolution introduced a series of changes producing gradual alteration of habitats and less favourable general climatic conditions. In addition, the fast-modernizing worlds, both animal and plant, were making new demands, and the old food supply was gradually but definitely failing. The ancient race, bowed under the weight of habit and unadaptability, could not meet the new demands; its vitality flickered, and was finally and irrevocably extinguished.

Quite recently new knowledge of variations in the earth's magnetic field and occasional reversals have led to the suggestion that an increase in cosmic-ray exposure might have proved

284

fatal to dinosaurs. Here again one wonders why the rays were so selective.

There was, therefore, no one particular cause (and perhaps it has been unrealistic to expect it), but rather a complex series of circumstances based on a fundamental geological change, complicated by racial old age (phylogeronty), lack of plasticity, both physical and mental, of the dinosaurs themselves, and with, maybe, the added factors of food deficiency, climatic variation, and possibly epidemic disease.

The career of the dinosaurs was far from brief, and far from a futile or vain attempt to snatch a permanent hold on the chain of life. Their passing was comparable with, and no less dramatic than, that of a mighty empire of world-wide extent. But that same passing was complete, and gave, no doubt, the all-important opportunity for development to the mammals, whose evolution has culminated in Man.

CHAPTER XIV

The Homes of the Dinosaurs

Shrine of the Mighty! can it be
That this is all remains of thee?
BYRON *The Giaour*

With the close of the last chapter we have finished with the living dinosaurs; as creatures of flesh and blood we shall know them no more, and our concern with them now must be not as we picture them to have been or to visualize their habitats, but to consider the evidences that remain, the bones, scutes, teeth and eggs, their collection, preservation, and exhibition. The whole tale, or vision, that is unfolded in these previous chapters rests upon the foundation of the collections in our museums. How were these preserved and found? Where can the collections be seen? These are the questions that may rise in the reader's mind.

In the introduction we have stressed the rarity of fossilization. Although we know many fossils the whole number is but a fraction of the population that lived, and it is rather by accident that the evidence is preserved for us. When an animal dies on land the chances are that a more or less rapid decay sets in destroying the skin and muscles where these are soft. Even the bony matter may not persist after the lapse of many years. If, however, by some means the bones become covered up and preserved, and the material enclosing them becomes consolidated, future excavation may rediscover them and they are then called 'fossils'.

In this connexion it is important to remember that where an animal is buried is not necessarily where it died, for various agencies may have disturbed the carcass. Similarly, the place of death and the living habitat are not necessarily alike either.

So far as dinosaurs are concerned none has been found in

286

anything like so complete a state of preservation as is the case of many mammoths frozen intact in the tundras of Siberia or in less complete condition in the frozen soil of Alaska. In the case of the bones they may be preserved by being covered up by wind-blown sand or by volcanic ash, and both these conditions are met with in the fossil vertebrates. Conditions are most favourable for fossilization when the animal dies in water or where its decaying body is washed away, for it is usually accompanied by an amount of sand and silt which will eventually cover it. The deposition of further material will be a gradual process and the animal's remains will thus be safely entombed, though it will be realized that the chances of subsequent discovery will be remote. Petrifaction or mineralization frequently occurs and this term may be defined as the gradual replacement of the original substance by some new material, silica, lime, or iron pyrites, for example, until the whole bone or tooth is changed, but still retains its original form and microscopic arrangement. If the original form is retained but the histological structure is altered or lost the fossil is said to be a pseudomorph. Very often, especially in sandstone or volcanic ash, the covering material has become more or less consolidated, but the organic matter has decayed so that the original of it is preserved only as an impression, and an idea of the creature can only be obtained by running plaster or artificial rubber or plastics into the natural mould and obtaining a cast of the original.

However the bones, scutes, teeth or eggs may have been protected the mere act of fossilization is no guarantee that they will remain preserved, for later geological processes may seriously affect them. The weight of subsequent deposits, often of great thickness, upon them may crush them, and folding and faulting may destroy them. If the deposit again becomes elevated erosion will once more commence, the bones may be exposed, weathered, scattered, and lost.

If they survive these trials it is only one chance in thousands that the area in which they lie concealed will be subjected to excavation of any sort, and again a very slight chance that they will be discovered. Thus there are many ifs in the making and collection of fossils. Far from it being surprising that so little is known about the past, a little reflection will show that it is truly

287

remarkable how the slow methods of scientific investigation have unravelled the long and tangled history and have produced so much of value.

In many parts of the world the remains of dinosaurs have been found; indeed some trace has been found in each of the continents with the exception of the Antarctic. Some areas have been prolific, and we may mention some of the more important of these.

The first dinosaur bones were found in Oxfordshire, in England, while many early specimens were discovered in the Wealden deposits of Sussex, and further localities of this age, especially in Dorset and the Isle of Wight, have produced abundant material. The reason is that the Wealden is the remains of a delta deposit of a great river that must have drained a large, almost continental, area. Thus, from the preliminary account of the requirements of fossilization, it will be seen that we might expect to find an appreciable number of fossils in such a site. It is perhaps remarkable that out of the large number of bones of dinosaurs found of Wealden age so few nearly complete skeletons have so far been found. By far the greater part of the bones obtained belong to *Iguanodon*, and casts of the footprints are also well known and by no means infrequently found on the Sussex and Dorset coasts and in quarries in these counties.

Elsewhere in Europe important finds have been made, as for example, in the Triassic sandstone quarries of Trossingen in Würtemberg, which have yielded the important remains of early forms such as *Plateosaurus*, *Zanclodon* and *Gresslyosaurus*. This area and its quarries have been described by von Huene (1928). The discovery of more than thirty specimens of *Iguanodon* which were entombed at Bernissart, near Mons, in Belgium, has frequently been alluded to in these pages, and has been described by Dollo (1884) and Casier (1960).

The 'dark' continent of Africa has not failed to disclose interesting and even numerous remnants of its dinosaurian inhabitants. The Stormberg Beds of the Orange Free State, Transvaal, and Cape Province have revealed many forms closely akin to the theropods of Würtemberg, and the first glimpses of ornithopods, while the great delta deposits at

Tendaguru, in Tanzania (formerly Tanganyika), have produced an immense number of bones. In this last field immediately before the First World War a series of German expeditions recovered excellent remains of all the main Sub-orders and, amongst the Sauropoda, the bones of the largest so far known. After the war, expeditions under the auspices of the British Museum continued the German work and produced important results. Janensch (1914) described the German work, and Parkinson (1930) published a book describing the British expeditions. Details of both these publications will be found in the bibliography at the end of this book.

Of all the localities in which dinosaur remains have been found the most important are those of North America, not only in point of the numbers of specimens excavated, but also in the literature upon them and the number of leading palaeontologists who have worked them. The principal localities, in which a splendid assembly of forms of late Jurassic age have been found, are those of Wyoming, Colorado, and Utah. These have been the scenes of numerous expeditions led by the pioneers of American palaeontology, such as Marsh, Cope, Williston, Lull, and Osborn. Despite the fact that it was in England that the first remains of dinosaurs were discovered by Buckland and Mantell and fully described later by Owen, it was in the heat of the summer sun, or round the camps during winter or unseasonable blizzards in these American outposts that the real structure of dinosaurian palaeontology was founded. The literature of the deposits there excavated is more than half that of the dinosaurs, and the results of these expeditions constitute the glory of the principal American museums.

Almost equally important are the discoveries which have been made in the Old Man Series and the Edmonton Formation, of Upper Cretaceous age, of the Red Deer River in Alberta, Canada, and the material there obtained by Charles Sternberg, W. E. Cutler, and W. A. Parks has enriched the museums of New York, Ottawa, Toronto, and London. An excellent and popular account of the vicissitudes of the collector and of the fossils obtained in this region was given by Sternberg (1932) and their history by Loris Russell (1966).

Remarkable discoveries of primary importance were made

289

by the American Museum Expeditions to the Gobi Desert in Mongolia. Some of this work has already been alluded to in the account of the Ceratopsia and the distribution of dinosaurs generally, but the discovery of the remarkable dinosaur nests and eggs is still often brought to memory. More recent works there by Russian and Polish expeditions has yielded important results.

In addition to these historical localities, of course, many sites of importance have been examined and have yielded good results. Von Huene broke almost fresh territory in Brazil, while Longman in Australia, Matley in India, and Nopcsa in Transylvania brought fresh finds to light. But it must not be thought that the discovery of dinosaur remains, or any practical interest therein, is the prerogative only of the well-equipped explorer or the expedition supported by a great museum. Much of the best work, particularly in England, has been done by the enthusiastic amateur. For example, the fine skeleton of *Iguanodon atherfieldensis*, now in the Dinosaur Gallery of the British Museum, was discovered, excavated, and described by the late Mr R. W. Hooley, a Winchester business man. Fortune may favour the well-equipped specialist, but much will come to the eye of the interested amateur, to say nothing of the pleasures of the chase, which is none the less worthy because the kill was made before the hunt comes to an end. The quarries of the Midlands and the south-east coasts of England may richly reward the searcher who, in addition to having all the pleasures of a holiday task, may well contribute handsomely to science.

The finding of dinosaur remains is not the end of the task, however, for they have to be excavated, hardened for transport, and conveyed to the museum. With any fossils of considerable size these processes are beyond the means of the ordinary amateur, and he may be well advised to leave the excavation and transport to skilled hands; at least, if the discovery is made within reasonable distance of a museum.

It seldom happens that the bones are free from adhering rock or in a condition for immediate removal. In most of the expeditions mentioned above the fossils were obtained only after intensive work over an area. Ditches and cross ditches, bores, pits, and even little quarries had to be dug. If the bone is found embedded in matrix (*i.e.*, the adherent or enclosing rock) some of this must be removed not only to reveal the nature of the bone itself but to lighten the load that must be carried. This can be done by chipping it off carefully with hammer and chisel; and it should be remembered that many light blows are better than a show of strength. While more and more of the bone is becoming revealed it is necessary to harden it so that the shocks due to development or excavation do not shatter it. For this purpose thin solutions of shellac in methylated spirit, or any of the many commercial products, such as Durofix or P.V.A. are useful. They are applied thinly so as to penetrate, and this naturally presupposes that the bone is not saturated with moisture. Should the bone be damp it must be carefully dried in the sun or the bone shed before the shellac or other solution is employed.

When the surface of the bone, skull, or vertebra is more or less exposed great care should be exercised in its movement. Probably it is already fractured in one or more places. Accordingly, pieces of fine paper are wetted and placed over the bone, and upon them are placed strips or bandages of cheese cloth or canvas cloth, particularly the kind known as burlap, which have been soaked in liquid plaster of Paris. If the bones are very small ordinary flour paste will do equally well. In both cases the preliminary casing of thin wet paper is important, as it prevents the overlying plaster bandages from adhering to the bone surface. When the plaster or paste bandages are set or dry, the bone may be turned over and the development of the other side proceeded with. Even a brief experience will show that care, patience, and no little skill are required in the performance of this apparently simple task. They are essential, however, if the trophy is to be brought to the study or workshop in a condition worthy of further treatment.

When sufficient of the bone or skeleton is thus excavated and treated, splints may be included in the final bandages or they may be tied to the completely bandaged specimen. The result has a surgical appearance, and, indeed, it was a surgeon who invented this useful process. The bandages and splints will sufficiently ensure that the specimen does not further disintegrate, while, in addition, the splints are useful if it has to be carried some distance to railhead or expedition headquarters.

291

The boxing of the bones is no less important, for inadequate packing means that they may move about in the case and pound upon one another. As a packing material hay, straw, or wood-wool are to be recommended, but earth or sawdust must never be used. The boxes, too, must be of adequate construction.

Labelling is of paramount importance. The contents of each box should be clearly stated on the package, and full details of the geographical and geological position of the find should accompany the specimen as well as be recorded in the field note book. Photographs make invaluable records.

Finally, from the collector's point of view, it should be remembered that the smaller the box, the easier it is to handle, and the less shock in transport it is likely to receive. When many boxes are in a collection some system of numbering should be devised, so that the preparator in the museum can open the boxes in due order, or select a particular one for preferential treatment. A suitable paint for marking specimens is white oil colour or sealing wax dissolved in spirit, while black paint is generally used upon the boxes. Many marking inks and special pens are now on the market.

On reaching the museum the boxes are unpacked as soon as the other work on hand, or other conditions permit. The selected boxes are opened and the packing removed. Despite the apparent simplicity of this process it should not be left to the unsupervised attention of inexperienced persons, and if the consignment has come from a tropical country it is wise to burn the packing material in case its storage for further use, or its placing on a dump, puts it in the way of spreading animal or plant disease.

In the workshop, the splints and bandages are removed by soaking off the latter. Further development, often a very lengthy process, is done by hammer and chisel, or in the larger museums, by pneumatic hammer or supersonic dental drill. Fractures are repaired and, in the case of large fractured bones, part of the centre has to be developed out and a piece of iron rod or piping plastered in to support the joined pieces of bone.

When all the bones are thus developed and repaired their final cleaning is accomplished, usually by such homely means as a scrubbing brush, a tooth-brush, or a small wire-brush. If part of a skeleton or bone is missing, for exhibition purposes it is often advisable to complete it in plaster, modelling the missing piece from some similar part of the same, or a like, skeleton. The bones must then be hardened, and many substances can be used for this purpose. The most common is amber shellac dissolved in methylated spirit, but gelatine was used by Dollo in the Brussels Iguanodons, or a solution composed of celluloid dissolved in equal parts of amyl acetate and acetone. There are also other processes in which special commercial products, fibreglass and other plastics are employed. For large specimens a substance called 'Fibrenyle' makes strong and satisfactory joints.

Conflicting views are held as to whether plaster or fibreglass restoration work should be coloured absolutely to match the true bone. The individual must please himself on the question, but any glaring differentiation is at once striking to the eye and spoils the whole effect, while the experienced palaeontologist can never fail to detect the difference in surface however well the colours may be matched.

These preparation and preservation methods take but a short time to describe and they do not seem to be involved, so that the uninitiated may well ask why it is that large skeletons take so long to prepare for exhibition. The answer is that even where the preparator has ample tools and time at his command the process is of necessity slow. The matrix is seldom removed with ease and each piece must be done with the greatest care and under the closest scrutiny. Otherwise, traces of skin, which are often represented by a mere brownish tinged layer of the matrix, would easily be overlooked and lost; and both the preparator and the curator must constantly be on the lookout for unusual features, ossified tendons, or the remains or traces of associated animals and plants embedded with the bone or skeleton being treated. Often there is great difficulty in deciding where matrix ends and bone begins, and in the unravelling of the delicate structure of skulls it is obvious that a slip of the chisel may do irretrievable damage. As each piece of bone is cleaned it must also be hardened. Finally comes the process of assembling the numerous pieces into one intelligible structure,

293

a piece of work that in many ways constitutes a very difficult jig-saw puzzle and demands a wide knowledge of comparative anatomy. No part of the process can be hurried if results either of scientific or exhibition value are to accrue.

Skeletons and large bones are usually mounted on iron supports screwed and bolted into wooden bases. Provision has to be made for both the safety of the public and the specimen because the bones of any moderately large fossil vertebrate are weighty. For example, a femur of *Argyrosaurus*, from the Argentine, in the Field Museum, Chicago, is 6′ 7″ long and weighs 930 lbs. Those of the young *Iguanodon* in the British Museum are 3 feet long and weigh separately 38 pounds, or just a pound per inch. Thus, although the weight varies, it is always considerable, and demands strength in the iron supports when bones are exhibited. In a museum gallery, however, the supporting framework is not an addition to the specimen's exhibition value and must therefore be as unobtrusive as possible. For this reason the iron work is always literally made to measure for the specimen and is applied to the bone or bones as closely as possible, and modelled to fit and support almost every little variation. This in itself is not simple work and calls for painstaking efforts on the part of a competent smith. As a rule also the various parts of a skeleton are mounted so as to be readily detachable for study by the experts who from time to time are bound to visit the museum.

It would be invidious to mention the more notorious examples of the old style of iron mounting in which the framework was often more conspicuous than the fossil, but, on the other hand, any interested person has only to examine the later exhibits in the dinosaur galleries of the natural history museums of Brussels, London, Washington or New York to appreciate the infinite pains which go to make the preparator's genius.

When to the time which must be allowed for preparation and mounting is added the time that must elapse before the fossil is studied scientifically, it will be apparent even to the most skilled and speedy workman who views the result that obviously he cannot read of a specimen's arrival at the museum one week and expect to find it on view the next. This may appear an unnecessary explanation, but, alas, such expectant visitors are common in every curator's experience.

The questions of keeping the exhibit exposed in the gallery, and of the type of labels to be set out, depend on the tastes of the curator, the humidity and cleanliness of the air in the town in question, or whether there is air-conditioning in the museum, and the liability to theft. Souvenir hunters penetrate into museums more often than is popularly imagined.

It has become the custom to illustrate the fossils for the public, wherever possible, by models or pictures which purport to give some idea of the creature in life. These restoration models or restoration-pictures as they are properly called, are generally to scale, often 1 inch to 1 foot, and sometimes look very charming. They have met, however, with displeasure in many quarters as it is alleged they present to the public a wholly false conception of the extent of our knowledge and tend to invest the lowly reptiles with mammalian expression.

It is true, as has been shown in previous pages, that we have but little knowledge of the skin of dinosaurs and no evidence at all of its coloration. Further, the thickness of the underlying tissue and musculature is unknown, and the misleading results from its estimation have been amply proved by reconstruction work on the skulls of human beings whose photographs were available for subsequent comparison. In many cases also our knowledge of the dinosaur's skeleton is inadequate. Thus any attempt at a picture of the living animal is only a guess and perhaps a bad one. As many of these pictorial 'crimes' are committed, and some appear in this book, perhaps some explanation may be allowed.

It is frankly conceded that any attempt to restore the appearance of an animal from inadequate material is wrong. Equally so would it be to apply a name to it. But if a knowledge of comparative anatomy and experience of animal mechanics be permitted in the elucidation of a skeleton, or a part of one, for a scientific paper, is their use any less permissible in an attempt to recreate the living appearance? However flexible may be the imagination of the palaeontologist there is no greater test of his understanding of the evidence than an attempt to illustrate it in two or three dimensions. Fresh and unlooked-for problems are

295

constantly arising and their solution materially advances knowledge, at least of the animal in question. If this modelling of ideas is of use to the scientist may it not be of interest to the public? If the plasticene conclusions of the expert satisfy the demands of the bony premises surely the error in imaginative logic cannot be too great. It is true that one restorer's conclusion may appear as another man's astigmatism, but the same might possibly be said of it as written.

Where skin is concerned there is a justifiable objection, but only when the artist deliberately falsifies. If skin texture or pattern is known some attempt at its modelling is not unwarranted. Colour is an insuperable problem, but if we accept the evidences of comparative anatomy for the bones we may not be entirely wrong in assuming that the large reptiles of the past were similar in coloration to the great reptiles of today.

For public exhibition we believe some illustration is useful. The hind leg of a dinosaur, however well preserved and charmingly mounted, is still but a hind leg to the public. But if an attempt to illustrate its true position in life is given, and is based on sources not available for exhibition in that particular museum, interest may be quickened and understanding be achieved. 'Can these bones live?' is the visitor's cry, and the curator with pen and plastics answers 'Yes!'

Now that we have discussed the recovery of dinosaurian remains and their treatment in the museum, it may be of some interest to mention the principal institutions in which good collections can be seen.

Nearly all the large state, city, or university museums in North America possess some exhibits worthy of inspection, while some are justly world-famous. Particularly may be mentioned the fine dinosaur series on view in the United States National Museum in Washington D.C. which have been described in the many scientific papers; those in the American Museum of Natural History in New York made famous by the writings of Osborn, Matthew, Barnum Brown, and E. H. Colbert; the collections at Harvard, Yale, and the Field Natural History Museum, Chicago; and in the museums of Nebraska, Michigan, Pittsburgh, Denver and California.

In Canada there are good collections well displayed in the

National Museum, Ottawa, and the Royal Ontario Museum, Toronto.

Amongst more fragmentary evidences of dinosaurian life preserved in museums, collections in the South African Museum, Cape Town, and the Queensland Museum, at Brisbane in Australia, may be mentioned.

In Europe the chief and best known collections are in Berlin, Frankfurt-am-Main, Brussels, London and Moscow. In Germany, the Geological and Palaeontological Institute and Museum, Berlin, has on view an excellent selection of the dinosaur material brought back by the expeditions to Tendaguru; while the first results of these expeditions are housed in the Würtemberg Natural History Museum in Stuttgart. The early Triassic theropodous dinosaurs and the results of historic excavation in Brazil are to be seen in the Geological and Palaeontological Institute of Tübingen University. The fine Senckenberg Museum in Frankfurt-am-Main has a notable and unusually mounted plaster cast of the skeleton of the great sauropod, *Brachiosaurus*.

Coming nearer to England, the traveller who is interested in dinosaurs must not fail to see the wonderful series of *Iguanodon bernissartensis* so excellently displayed in the Institut royal des Sciences naturelles in Brussels. Here can be seen mounted some of the twenty-nine skeletons found in 1878, while, in a specially constructed pit, others lie in the position in which they were found.

In England, the University Museum in Oxford has an interesting skeleton of the carnivorous *Eustreptospondylus cuvieri*. In London, the British Museum (Natural History) has one of the most important collections in the world, not in respect of size, which is greatly overshadowed by the American collections, but in the fact that the earliest-known specimens are here preserved, and in the variety of the general collection. Apart from the plaster reproductions of *Iguanodon bernissartensis*, *Diplodocus carnegii*, and *Triceratops prorsus*, which never fail to interest and delight the public, there are numerous skeletons of great scientific value. Among these may be mentioned the unique armoured *Scelidosaurus*, the curious and also armoured *Polacanthus*, the exceptionally fine and only known specimen

297

of *Scolosaurus*, which is perhaps the best armoured dinosaur so far found, the young *Iguanodon* from the Isle of Wight, *I. atherfieldensis*, and many other *Iguanodon* remains, the small Ornithopod, *Hypsilophodon foxi*, and the imposing remains of the large sauropod, *Cetiosaurus leedsi*.

A mere list of the other material in the Palaeontology Department of the British Museum would need a book for itself, but these are the salient points of a notable collection which is always popular with visitors, but is, none the less, inadequately known.

It is impossible to give within the narrow limits of this history anything like an adequate list of the museums which contain some reminder of the dinosaurian world, but enough has been said to show that in most of the countries visited by tourists and students there are splendid collections which demand at least one visit and deserve a great many more.

Finally, there are also such outdoor 'shrines' as the Crystal Palace restoration models at Sydenham, South London, England and the Dinosaur National Monument, near Vernal, Utah, U.S.A. A series of life-size models is exhibited at the Zoological Gardens, Calgary, Alberta, Canada.

APPENDIX I

Collections

A list of museums with *good* collections is quite extensive and the following is not exhaustive.

England. British Museum (Natural History), London, and the Geological Museum, London
The University Museum, Oxford has important historical specimens.

France. Musée National d'histoire naturelle, Paris.

Germany. Museums in Berlin, Frankfurt-am-Main, and the natural history collections of Munich and Stuttgart.

Belgium. Institut royal des Sciences naturelles, Brussels.

Sweden. Palaeontological Museum of Uppsala University.

Moscow. The Palaeontological Institute of the Academy of Science of the U.S.S.R.

Canada. National Museum, Ottawa; Royal Ontario Museum, Toronto.

U.S.A. Buffalo, New York State, Natural History Museum.
Boulder, Colorado, University Natural History Museum.
Chicago, Illinois, Field Natural History Museum.
Cleveland, Ohio, Natural History Museum.
Denver, Colorado, Museum of Natural History.
Lincoln, Nebraska, State Museum.
Los Angeles, California.
New York City, American Museum of Natural History.
Philadelphia, Academy of Natural Sciences.
Pittsburgh, Carnegie Museum.
Salt Lake City, Utah, University Museum.
Yale University, Peabody Museum.
Washington, US National Museum.

Maps of Dinosaur Localities in Britain

The first edition contained an appendix, 'An alphabetical list of British dinosaurs', which was thought to be of advantage to non-British students. The advances of the intervening years have made this of historical value only and it seems wiser to include another kind of information—the historic sites in England from which dinosaurs have come or have been alleged to come. Thanks to the cartographic skill and geological knowledge of Mr Justin B. Delair, these maps have been specially prepared in the hope they will lead to a revival of field interest in some of these quarries and localities.

   I   Kent, Surrey and Sussex.
   II   Buckinghamshire, Hertfordshire, Bedfordshire, Huntingdonshire and Cambridgeshire.
  III   Wiltshire, Hampshire and Isle of Wight.
  IV   Dorset, Somerset and Glamorgan.
   V   Gloucestershire, Oxfordshire and Berkshire.
  VI   Warwickshire, Leicestershire, Nottinghamshire, Rutland and Northamptonshire.
 VII   Yorkshire.

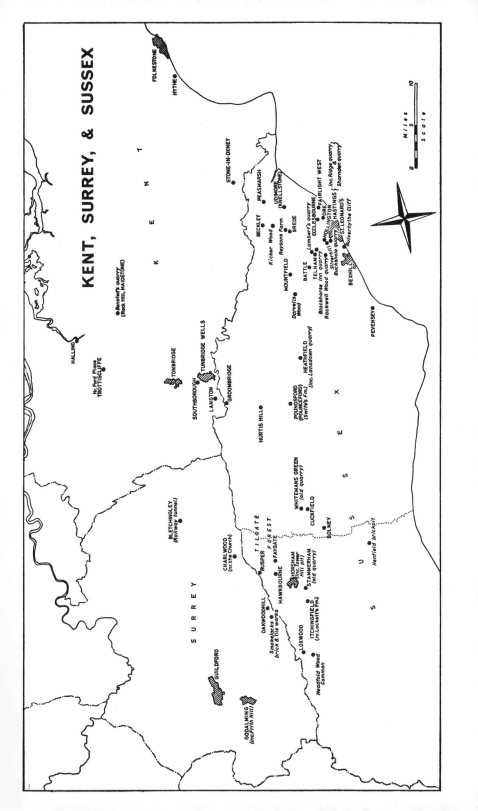

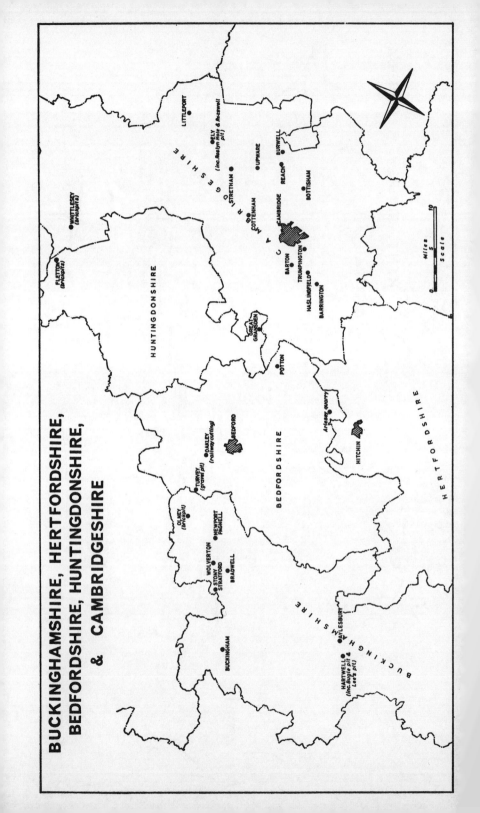

BUCKINGHAMSHIRE, HERTFORDSHIRE, BEDFORDSHIRE, HUNTINGDONSHIRE, & CAMBRIDGESHIRE

CAMBRIDGESHIRE

HUNTINGDONSHIRE

BEDFORDSHIRE

HERTFORDSHIRE

BUCKINGHAMSHIRE

Scale
Miles
0 5 10

LITTLEPORT

ELY
(inc.Roslyn Hole & Roswell pit)

WHITTLESEY
(brickpits)

FLETTON
(brickpits)

UPWARE

BURWELL

STRETHAM

REACH

BOTTISHAM

COTTENHAM

CAMBRIDGE

BARTON

TRUMPINGTON

HASLINGFIELD

BARRINGTON

GREAT GRANSDEN

POTTON

Arlesey Quarry

HITCHIN

BEDFORD

OAKLEY
(railway cutting)

TURVEY
(gravel pit)

OLNEY
(brickpits)

NEWPORT PAGNELL

WOLVERTON

BRADWELL

STONY STRATFORD

BUCKINGHAM

AYLESBURY

HARTWELL
(inc.Bugle pit & Lee's pit)

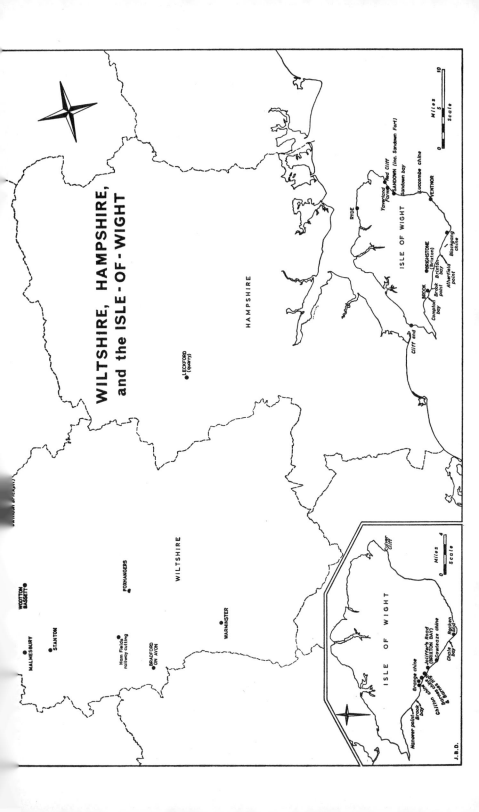

WILTSHIRE, HAMPSHIRE, and the ISLE-OF-WIGHT

HAMPSHIRE

WILTSHIRE

ISLE OF WIGHT

Scale
Miles
0   5   10

WOOTTON
BASSETT
MALMESBURY
STANTON
FOXHANGERS
Ham Fields
railway cutting
BRADFORD
ON AVON
WARMINSTER

LECHFORD
(quarry)

RYDE
Yaverland
Farm
Red Cliff
SANDOWN (inc. Sandown Fort)
Sandown bay
Luccombe chine
VENTNOR
SHIDESTONE
(Brixton)
Brixton
point
Atherfield
point
Blackgang
chine
BROOK
Brook
point
Compton
bay
Cliff end

ISLE OF WIGHT

Scale
Miles
0   4

Culver
Cliff

Hanover point
Brook
bay
Grange chine
Chilton
chine
Cowleaze chine
Chale
bay
Rocken
bay
Jolliffe's Road
(BRIXTON BAY)

J.B.D.

DORSETSHIRE, SOMERSETSHIRE, & GLAMORGANSHIRE.

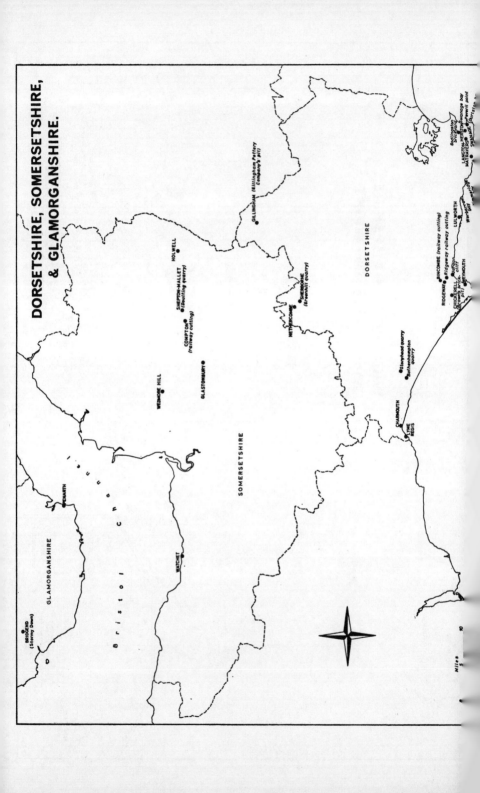

GLAMORGANSHIRE

BRIDGEND
(Stormy Down)

PENARTH

Bristol Channel

WATCHET

SOMERSETSHIRE

WEDMORE HILL

GLASTONBURY

SHEPTON-MALLET
(Dowlting quarry)

HOWELL

COMPTON
(railway cutting)

HETHERCOMBE

SHERBORNE
(Brownhill quarry)

GILLINGHAM (Gillingham Pottery
Company's pit)

DORSETSHIRE

CHARMOUTH

LYME
REGIS

Stonyhead quarry

Gothenhampton
quarry

RIDGEWAY

INCOMBE   Ridgeway railway cutting

Osmington
Brown's pit
cliff

CHICKERELL

WEYMOUTH

LULWORTH

Worbarrow
bay

Bollington
Knolinsea
LANGTON-HERRING Kimmeridge bar
MATRAVERS   Durwell point
SWANAGE   fountain bay

Miles
5   10

DORSETSHIRE

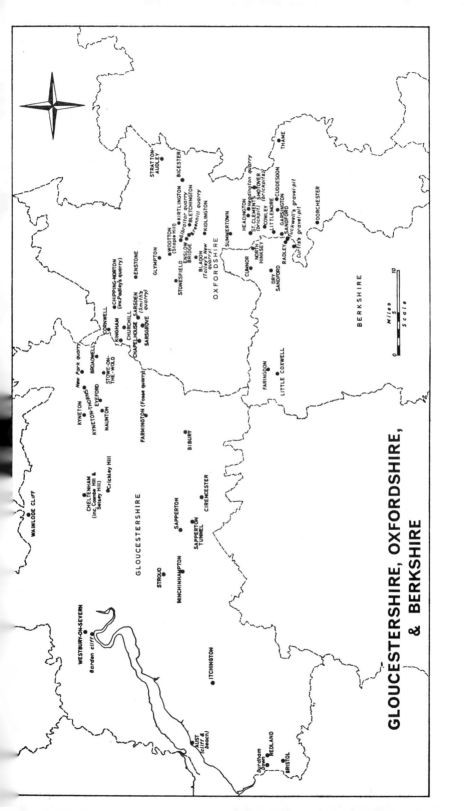

GLOUCESTERSHIRE, OXFORDSHIRE, & BERKSHIRE

WAINLODE CLIFF

GLOUCESTERSHIRE

WESTBURY-ON-SEVERN
Garden cliffs

ITCHINGTON

STROUD

MINCHINHAMPTON

SAPPERTON

SAPPERTON
TUNNEL

CIRENCESTER

CHELTENHAM
(inc. Coombe Hill &
Selsey Hill)

Cricksey Hill

AUST
(cliff &
beach)

Durdham
Down

REDLAND

BRISTOL

BIBURY

FARMINGTON (Fosse quarry)

NAUNTON

KYNETON
KYNETON-THORNS
EYFORD

New Park quarry

BROADWELL

STOWE-ON-
THE-WOLD

KINGHAM

CORNWELL

CHURCHILL

CHAPEL HOUSE

SARSGROVE

SARSDEN
(Smith's
quarry)

CHIPPING-NORTON
(McPladley's quarry)

ENSTONE

GLYMPTON

WOOTTON
(Slape Hill)

STONESFIELD

ENSLOW
BRIDGE

BLADON
(Tolley's New
quarry)

Glympton quarry

KIRTLINGTON
quarry

Sewhill quarry

KIDLINGTON

BLETCHINGTON

STRATTON-
AUDLEY

BICESTER

SUMMERTOWN

CLANOR

NORTH
HINKSEY

DRY
SANDFORD

RADLEY

HEADINGTON

ST. CLEMENTS
(brickpit)

Headington quarry

SHOTOVER
(brickpits)

LITTLEMORE

COWLEY

GARSINGTON

SANDFORD

CUDDESDON

Buckwell's gravel-pit

Curtis's gravel-pit

DORCHESTER

THAME

OXFORDSHIRE

BERKSHIRE

FARINGDON

LITTLE COXWELL

Scale

0   5   10
Miles

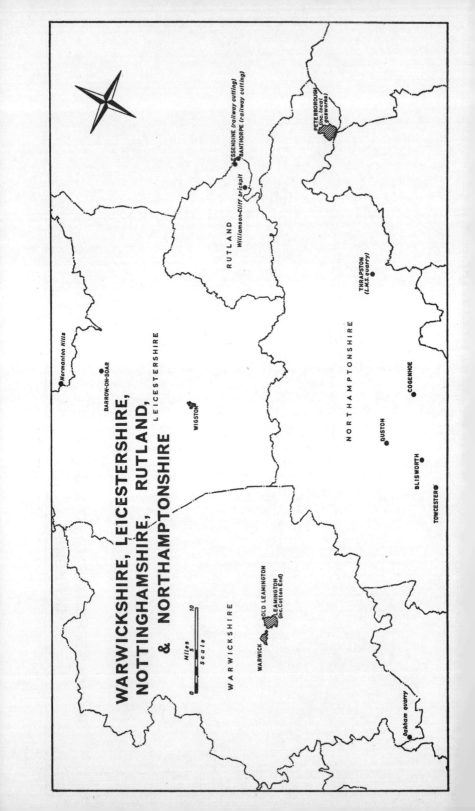

WARWICKSHIRE, LEICESTERSHIRE, NOTTINGHAMSHIRE, RUTLAND, & NORTHAMPTONSHIRE

Scale

Miles

0 5 10

North

RUTLAND

LEICESTERSHIRE

WARWICKSHIRE

NORTHAMPTONSHIRE

Normanton Hills

BARROW-ON-SOAR

WIGSTON

ESSENDINE (railway cutting)
BARNTHORPE (railway cutting)

Williamson-Cliff brickpit

PETERBOROUGH (inc. local gasworks)

THRAPSTON (L.M.S. quarry)

COGENHOE

QUSTON

BLISWORTH

TOWCESTER

WARWICK
OLD LEAMINGTON
LEAMINGTON (inc. Cotton End)

Oakham quarry

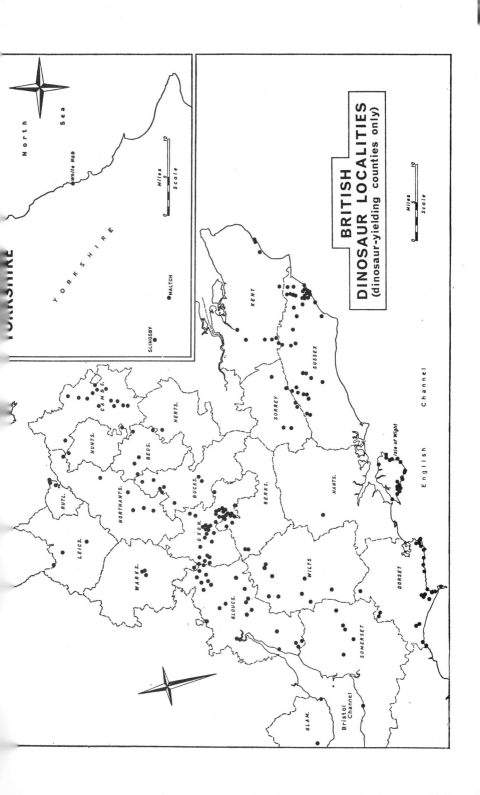

BRITISH
DINOSAUR LOCALITIES
(dinosaur-yielding counties only)

YORKSHIRE

White Nab

North Sea

MALTON

SLINGSBY

Miles
Scale
0 5 10

CAMBS.

HERTS.

HUNTS.

BEDS.

RUTL.

NORTHANTS.

BUCKS.

KENT

SUSSEX

SURREY

LEICS.

OXON.

BERKS.

HANTS.

Isle of Wight

WARKS.

GLOUCS.

WILTS

DORSET

SOMERSET

GLAM.

Bristol
Channel

English Channel

Miles
Scale
0 5 10

BIBLIOGRAPHY

ABEL, O. 1910. 'Die Rekonstruktion des *Diplodocus.*' *Abh. zool.-bot. Ges. Wien.* Bd. V, Heft 3, pp. 1–60.
—— 1922. *Lebensbilder aus der Tierwelt der Vorzeit.* Jena, Gustav Fischer.
—— 1925. *Geschichte und Methode der Rekonstruktion vorzeitlicher Wirbeltiere.* Jena, Gustav Fischer.
ANDREWS, R. C. 1953. *All About Dinosaurs.* New York, Random House.
ARLDT, T. 1919, 1922. *Handbuch der Palaeogeographie.* Vol. I. 1919, vol. II, 1922. Leipzig, Gebrüder Borntraeger.
AXELROD, D. I. and BAILEY, H. P. 1968. 'Cretaceous Dinosaur Extinction.' *Evolution.* Vol. 22, Sept., No. 3, pp. 595, 611.

BALDWIN, E. 1964. *Introduction to Comparative Biochemistry,* 4th edn Cambridge U.P.
BEER, SIR GAVIN DE and SWINTON, W. E. 1958. 'Prophetic Fossils.' *Studies in Fossil Vertebrates.* Ed. T. S. Westoll, London, pp. 1–14.
BELLAIRS, A. 1957. *Reptiles.* London, Hutchinson.
BRANCA, W. 1914. 'Die Riesengrösse sauropoder Dinosaurier vom Tendaguru, ihr Aussterben und die Bedingungen ihrer Entstehung.' *Archiv. für Biontologie, Berlin.* III Bd., 1 Heft, pp. 71–78.
BROOKS, C. E. P. 1926. *Climate throughout the Ages.* London, Ernest Benn.
BROWN, B. 1908. 'The Ankylosauridae.' *Bull. Amer. Mus. Nat. Hist. N.Y.* Vol. XXIV, p. 187.
—— 1914. '*Leptoceratops*, a New Genus of Ceratopsia from the Edmonton Cretaceous of Alberta.' *Bull. Amer. Mus. Nat. Hist., N.Y.* Vol. XXXIII, pp. 567–580.
BROWN, BARNUM and SCHLAIKJER, E. M. 1937. 'The skeleton of *Styracosaurus* with the description of a new species.' *Amer. Mus. Novitates.* No. 955, Oct. 30, Amer. Mus. Nat. Hist., N.Y.
—— 1940. 'The origin of Ceratopsian horn-cores.' *Amer. Mus. Novitates.* No. 1065, May 3, Amer. Mus. Nat. Hist., N.Y.
BUCKLAND, W. 1824. 'Notice on the Megalosaurus or great Fossil Lizard of Stonesfield.' *Trans. Geol. Soc., London.* Ser. II, Vol. I, p. 390.

BULLARD, SIR E. C., 1964. 'Continental Drift.' *Q. J. Geol. Soc. London*. Vol. 120, pp. 1–33.

CABRERA, A. 1947. 'Un Sauropodo nuevo del Jurassico de Patagonia.' *Nat. Mus. la Plata*, 12, (*Amygdalodon*).

CASIER, E. 1960. *Les Iguanodons de Bernissart*. Brussels. 134 pp.

CHARIG, A. J., ATTRIDGE, J. and CROMPTON, A. W. 1965. 'On the origin of the sauropods and the classification of the Saurischia.' *Proc. Linn. Soc. Lond.* 176, pt. 2, pp. 197–221.

COLBERT, E. H. 1945. 'The hyoid bones in *Protoceratops* and in *Psittacosaurus*.' *Amer. Mus. Novitates*, No. 1301. Nov. 6. Amer. Mus. Nat. Hist., N.Y.

1947. *Dinosaurs*. Science Guide No. 70., Amer. Mus. Nat. Hist., N.Y.

1948. 'Evolution of the horned Dinosaurs.' *Evolution*. Vol. II, No. 2, June, pp. 145–163.

1949. 'Evolutionary Growth Rates in the Dinosaurs.' *Sci. Monthly*. Vol. LXIX, No. 2, Aug., pp. 71–79.

1952. 'Breathing habits of the Sauropod Dinosaurs.' *Ann. Mag. Nat. Hist.* Ser. 12, 5, pp. 708–710.

1958. 'The Beginning of the Age of Dinosaurs.' *Studies in Fossil Vertebrates*. Ed. T. S. Westoll, London, pp. 39–58.

1961. *Dinosaurs. Their Discovery and Their World*. New York, Dutton, pp. xiv + 300.

1962. 'The Weights of Dinosaurs.' *Amer. Mus. Novitates*. No. 2076, Feb. 28, Amer. Mus. Nat. Hist., N.Y.

1964. 'Relationship of the saurischian dinosaurs.' *Amer. Mus. Novitates*, No. 2181, pp. 1–24.

1964. 'The Triassic Dinosaur Genera *Podokesaurus* and *Coelophysis*,' *Amer. Mus. Novitates*, No. 2168. Feb. 21, pp. 1–11.

1968. *Men and Dinosaurs. The Search in Field and Laboratory*. New York, Dutton, pp. xviii + 284.

COLBERT, E. H. and BAIRD, D. 1958. 'Triassic Coelurosaur Bone Casts from the Connecticut Valley.' *Amer. Mus. Novitates*, No. 1901, July 22.

COLBERT, E. H., COWLES, R. B., and BOGERT, C. M. 1946. 'Temperature tolerances in the American alligator and their bearing on the habits, evolution and extinction of the dinosaurs.' *Bull. Amer. Mus. Nat. Hist.* 86, New York, pp. 327–373.

COLBERT, E. H. and OSTROM, J. H. 1958. 'Dinosaur Stapes.' *Amer. Mus. Novitates*, No. 1900, July 22, pp. 1–20.

CROMPTON, A. W. and CHARIG, A. J. 1962. 'A new Ornithischian from the Upper Triassic of South Africa.' *Nature*. V, 196, No. 4859, pp. 1074–1077, Dec. 15.

CURWEN, E. C. 1940. *The Journal of Gideon Mantell*. Oxford.

CYS, J. M. 1967. 'The inability of dinosaurs to hibernate as a possible key factor in their extinction.' *Journ. Paleont.* Vol. 41, No. 1, Jan., p. 266 (comment by L. S. Russell, *ibid.*, p. 267.)

DOLLO, L. 1882–4. 'Premiere-Cinquieme Note sur les Dinosauriens de Bernissart.' *Bull. Mus. Roy. Hist. Nat. Belg.* Vol. I, 1882, Vol. II, 1883, Vol. III, 1884.
1884. 'Les Découvertes de Bernissart.' *Ann. Sci. Geol. Paris.* Tom. XVI, Art. No. 6, pp. 14.
1914. *Guide illustré des Musées de Bruxelles*, édité par le Touring Club de Belgique.

DUNKLE, D. H. 1966. *The World of the Dinosaurs.* Smithsonian publication, Smithsonian Institution, Washington 4296 D.C., USA, pp. 1–22.

FRAAS, O. 1866. *Vor der Sündfluth!* Stuttgart. Plate at p. 306.

GILMORE, C. W. 1909. 'Osteology of the Jurassic Reptile *Camptosaurus.* ...' *Proc. United States National Museum*, Vol. XXXVI, pp. 197–332.
1914. 'Osteology of the Armored Dinosauria in the United States National Museum, with Special Reference to the Genus *Stegosaurus*.' *Bulletin 89, United States National Museum.*
1920. 'Osteology of the Carnivorous Dinosauria in the United States National Museum, with Special Reference to the Genera *Antrodemus* (*Allosaurus*) and *Ceratosaurus*.' *Bulletin 110, United States National Museum.*
1924. 'On *Troodon validus.* An Orthopodous Dinosaur from the Belly River Cretaceous of Alberta, Canada.' *Dept. Geol. Univ. Alberta. Bull No. 1.*
1925. 'A nearly complete articulated skeleton of *Camarasaurus.* ...' *Mem. Carnegie Mus. Pittsburgh.* Vol. IX, No. 3, pp. 347–384.
1930. 'On Dinosaurian Reptiles from the Two Medicine Formation of Montana.' *Proc. U.S. Nat. Mus.* Vol. LXXVII, Art. 16, pp. 1–39.
1931. 'A new species of Troödont dinosaur from the Lance Formation of Wyoming.' *Proc. U.S. Nat. Mus.* Vol. LXXIX, Art. 9, pp. 1–6.
1932. 'On a newly mounted skeleton of *Diplodocus* in the United States National Museum.' *Proc. U.S. Nat. Mus.* Vol. LXXXI, Art. 18, pp. 1–21.

GINSBURG, L. 1964. 'Decouverte d'un scelidosaurien (dinosaure ornithischien), dans le Trias supérieur du Basutoland.' *C. V. Hebd Séanc. Acad. Sci. Paris*, 258, 2366–2368.

GOOD, J. M., WHITE, T. E., and STUCKER, G. F. 1958. *The Dinosaur Quarry*, Colorado, Utah. National Park Service, Washington, D.C., pp. 1–46.

GRANGER, W. and GREGORY, W. K. 1923. '*Protoceratops andrewsi*, a Pre-Ceratopsian Dinosaur from Mongolia.' *Amer. Mus. Nov.*, N.Y., No. 72.

GREGORY, W. K. and MOOK, C. C. 1925. 'On *Protoceratops*, a primitive

Ceratopsian Dinosaur from the Lower Cretaceous of Mongolia.'
Amer. Mus. Nov., N.Y., No. 156.
GREGORY, J. W., F.R.S. and BARRETT, B. H. 1931. *General Strati-graphy.* London, Methuen & Co.

HARLAND, W. B. *et al.* (Eds.) 1967. *The Fossil Record.* London (Geological Society), pp. xii + 828.
HATCHER, J. B. 1901. '*Diplodocus* (Marsh): Its osteology, taxonomy and probable habits with a restoration of the skeleton.' *Mem. Carnegie Mus. Pittsburgh.* Vol. I, No. 1, pp. 1–61.
HATCHER, J. B. 1907. 'The Ceratopsia.' *Monog. U.S. Geol. Surv.* No. 49.
HAUGHTON, S. H. 1928. (*Gigantosaurus dixeyi*). *Trans. Roy. Soc. S. Afr.* Vol. XVI, p. 70.
HAY, O. P. 1908. 'On the Habits and the Pose of the Sauropodous Dinosaurs, especially of *Diplodocus.*' *Amer. Nat. N.Y.* Vol. XLII, pp. 672–681.
1911. 'Further observations on the Pose of the Sauropodous Dinosaurs.' *Loc. cit.,* Vol. XLV, July, p. 398.
HEILMANN, G. 1916. *Fuglenes Afstamning.* Copenhagen.
1926. *The Origin of Birds.* London, Witherby.
HOLLAND, W. J. 1924. 'The Skull of Diplodocus.' *Mem. Carnegie Mus.* Vol. IX, No. 3, pp. 379–403.
HOOLEY, R. W. 1925. 'The Skeleton of *Iguanodon atherfieldensis.*' *Q.J. Geol. Soc., London.* Vol. LXXXI, pp. 1–61.
HOTTON III, NICHOLAS. 1963. *Dinosaurs.* New York, Pyramid Publications.
HUENE, FREIHERR F. VON. 1925. 'Eine neue Rekonstruktion von *Compsognathus.*' *Central f. Min., etc.* Abt. B. p. 157.
1926. 'Vollständige Osteologie eines Plateosauriden aus dem schwäbischen Keuper.' *Geol. paläont. Abh. Berlin.* N.f. Bd. XV, p. 178.
1926. 'The Carnivorous Saurischia in the Jura and Cretaceous Formations principally in Europe.' *Rev. Mus. La Plata.* Vol. XXIX, pp. 35–167.
1926. 'Reptiles of the Order Saurischia from England and France.' *Ann. Mag. Nat. Hist.* [9], Vol. XVII, p. 473.
1928. 'Lebensbild des Saurischier-Vorkommens im obersten Keuper von Trossingen.' *Palaeobiologica.* Vol. I, p. 103.
1926. (Osteology of *Plateosaurus*). *Geol. paläont. Abh. Berlin.* N.f. Bd. XV, p. 178.
1927a. 'Short review of the present knowledge of the Sauropoda.' *Mem. Qd. Mus. Brisbane.* Vol. IX, pt. 1, p. 121.
1927b. 'Sichtung der Grundlagen der jetzigen Kenntnis der Sauropoden.' *Ecl. geol. Helv.* Vol. XX, No. 3, pp. 444–470.
1928. 'Lebensbild des Saurischier-Vorkommens im obersten Keuper von Trossingen.' *Palaeobiol. Wien.* Bd. I, p. 103.
1929. 'Los Saurisquios y Ornithisquios del Cretáceo Argentino.' *Ann. Mus. La Plata, Buenos Aires.* Tome III, Ser. 2a.

312

BIBLIOGRAPHY

1932. 'Die fossile Reptil-Ordnung Saurischia, ihre Entwicklung und Geschichte.' pp. viii+360. 2 parts. *Monog. Geol. Palaeont. Berlin.*

1950. 'Die Entstehung der Ornithischia schon früh in der Trias.' *Jahrb. Geol. Paläont. Monatsheft Jahrg.* 1950. Heft 2, pp. 53–58.

HUENE FREIHERR F. VON and MATLEY, C. A. 1933. 'The Cretaceous Saurischia and Ornithischia of the Central Provinces of India.' *Pal. Indica.* N.S. XXI, No. 1, p. 74, 24 pls.

HULKE, J. W. 1881. '*Polacanthus Foxii*, a large undescribed Dinosaur from the Wealden Formation in the Isle of Wight.' *Philos. Trans. London.* Vol. 172, pp. 653–662.

1882. 'An attempt at a complete Osteology of *Hypsilophodon foxii.*' *Philos. Trans. London.* Vol. CLXXIII, p. 1035.

HUTCHINSON, H. N. 1910. *Extinct monsters and creatures of other days.* 2nd edition. London, Chapman & Hall.

1917. 'Observations on the reconstructed skeleton of *Diplodocus carnegiei.*' *Geol. Mag.* Dec. VI. Vol. IV, pp. 356–370.

HUXLEY, T. H. 1870. 'On *Hypsilophodon foxii*; a new Dinosaur from the Isle of Wight.' *Q.J. Geol. Soc., London.* Vol. XXVI, p. 3.

1870. 'On the classification of the Dinosauria.' *Q.J. Geol. Soc., London.* Vol. XXVII, p. 32.

JAEKEL, O. 1910. 'Fusstellung und Lebensweise der grossen Dinosaurier.' *Monatsb. deutsch geol. Ges.* No. 4, pp. 270–277.

JANENSCH, W. 1914. 'Kurze Charakterisierung der neu aufgestellten Arten von Sauropoden.' *Archiv. für Biontologie, Berlin.* III Bd., 1 Heft, pp. 86–110.

1914. 'Bericht über den Verlauf der Tendaguru Expedition.' *Archiv. für Biontologie.* III Bd., 1 Heft. Teil 1.

1929. 'Die Wirbelsaule der Gattung Dicraeosaurus.' *Palaeontographica.* Suppl. VII, Erste Reihe; Teil II, pp. 35–133

1929. 'Ein aufgestelltes und rekonstruiertes Skelett von Elaphrosaurus bambergi.' *Palaeontographica.* Supp. VII.

1935–36. 'Die Schädel der Sauropoden Brachiosaurus, Barosaurus und Dicraeosaurus aus den Tendaguru Schichten Deutsch–Ostafrikas.' *Palaeontographica.* Suppl. VII. Erste Reihe; Teil II, pp. 145–298.

1936. Ein aufgestelltes Skelett von Dicraeosaurus Hansemanni. *Palaeontographica.* Suppl. VII. Erste Reihe; Teil II, pp. 299–308.

1938. 'Vom Urveltnesen *Brachiosaurus*. *Aus der Natur*, Heft 4, Jahrg. 15, July. Berlin. 4 pp.

1939. 'Der sakrale Neural Kanal, einiger Sauropoden und anderer Dinosaurier.' *Palaeont. Z. 21*, pp. 171–191.

1947. 'Pneumatizität bei Wirbeln von Sauropoden und anderen Saurischiern.' *Palaeontographica.* Suppl. VII, pp. 1–25.

JENSEN, J. A. 1966. 'Dinosaur Eggs from the Upper Cretaceous North Horn Formation of Central Utah.' *Brigham Young University Geology Studies.* Vol. 13.

313

JEPSEN, G. L. 1964. 'Riddles of the Terrible Lizards.' *Amer. Scientist*, 52, pp. 227–246.

KERMACK, K. A. 1951. 'A note on the habits of Sauropods.' *Ann. Mag. Nat. Hist.* Ser. 12, *4*, p. 830.

KNOWLTON, F. H., SC.D. 1927. *Plants of the Past*. Princeton, Princeton University Press.

KUHN, O. 1965. *Fossilium Catalogus* 1. Animalia; Pars 109 Saurischia (Supplementum 1). 's—Gravenhage. 30. iv. 1965.

KURTÉN, B. 1968. *The Age of Dinosaurs*. London, World University Library.

LAMBE, L. 1915. 'On *Eoceratops canadensis*, gen. nov. with Remarks on Other Genera of Cretaceous Horned Dinosaurs.' *Bull. Canada, Dept. Mines, Ottawa*. Mus. Bull. No. 12. Geol. Ser. No. 24.

1917. 'The Cretaceous Theropodous Dinosaur *Gorgosaurus*.' *Memoir* 100, *Geol. Survey of Canada, Ottawa*.

1920. 'The Hadrosaur *Edmontosaurus* from the Upper Cretaceous of Alberta.' *Canada, Dept. Mines, Geol. Surv. Mem.* 120.

LAPPARENT, A. F. DE. 1958. 'Sur les Dinosauriens du "Continental Intercalaire" du Sahara central.' *C. R. Acad. Sci. Paris.* C. 246, pp. 1237–1240.

1960. 'Los dos Dinosaurios de Galve.' *Teruel*, No. 24, pp. 1–22.

1962. 'Footprints of Dinosaur in the Lower Cretaceous of Vest-Spitsbergen-Svalbard.' *Norsk Polarinstitutt Årbok 1960*. Oslo, 1962, pp. 14–2.

LAPPARENT, A. F. DE, MONTENAT, C., and DESPARMET, R. 1966. 'Nouvelles pistes de Dinosauriens dans l'infralias de Vendée.' *C. R. Soc. Géol. France*. fasc. 1, p. 20.

LAPPARENT, A. F. LE and ZLBYSZEWSKI, G. 1957. 'Les Dinosauriens du Portugal.' *Services Géol. du Portugal*. Memoire No. 2, N.S., pp. 7–63. XXXVI Pls.

LEIDY, J. 1856. 'Notice of remains of extinct Reptiles and Fishes.' *Proc. Acad. Nat. Sci. Philad.* Vol. VIII, p. 72.

1870. 'Remarks on *Poicilopleuron* (*Antrodemus*) *valens*, etc.' *Proc. Acad. Nat. Sci. Philad.* p. 3.

LONGMAN, H. A. 1926. 'A Giant Dinosaur from Durham Downs, Queensland.' *Mem. Qd. Mus. Brisbane*. Vol. VIII, pt. 3, pp. 183–194.

1927. 'The Giant Dinosaur: *Rhoetosaurus brownei*.' *Loc. cit.* Vol. IX, pt. 1, pp. 1–18.

LOWE, P. 1935. 'On the relationship of the Struthiones to the Dinosaurs and the rest of the Avian Class, with special reference to *Archaeopteryx*.' *Ibis*, London (13), *5*, pp. 398–432.

LUCAS, F. A. 1901. *Animals of the Past*. New York, Amer. Mus. Nat. Hist. Handbook Ser. No. 4, p. 91.

LULL, R. S. 1910. 'Dinosaurian Distribution.' *Amer. Journ. Sci. New Haven*. IV Ser., Vol. XXIX, p. 1.

BIBLIOGRAPHY

1910. '*Stegosaurus ungulatus* Marsh, recently mounted at the Peabody Museum of Yale University.' *Amer. Journ. Sci. New Haven.* IV Ser., Vol. XXX, pp. 361–377.

1915. 'Triassic Life in the Connecticut Valley.' *Bull. No. 24 Connecticut Geol. and Nat. Hist. Survey.* Hartford.

1917. 'On the Functions of the "Sacral Brain" in Dinosaurs.' *Loc. cit.* IV Ser., Vol. XLIV, pp. 471–477.

1924. 'Dinosaurian Climatic Response.' Chap. VII. *Organic Adaptation to Environment*, New Haven, Yale Univ. Press.

1930. Skeleton of *Camarasaurus lentus* recently mounted at Yale. *Amer. Journ. Sci. New Haven.* V Ser., Vol. XIX, pp. 1–5.

1933. 'A Revision of the Ceratopsia or Horned Dinosaurs.' *Mem. Peabody Mus. Nat. Hist.* Vol. III, Pt. 3, New Haven, pp. 1–175.

LULL, R. S. and WRIGHT, N. E. 1942. 'Hadrosaurian Dinosaurs of North America.' *Geol. Soc. Amer. Special Paper* No. 40, August 31.

MACGREGOR, A. H. 1948. 'The Grampian Highlands.' *British Regional Geology.* 2nd edn H.M.S.O., pp. viii + 83.

MANN, IDA and PIRIE, ANTOINETTE. 1950. *The Science of Seeing.* London. Pelican Books.

MANTELL, G. A. 1822. *The Fossils of the South Downs.* London.

1825. 'Notice on *Iguanodon*.' *Philos. Trans. London*, 1825, p. 184.

1825. 'On the teeth of the Iguanodon, a newly-discovered fossil herbivorous reptile.' *Philos. Trans. London.* Vol. CXV, pp. 179–186.

1833. '*Geology of the South-East of England.*' London.

MARSH, O. C. 1877. 'Notice of New Dinosaurian Reptiles from the Jurassic formation.' *Amer. Journ. Sci. New Haven.* III Ser. Vol. XIV, p. 514.

1892. 'Restorations of *Claosaurus* and *Ceratosaurus*. *Amer. Journ. Sci. New Haven.* III Ser. Vol. XLIV, pp. 343–350.

1891. 'Restoration of *Stegosaurus*.' *Amer. Journ. Sci. New Haven.* III Ser., Vol. XLII, pp. 179–181. Reprinted *Geol. Mag. London.* Dec. III, Vol. VIII, pp. 385–387.

1896. '*The Dinosaurs of North America.*' 16th Annual Report of the U.S. Geol. Survey, 1896.

MATSCHIE, P. 1910. 'Wahngebilde der Urweltkunde.' *Mode und Haus*, Berlin. Aug. 18th issue.

MATTHEW, W. D. 1905. 'The mounted skeleton of *Brontosaurus*.' *Amer. Mus. Journ.* Vol. V, pp. 63–70.

1910. 'The Pose of Sauropodous Dinosaurs.' *Amer. Nat. N.Y.* Vol. XLIV, pp. 547–560.

1915. *Dinosaurs.* New York, American Museum of Natural History.

MOODIE, ROY L., PH.D. 1923a. *The Antiquity of Disease.* pp. xiv + 148. Chicago, Univ. of Chicago Press.

1923b. *Palaeopathology*, pp. 568. Pls. CXVII. Urbana, Ill., University of Illinois Press.

1928. 'The histological nature of ossified Tendons found in Dinosaurs.' *Amer. Mus. Nov. N.Y.* No. 311.

315

THE DINOSAURS

MOOK, C. C. 1914. 'Notes on *Camarasaurus* Cope.' *Ann. N.Y. Acad. Sci.*
Vol. XXIV, pp. 19–22.
1918. 'The Habitat of the Sauropod Dinosaurs.' *J. Geol. Chicago.*
Vol. XXVI, No. 5, pp. 459–470.

NAGAO, T. 1936. '*Nipponosaurus sachalinensis.* A new genus and species
of Trachodont Dinosaur from Japanese Saghalien.' *Journ. Fac. Sci.*
Hokkaido Univ. Ser. IV. Vol. 3, No. 2, pp. 185–220.

NOPCSA, BARON F. 1903. 'Neues über *Compsognathus.*' *N. Jahrb. Min.
Geol. Paläont. Stuttgart.* Beil. Bd. XVI, p. 476.
1922. 'Probable Habits of *Struthiomimus.*' *Ann. Mag. Nat. Hist.* [9].
Vol. X, p. 152.
1905. 'Notes on British Dinosaurs. Part. II. *Polacanthus.*' *Geol. Mag.
London.* Dec. V. Vol. II, pp. 241–250.
1905. 'Notes on British Dinosaurs. I. *Hypsilophodon.*' *Geol. Mag.* Dec. V.
Vol. II, p. 203.
1918. Neues über Geschlechtsunterschiede bei Orthopoden. *Centralbl. f.
Min.*, *etc.*, p. 186.
1925. 'On Some Reptilian Bones from the Eocene of Sokoto.' *Occ. Pap.
Geol. Surv. Nigeria.* No. 2.
1928. 'Palaeontological Notes on Reptiles.' *Geol. Hungarica.* Ser.
Palaeont. Tom. 1, fasc. 1, p. 73.
1929a. 'Sexual Differences in Ornithopodous Dinosaurs.' *Palaeobiol.
Wien.* II Bd., p. 187.
1929b. 'Dinosaurierreste aus Siebenburgen.' V. *Geol. Hungarica.* Ser.
Palaeont. fasc. 4, p. 65.
1930. 'Zur Systematic und Biologie der Sauropoden.' *Palaeobiol. Wien.*
III Band, pp. 40–52.
1931. 'On *Troödon.*' *Ann. Mag. Nat. Hist.* [10]. Vol. VIII, pp. 70–73.
1926 and 1931. *Fossilium Catalogus.* Pars 27, pp. 391 and Pars 50,
pp. 62.

OSBORN, H. F. 1899. 'A skeleton of *Diplodocus.*' *Mem. Amer. Mus. Nat.
Hist. N.Y.* Vol. I, pt. 5, pp. 168–214.
1905. '*Tyrannosaurus* and other Cretaceous Carnivorous Dinosaurs.'
Bull. Amer. Mus. Nat. Hist. Vol. XXI, p. 259.
1911. 'A Dinosaur mummy.' *Amer. Mus. Journ.* Vol. XI, p. 7.
1917. 'Restudy of *Ornitholestes hermanni.*' *Bull. Amer. Mus. Nat. Hist.*
Vol. XXXV, p. 735.
1917. 'Skeletal Adaptations of *Ornitholestes, Struthiomimus, Tyrannosaurus.*' *Bull. Amer. Mus. Nat. Hist.* Vol. XLVIII, p. 733.
1923. 'Two Lower Cretaceous Dinosaurs of Mongolia.' *Amer. Mus.
Nov. N.Y.* No. 95.
1924. '*Psittacosaurus* and *Protiguanodon:* two Lower Cretaceous
Iguanodonts from Mongolia.' *Amer. Mus. Nov. N.Y.* No. 127.
1924. '*Oviraptor philoceratops.*' *Amer. Mus. Novit.* No. 144, p. 7.

316

1929. 'The Titanotheres of Ancient Wyoming, Dakota, and Nebraska.' *Monog. U.S. Geol. Surv.* No. 55, p. 852.

OSBORN, H. F. and MOOK, C. C. 1919. 'Characters and Restoration of the Sauropod genus *Camarasaurus* Cope.' *Proc. Amer. Phil. Soc. Philad.* Vol. LVIII, pp. 386–396.

1921. '*Camarasaurus, Amphicoelias,* and other Sauropods of Cope.' *Mem. Amer. Mus. Nat. Hist.* N.S. Vol. III, pt. III, pp. 249–387. Jan. 1921.

OSTROM, J. H. 1962. 'The cranial crests of hadrosaurian dinosaurs.' Postilla, No. 62, June *Yale Peabody Mus. Nat. Hist.* New Haven, pp. 1–29.

1964. *The Strange World of Dinosaurs.* New York, Putnam's & Sons. 128 pp.

1964. 'A reconsideration of the Paleocology of Hadrosaurian Dinosaurs.' *Amer. Journ. Sci.* Vol. 262, Oct. pp. 975–997.

1964. 'A functional analysis of jaw mechanics in the Dinosaur *Triceratops*', Postilla. No. 88, Dec. 24, pp. 1–35. Peabody Mus. Nat. Hist., Yale U.

1966. 'A Study in Dinosaur Evolution.' *Discovery.* Vol. 1, No. 2, Spring. Peabody Mus. Nat. Hist., Yale U.

1966. 'Functional Morphology and Evolution of the Ceratopsian Dinosaurs,' *Evolution.* Vol. 20, No. 3, Sept., pp. 290–308.

OSTROM, J. H. and MCINTOSH, J. E. 1966. *Marsh's Dinosaurs. The Collections from Como Bluff.* Yale University Press. pp. xiv + 64, 65 pls.

OWEN, R. 1841. *Odontography. (Cardiodon,* p. 291).

1842. 'Report on British Fossil Reptiles.' *Rep. Brit. Assoc.* (1841).

1861. 'A Monograph of the Fossil Reptilia of the Liassic Formations.' Part I. *Palaeontogr. Soc. (Monog.) London.* 1861, p. 1.

1875. 'Reptilia of the Mesozoic Formations.' Part II. *Loc. cit.,* 1875, p. 75.

1861. *Palaeontology,* 2nd edn. Edinburgh, pp. xvi + 463.

PARKINSON, JAMES. 1822. *Outlines of Oryctology: An Introduction to the study of fossil organic remains.* London.

PARKINSON, J. 1930. *The Dinosaur in East Africa.* Witherby, London.

PARKS, W. A. 1920. 'The Osteology of the Trachodont Dinosaur *Kritosaurus incurvimanus.*' *Univ. Toronto Stud. Geol.* No. 11.

1922. '*Parasaurolophus walkeri.*' *Loc. cit.* No. 13.

1924. '*Dyoplosaurus acutosquameus,* a New Genus and Species of Armoured Dinosaur.' *Loc. cit.* No. 18.

1925. '*Arrhinoceratops brachyops,* a New Genus and Species of Ceratopsia from the Edmonton Formation of Alberta.' *Loc. cit.* No. 19.

1926. '*Thescelosaurus warreni,* a new species of Orthopodous Dinosaurs from the Edmonton Formation of Alberta.' *Loc. cit.* No. 21.

1931. 'A new genus and two new species of Trachodont Dinosaurs from the Belly River Formation of Alberta.' *Loc. cit.* No. 31.

1933. 'New Species of Dinosaurs, etc. (*Struthiomimus currelli*.)' *Univ. Toronto Studies Geol. Ser.* No. 34.

1935. 'Dinosaurs in the Royal Ontario Museum.' *Univ. Toronto Quarterly.* Vol. IV, No. 2, Jan.

PARSONS, T. S. 1967. 'Evolution of the nasal structure in the Lower Tetrapods.' *Amer. Zoologist.* Vol. 7, No. 3, pp. 397–413.

PHILLIPS, JOHN. 1871. *Geology of Oxford and the Valley of the Thames.* Oxford, pp. xxiv + 523.

PLOT, ROBERT. 1677. *The Natural History of Oxford-Shire* . . . . Oxford, pp. 358.

QUENSTEDT, F. A. 1856. *Sonst und Jetzt!* Tübingen, p. 131.

RAYNER, D. H. 1967. *The Stratigraphy of the British Isles.* Cambridge, pp. x + 453.

RIABININ, A. 1925. 'A mounted skeleton of the gigantic reptile *Trachodon amurense*' nov. sp. *Isv. Geol. Committee*, Moscow, (In Russian.)

RIGGS, E. S. 1902. '*Brachiosaurus altithorax*, the largest known dinosaur.' *Amer. Journ. Sci. New Haven.* Ser. IV, Vol. XV, p. 299.

1903. 'Structure and Relationships of Opisthocoelian Dinosaurs. I. *Apatosaurus* Marsh.' *Field Columbian Mus., Chicago.* Publ. 82, Geol. Ser., Vol. II, No. 4.

1904. 'Structure and Relationships of Opisthocoelian Dinosaurs. II. The Brachiosauridae.' *Loc. cit.* Publ. 94, Vol. II, No. 6.

ROMER, A. S. 1956. *Osteology of the Reptiles.* Univ. of Chicago Press, pp. xxi + 772.

1966. *Vertebrate Paleontology.* 3rd edn. Univ. of Chicago Press, pp. x + 468.

ROZHDESTVENSKY, A. K. 1957. *With Dinosaurs in Gobi.* Moscow. (In Russian.)

1957. 'Duck-billed Dinosaurs—*Saurolophus* from Upper Cretaceous of Mongolia.' *Vertebrata Palasiatica* Vol. 1, No. 2, June, pp. 129–149. (Russian with English summary.)

1965. 'Age variation and some problems in classification of dinosaurs of Asia.' *Palaeont. Journ. Acad. Sci. U.S.S.R.* No. 3, pp. 95–109. (In Russian.)

1966. 'New Iguanodontidae from Central Asia. Phylogenetic and taxonomic interrelationships of the late Iguanodontidae and early Hadrosauridae.' *Palaeont. Journ. Acad. Sci. U.S.S.R.* No. 3, pp. 103–116. (In Russian.)

RUSSELL, DALE A. 1967. *The Dinosaurs of Canada.* Nat. Mus. Canada, Aug., pp. 1–11.

1967. 'A Census of dinosaur specimens collected in Western Canada.' *Nat. Mus. Canada. Nat. Hist. Papers.* No. 36, Nov. 8, pp. 1–13.

RUSSELL, DALE A. and CHAMNEY, T. P. 1967. 'Notes on the Biostratigraphy of Dinosaurian and Microfossil Faunas in the Edmonton

Formation (Cretaceous), Alberta.' *Nat. Mus. Canada. Nat. Hist. Papers.* No. 35, Sept. 30, pp. 1–22.

RUSSELL, L. S. 1930. 'Upper Cretaceous Dinosaur Faunas of North America.' *Proc. Amer. Phil. Soc. Philad.* Vol. LXIX, p. 159.

1932. 'On the Occurrence and Relationships of the Dinosaur *Troödon.*' *Ann. Mag. Nat. Hist.* [10]. Vol. IX, p. 334.

1935. 'Musculature and Functions in the Ceratopsia.' *Nat. Mus. Canada Bull. 77. Geol. Ser.* No. 52., pp. 39–48.

1940. '*Edmontonia rugosidens* (Gilmore) an armoured dinosaur from the Belly River Series of Alberta.' *Univ. of Toronto Studies Geol. Series.* No. 43. Toronto.

1965. 'Body temperature of dinosaurs and its relationships to their extinction.' *Journ. Palaeont.* Vol. 39, No. 3, pp. 497–503.

1966. 'Dinosaur Hunting in Western Canada.' *Contribution No. 70, Life Sciences, Royal Ontario Museum.* Toronto, p. 37.

SCHATZ, A. 1957. 'Some biochemical and physiological considerations regarding the extinction of the dinosaurs' *Proc. Penn. Acad. Sci.* Vol. XXXI, pp. 26–36.

1958. 'A reply to Cowles "Comments on the Schatz theory of dinosaurian extinction".' *Proc. Penn. Acad. Sci.* Vol. XXXII, pp. 267–269.

SCHUCHERT, C. 1915. *A Text-Book of Geology.* Pirsson and Schuchert. Vol. II. New York, J. Wiley & Sons.

SEELEY, H. G. 1887. 'Classification of the Fossil Animals commonly named Dinosauria.' *Proc. Roy. Soc.* Nov. 24, pp. 165–171.

1888. The Classification of the Dinosauria. *Rep. Brit. Assoc.* (1887), pp. 698–99.

SEITZ, ADOLF L. L., M.D. 1907. 'Vergleichende Studien über den mikroskopischen Knochenbau fossiler und rezenter Reptilien.' *Nova Acta, Abh. d. k. Leop. Carol. deutsch. Akad. Naturforscher Halle.* Vol. LXXXVII, 2, pp. 229–400.

STEGNER, W. (ed.) 1955. *This is Dinosaur.* New York, A. A. Knopf.

STERNBERG, C. M. 1932.

1933. 'A new *Ornithomimus* with complete abdominal cuirass.' *Canad. Field. Nat.* Vol. XLVII, No. 5, pp. 79–83, May, 1933.

1933. 'Relationships and Habitat of *Troödon* and the Nodosaurs.' *Ann. Mag. Nat. Hist.* [10], Vol. XI, pp. 231–233.

1935. 'Hooded Hadrosaurs of the Belly River Series of the Upper Cretaceous.' *Nat. Mus. Canada Bull. 77, Geol. Ser.* No. 52, pp. 1–37.

1949. 'The Edmonton Fauna and Description of a New Triceratops from the Upper Edmonton Member; Phylogeny of the Ceratopsidae.' *Bull. 113. Ann. Report Nat. Mus. Canada 1947–48,* pp. 33–46.

1950. '*Pachyrhinosaurus canadensis,* representing a new family of the Ceratopsia, from Southern Alberta.' *Bull. 118. Nat. Mus. Canada Ann. Report 1948–49,* pp. 109–120.

1963. 'Early Discoveries of Dinosaurs' *Nat. Hist. Papers, National Mus. Canada,* No. 21, Sept., pp. 1–4.

1965. 'New Restoration of Hadrosaurian Dinosaur.' *Nat. Mus. Canada. Nat. Hist. Papers.* No. 30, August.

1966. 'Canadian Dinosaurs.' *Nat. Mus. Can. Geol. Ser.* No. 54,

STERNBERG, R. M. 1940. 'A Toothless Bird from the Cretaceous of Alberta.' *J. Palaeont* Menasha. 14, pp. 81–85.

STRAELEN, V. VAN 1925. 'The Microstructure of the Dinosaurian Eggshells from the Cretaceous beds of Mongolia.' *Amer. Mus. Nov. N.Y.* No. 173.

1928. 'Les oeufs de Reptiles fossiles.' *Palaeobiol. Wien.* I Bd., p. 295.

STROMER, E. VON 1915. '*Spinosaurus oegyptiacus* n. gen. und n. sp.' *Abh. bayer Akad. Wiss.* Vol. XXVIII, p. 32.

SWINTON, W. E. 1929. 'A Canadian Armoured Dinosaur.' *Nat. Hist. Mag. London.* Vol. II, pp. 67–74.

1930. 'On Fossil Reptilia from Sokoto Province.' *Bull. Geol. Surv. Nigeria.* No. 13.

1933. 'A New Exhibit of *Iguanodon*.' *Nat. Hist. Mag. London.* Vol. IV, No. 26, p. 66.

1936. 'Notes on the osteology of *Hypsilophodon* and on the family Hypsilophodontidae,' *Proc. Zool. Soc. London*, pt. 2, pp. 555–578.

1939. 'Observations on the Extinction of Vertebrates.' *Proc. Geol. Assn.* London, Vol. L, pt. 2, pp. 135–146.

1951. 'Gideon Mantell and the Maidstone *Iguanodon*.' *Notes & Rec. Roy. Soc. Lond.* Vol. 8, No. 2, April, pp. 261–276.

1954. 'The Causes of Extinction.' *Discovery*, March, pp. 116–120.

1965. *Fossil Amphibians and Reptiles*, 4th edn. Brit. Mus. Nat. Hist. London, pp. x + 134.

1966. *Giants, Past and Present.* London, R. Hale, pp. 192.

1967. *Dinosaurs*, 3rd edn. Brit. Mus. Nat. Hist. London, pp. xiv + 44.

TORNIER, T. 1909. 'Wie war der *Diplodocus carnegii* wirklich gebaut?' *SitzBer. Ges. naturf. Fr. Berlin.* No. 4, April, pp. 193–209.

WAGNER, A. 1864. (On *Compsognathus*.) *Abh. bayer. Akad. Wiss.* Vol. IX, p. 94.

WALKER, A. D. 1964 'Ornithosuchus and the origin of Carnosaurs.' *Phil. Trans. R. Soc.* 248B, pp. 53–124.

WATSON, D. M. S. 1962. Article on Reptiles. *Encyclopaedia Britannica.* 14th Edition.

WELLES, S. 1954. (*Megalosaurus wetherilli*) *Bull. Geol. Soc. Amer.* 65, p. 591.

WHITE, F. N. 1968. 'Functional Anatomy of the Heart of Reptiles.' *American Zoologist.* Vol. 8, No. 2, May, pp. 211–219.

WHITE, T. E. 1967. *Dinosaurs—At Home.* New York, Vantage Press, pp. 232.

WILFARTH, M. 1949. *Die Lebensweise der Dinosaurier.* Stuttgart, pp. 95, 3 pls.

BIBLIOGRAPHY

WILLISTON, S. W. 1925. *The Osteology of the Reptiles.* Cambridge, Mass., Harvard Univ. Press.

WIMAN, C. 1929. 'Die Kreide-Dinosaurier aus Shantung.' *Palaeont. Sinica.* Ser. C, Vol. VI, Fasc. 1, pp. 6–37.

WOODWARD, A. S. 1907. 'On a New Dinosaurian Reptile (*Scleromochlus taylori*, gen. et sp. nov.) from the Trias of Lossiemouth, Elgin.' *Quart. J. Geol. Soc. London.* Vol. LXIII, p. 140.

1910. 'On a skull of *Megalosaurus* from the Great Oolite of Minchin-hampton (Glos.).' *Quart. J. Geol. Soc., London.* Vol. LXVI, p. 111.

in ZITTEL KARL A. VON, 1932. *Text-Book of Palaeontology.* Vol. II. Fishes to Birds. Revised by Sir A. Smith Woodward. London, Macmillan & Co.

YOUNG, C. C. 1936. 'On a new Chasmatosaurus from Sinkiang.' *Bull. Geol. Soc. China.* Vol. XV, No. 3.

1947. 'On *Lufengosaurus magnus* Young (sp. nov.) and additional finds of *Lufengosaurus huenei* Young.' *Pal. Sinica.* N.S. C. 12. Nanking, pp. 1–53.

YOUNG, C. C. and SUN, A. L. 1957. 'Note on a fragmentary mandible from Turfan, Sinkiang.' *Vert. Palasiatica.* Vol. 1, No. 2, June, pp. 159–162.

ZITTEL, KARL A. VON 1932. *Text-Book of Palaeontology.* Vol. II. Fishes to Birds. Revised by Sir A. Smith Woodward. London, Macmillan & Co.

1933a. 'Discussion on Deficiency Diseases.' *Journ. Roy. Soc. Med. London.* Vol. XXVI, No. 8, pp. 983–994.

1933b. 'Discussion on Plant Poisoning in Man and Animals.' *Loc. cit.* Vol. XXVI, No. 9, pp. 1267–1278.

ADDENDA

KIELEN-JAWOROWSKA, ZOFIA. 1969. 'Fossils from the Gobi Desert.' *Science Journal,* July 1969, pp. 32–38.

KIELEN-JAWOROWSKA, Z. and DOVCHIN, N. 1968. 'Results of the Polish-Mongolian Palaeontological Expeditions, Part 1, Narrative 1963–1965.' *Pal. Polonica,* No. 19, issued March 1969.

INDEX

323

Bavarian Academy of Sciences, 124
Bellairs, A., 102
Bensted, W. H., 203, 204, 205, 206,
207, 208
Berlin Museum, 172
Bernissart, Belgium, 30, 208, 209
Birds, 63
Blood corpuscles, 270
Bothriospondylus, 113
Brachiosaurus, 170, 171, 296, 297
B. altithorax, 172
B. brancai (fig.), 170, 172
B. fraasi, 172
Brachyceratops, 259, 260
Brachyceratops skull (fig.), 260
Brachyrhinodon, 120
Branca, W., 165
Brazil, 35, 59
Brighton, 32
British Museum (Natural History),
28, 33, 144, 152, 168, 172, 197,
227, 241, 261, 269
Brontosaurus, 113, 149, 150, 175,
176, 177, 178
Broom, R., 56, 108
Brown, Barnum, 108, 157
Buckingham, 33
Buckland, W., 32, 106, 108, 140
Bullard, Sir Edward, 38
Burian, Zdenek, 189

Caenagnathus, 130
C. collinsi, 136
Camarasaurus, 68, 96, 113, 167, 174
Camarasaurus brain (fig.), 97
Camarasaurus skull (fig.), 174
C. lentus, 173
C. supremus, 173
Cambridge, University Museum,
173
Campbell, J. G., 268
Camptonotus, 113
Camptosaurus, 69, 82, 214, 215, 267
Canada, 130
Canadian Maritimes, 37
Canadian Shield, 38
Carbon dioxide, use, 228

Cardiodon, 169
Carnegie Museum, Pittsburgh, 152,
173, 176, 269
Carnosauria, 139
Carpals, 81
Casier, E., 30
Cenomanian transgression, 283
Ceratops, 254, 255
Ceratopsia, 58, 68, 71, 236
Ceratopsian sacrals, 76
Cetiosauriscus greppini, 169
Ceratosaurus, 116, 128, 144, 145,
149, 151, 157, 158
Ceratosaurus pelvis (fig.), 83
C. nasicornis, 139,
C. nasicornis femur (fig.), 86
C. nasicornis tibia and fibula (fig.),
87
Cetiosaurus, 33, 34, 108, 111, 112,
113, 160, 168, 169, 170
C. leedsi, 169, 269, 298
Chalk, 51
Charig, A. J., 60, 117, 161, 167, 196
Chasmosaurus, 259
Chasmosaurus musculature (fig.),
18, 89
Chasmosaurus skull (fig.), 259
C. belli, 259
Chialingosaurus, 161, 244
Chicago Natural History Museum,
172, 296
China, 161, 174
Chondrosteosaurus, 113, 173
Christman, E. S., 133
Cionodon, 113
C. stenopsis, 25
Classification: 116, 117
Cope 1866
Huxley 1870
Seeley 1874
Marsh 1878–84
Cope 1883
Seeley 1887
Clepsysaurus, 114
Coelophysis, 122
Coelurosaurus, 110
Coelurus, 82, 114, 122, 130

324

325

326